EDUCATION ABROAD AND THE
UNDERGRADUATE EXPERIENCE

D1501008

EDUCATION ABROAD AND THE UNDERGRADUATE EXPERIENCE

Critical Perspectives and Approaches
to Integration With Student Learning
and Development

Edited by Elizabeth Brewer and

Anthony C. Ogden

Foreword by Brian Whalen

Copublished with

STERLING, VIRGINIA

Published by Stylus Publishing, LLC.
22883 Quicksilver Drive
Sterling, Virginia 20166-2019

Library of Congress Cataloging-in-Publication Data
Names: Brewer, Elizabeth, editor. | Ogden, Anthony C., editor.
Title: Education abroad and the undergraduate experience : critical perspectives
   and approaches to integration with student learning and development
   \ Edited by Elizabeth Brewer and Anthony Ogden ; Foreword by Brian
   Whalen.
Description: First edition. | Sterling, Virginia : Stylus Publishing, [2019] |
   Includes bibliographical references and index.
Identifiers: LCCN 2019017000 (print) | LCCN 2019019563 (ebook) | ISBN
   9781620368282 (library networkable e-edition) | ISBN 9781620368299
   (consumer e-edition) | ISBN 9781620368268 (cloth : alk. paper) | ISBN
   9781620368275 (pbk. : alk. paper)
Subjects: LCSH: Foreign study--United States. | Undergraduates--United States.
   | Universities and colleges--Curricula--United States. | American students--
   Foreign countries.
Classification: LCC LB2376 (ebook) | LCC LB2376 .E28 2019 (print) | DDC
   370.116--dc23
LC record available at https://lccn.loc.gov/2019017000

13-digit ISBN: 978-1-62036-826-8 (cloth)
13-digit ISBN: 978-1-62036-827-5 (paperback)
13-digit ISBN: 978-1-62036-828-2 (library networkable e-edition)
13-digit ISBN: 978-1-62036-829-9 (consumer e-edition)

Printed in the United States of America

All first editions printed on acid-free paper
that meets the American National Standards Institute
Z39-48 Standard.

Bulk Purchases

Quantity discounts are available for use in workshops and for staff development.

Call 1-800-232-0223

First Edition, 2019

CONTENTS

FOREWORD

The publication of a book that offers critical perspectives on the field signals that the relatively short history of education abroad has caught up with its long past. International education journeys have transformed people for many centuries; but theory has informed practice only within the past few decades, giving rise to what is now a mature, formalized activity. The critical perspectives on education abroad in this book take us even farther along, providing sharp analyses of the meanings, purposes, contexts, and future of this established field.

These perspectives are rooted within the personal knowledge of the leading education abroad professionals who are the editors and contributors of this book. They share a broad and deep experience in the field, the ability to step outside of it to view it from afar, and the skill to articulate what is critically important at this point in its history. While these are essential shared qualities, it is each contributor's distinctive viewpoint that provides the real meaning and value for the reader. These perspectives reflect the essential, evolving diversity of the education abroad field itself.

When a field voices critical perspectives it often signals that a paradigm shift is under way. The progressive improvement of education abroad depends on these adjustments in thinking, which will impact practices over time. The power of this book and its contributors is in how it propels the education abroad field forward by (a) questioning its inherited structures and actions, (b) critically examining current challenges and opportunities, and (c) positing new ways to think about and conduct the work of education abroad.

Education abroad is a multidisciplinary enterprise that intersects with virtually all areas of higher education. This book informs and is useful to the multiple stakeholders who have varied interests in and concerns about education abroad. These include higher education administrators, education abroad researchers, faculty members, policymakers, graduate students, and of course education abroad professionals. Each reader will incorporate the insights contained in these pages into their work and, in turn, shape the education abroad field.

A unifying focus of the book is the idea that education abroad is best understood and practiced as part of an educational continuum embedded thoughtfully within a student's curriculum and overall learning experience.

This notion, which seems obvious, further signals the maturation of the education abroad field, which over the past decade or so has progressed in establishing that it offers a distinctive form of teaching and learning.

In this regard, this book is similar to how students themselves prepare for, experience, and learn from their education abroad sojourns. The way that students think about what their experience will be like and how they critically examine what happened afterward, gives meaning and shape to the experience itself. Herein lies the key to both student learning abroad and the importance of this book for the education abroad field.

—Brian Whalen
President and CEO
The Forum on Education Abroad
2006–2018

INTRODUCTION

The Case for Integrating Education Abroad Into Undergraduate Education

Elizabeth Brewer and Anthony C. Ogden

This volume focuses on two questions. First, how can education abroad be embedded into undergraduate education so that students experience it as an integral component of their education and something they help shape, rather than as time away from their education and as a commodity to be consumed? In other words, how can education abroad not only contribute to student learning and development but also serve as a catalyst to help students find connections across undergraduate education and advance their learning and development toward lifelong learning? Second, how can colleges and universities maximize the educational value of education abroad by forging stronger connections between it and other undergraduate experiences, including other high-impact educational practices? Just as student mobility is part of an interconnected, iterative institutional process of internationalization (American Council on Education, n.d.), so must learning abroad be positioned within the work of the larger institution and students' overall education.

Within higher education, education abroad is often seen as adding an important international, intercultural, or global perspective to undergraduate education. Once closely associated with a narrow segment of an institution's curricular offerings (foreign languages and area/international studies), education abroad is increasingly valued as a high-impact educational practice that can take place within and/or across disciplinary boundaries. Further, the learning outcomes often associated with higher education (critical thinking, problem-solving, perspective taking, confidence, curiosity, flexibility, adaptability, etc.) can be enhanced when students study abroad (Farrugia & Sanger, 2017).

Meanwhile, students study abroad for many reasons. Some want to broaden their horizons, become more independent, and/or simply have an international adventure. Others want to experience the context of questions raised in their studies; apply their learning through activities such as clinical rotations, service-learning, teaching, and internships; and/or become more versatile in their studies by taking courses not available at home. Students may be heritage seekers, desire to become more cosmopolitan, or see studying abroad as enhancing their prospects for employability or admission to graduate or professional schools. In fact, students have multiple, intersecting motivations and go abroad as whole selves, thinking, feeling, and behaving. To their detriment, however, students have often been conditioned to think of education as solely a cognitive activity; this diminishes their capacity to take meaning from studying abroad.

This volume argues that if studying abroad is to have lasting educative value, than colleges, universities, and international education organizations must make a concerted effort to better integrate student learning and development abroad into the undergraduate curriculum and cocurriculum at home. Ethics must be considered, no matter the length or location of education abroad. Who contributes to and benefits (and who does not) from education abroad practice and the education abroad industry? How? And when? Helping students to anticipate and address such complex questions can help them approach their time abroad self-reflexively and ethically. Further, students must be afforded multiple opportunities and ongoing support to enable them to draw connections between their learning abroad and other dimensions of their undergraduate education. This introduction begins with two student profiles, introduces a model for integrating education abroad into undergraduate education, then discusses the student profiles in relation to the model. The introduction concludes with an overview of the volume and the differing perspectives its contributors provide on integrating education abroad into undergraduate education.

Two Student Profiles: Prospects and Challenges for Leveraging the Educational Continuum

Consider the following profiles of two students who have studied abroad and the extent to which they have succeeded in leveraging education abroad for their continued learning and development. What factors seem to inhibit this? What might the students' institutions have done differently to amplify the contribution of the students' time abroad to their on-going learning and development? Their examples illustrate both the prospects and challenges of integrating education abroad into undergraduate education.

Student X

Student X grew up in a bilingual household with parents who had immigrated to the United States. X studied a third language in high school and made visits to the parents' home country as a child and teenager. At college, X easily forms bonds with both domestic and international students, continues to study the third language, and begins to focus on international politics. X is active in Amnesty International and Model UN. As a junior, X studies abroad for a semester, taking courses taught in the third language. In the application to study abroad, X discussed connections to studies pre– and post–study abroad, and referred to papers X had written that focused on the host country. Abroad, X undertakes a project focused on young adult unemployment, for which X is paired with a local student to conduct interviews. X and X's partner struggle to find common ground; they disagree on how to proceed and about their roles. Still, X finds the interviews fascinating, as they provide insights from young adults' actual experiences attempting to find employment, and the discrimination they face based on race, gender, and class. When X leaves for home, the project write-up is not complete; the partner is to add final commentary. When the partner does not follow through, X complains to the host national program director, who, to X's surprise, reprimands X for blaming the partner. Although X feels wronged, X apologizes on the advice of an education abroad adviser at X's home institution. The program director accepts the apology and assigns a grade for X's work on the project.

The following summer, X interns at a nonprofit, doing research and writing briefing papers. Back on campus, X's faculty adviser encourages X to take a development studies course to better frame the research conducted abroad, and to incorporate the interview data into a capstone paper. X also tutors local English-learner adults preparing for citizenship exams. Applying to graduate school, X chooses a master's program that requires field research in another country; X wants to work internationally and knows that the more field research X has conducted before looking for work, the better positioned X will be. Looking back, X ponders if X's project partner abroad felt that X could only see the problems in the host country at the expense of seeing anything that was good. X also wonders if the partner felt disrespected by X. X did make repeated references to X's textbook knowledge of the country and its challenges.

Student Y

Student Y grew up two hours from the college. A first-year student, Y has never traveled outside the country and does not speak another language, nor is Y studying one in college. Y has casual contact with a diversity of students in classes, the dormitory Y lives in, and the college cafeteria. Y's main social group, however, consists of Y's teammates, many of whom come from similar backgrounds. The opportunity to continue to play the sports Y played in junior high and high school was a factor in choosing the college. Y and a friend see a flyer for a three-week summer course that includes travel to Italy. There is no application for this particular course; students just need to register.

While in Italy, Y and the friend room together with a host family and take a course on Italian history and culture. Y finds the discussions of intercultural communication helpful while in Italy for figuring out how to understand cultural norms and behavior. A highlight of the three weeks is taking a bus with the friend from home on their own to a town an hour's distance from the city where they are studying; it feels empowering to travel on their own, explore, order food, and share in local routines. Y really enjoys the sojourn in Italy and returns home invigorated. With a passport and experience navigating in a foreign country, future international travel seems in reach. Back on campus, Y focuses on a business major. Although the course instructors recommended further language study, Y cannot pursue it; other obligations and interests intervene. However, Y is glad to have earned credit by studying abroad and to have had a fresh experience. Further, after returning from Italy, Y had the rest of the summer to work to help cover expenses in the following academic year.

Preliminary Discussion

These two composite students are typical of today's undergraduates. They are not meant to be stereotypes, but rather to suggest the diversity of backgrounds, life experiences, and perspectives that undergraduates bring to their educations. They reinforce the idea that students approach education abroad with different sets of assumptions and goals, and with different backgrounds and levels of preparation. They also demonstrate the complex roles their respective institutions, whether through faculty members, advisers, or curriculum structures, can have in providing opportunities, support, and pathways for integrating education abroad into undergraduate education. The model introduced next can help guide thinking about the integration of education abroad into undergraduate education. The discussion then returns to X and Y to illustrate the model's application.

Introducing the Education Abroad Integration Model

Student learning and development in undergraduate education has long been the focus of higher education researchers and scholars. Numerous theoretical perspectives have contributed to understanding the college student development and learning process (Astin, 1984; Dewey, 1938; Kolb, 1984; Magolda, 2007; Newell, 2001). The liberal arts in practice development model (LAPD) developed by Westerberg and Wickersham (2015), which draws on these perspectives, serves as the foundational model in this volume, as it best illustrates the potential for effectively leveraging education abroad in undergraduate education (see Figure I.1).

Developed at Beloit College, the LAPD model is a context-based advising tool designed to help students conceptualize their individualized progression over a four-year liberal arts education. It has evolved based on assessment data gathered from reflective writing on experiential learning experiences; the model's application in different advising settings; and changes in student demographics, the curriculum, and the cocurriculum.

As depicted in Figure I.1, students enter undergraduate education with different life experiences, skills and assets, and identities. Over the next four years, students engage in new experiences and develop meaning from these through active reflection and further study and engagement. During their first year of study, students "explore" by taking entry-level courses in several disciplines and joining cocurricular activities. In the second year, they "experiment" as they begin to satisfy general education requirements, engage in higher order cocurricular activities, and begin to identify their primary areas of interest. Then in the third, they begin to "cultivate" their education by acquiring greater depth in a major. Internships, community-based learning placements, education abroad, and other sustained activities help bring

Figure I.1. The LAPD model.

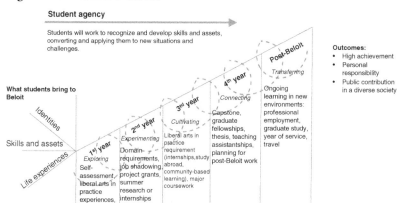

classroom learning into dialogue with out-of-classroom, experiential learning. In fact, the more students engage in out-of-classroom experiences and find ways to connect them with each other and their "academic" learning, the more adept learners they become.

Learning beyond the classroom in unfamiliar settings is challenging. It requires that students exercise critical thinking skills, to recall not only what they know but also how to "cultivate" this knowledge in relation to the new context. What may have seemed certain—concepts, theories, ways of doing things—becomes less certain when these do not neatly fit into new situations. Students must also acknowledge the limits of their skills and knowledge and defer to and learn from hosts whose expertise has more immediate relevance and utility. In this sense, any number of people (and situations) students encounter can "teach." However, transforming the new experiences into learning requires self-reflection and self-assessment, and a willingness to engage even when experiences may be challenging or uncomfortable. This is key to students' investing in learning, as opposed to thinking of education as something purchased and consumed.

In their senior year, students begin "connecting" their learning across ideas, concepts, and contexts, often through capstone projects, theses, teaching assistantships, and so on. This requires students to exercise individual agency, learn collaboratively with others, reflect on learning, and transfer learning into new contexts. "Connecting" is not "repetition toward mastery" but rather teaches students to transfer knowledge and skills acquired in one setting to new settings and, in so doing, to continue to acquire knowledge and skills. In this way, "connecting" becomes a "habitual way of being in the world" (Westerberg & Wickersham, 2015, p. 72). Just as students develop over time, so do educator roles, from exercising control over what is to be learned and how, to coaching/mentoring and helping students ask themselves questions, consider alternative hypotheses, and identify gaps in knowledge and skills. Students then begin to transition out of undergraduate education. Significantly, the looping spiral suggests that students will move back and forth along the continuum depending on who they are, their precollegiate experiences, and their particular pathways through college.

Figure I.2 contains an adaptation of the LAPD model to illustrate how education abroad can intersect with student learning and development along different points in the undergraduate years. The education abroad integration model builds on the theoretical underpinnings of the LAPD model and includes elements from Astin's student involvement model. However, rather than locating education abroad as one distinct way to "cultivate" knowledge and skills acquired in the first two years of college by applying them in new

Figure I.2. Education abroad integration model.

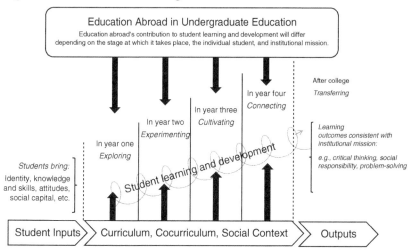

Note. Adapted from Astin, 1984; Dewey, 1938; Kolb, 1984; Magolda, 2007; Newell, 2001; Westernberg & Wickersham, 2015; with the help of Josh Morre.

contexts, this adaptation illustrates that studying abroad can enhance student learning and development at multiple points during undergraduate education. The model takes into account that students may study abroad as first-year students, in the summer between the first and second years, in their third and fourth years as bachelor degree students, or even after graduation as a bridge to future endeavors. (While the model depicts a four-year education, it can be adapted to shorter or longer educational programs.) Depending on when education abroad takes place, and what students bring to the experience, however, the students may be positioned more to explore than experiment, or to experiment rather than cultivate, and so on. Thus, student Y might be thought of as largely at the exploring stage while studying abroad, while at times X is cultivating and connecting knowledge and experience.

As is the case with the LAPD model, the looping spiral across a four-year education and beyond acknowledges that while the model suggests an upward trajectory as students develop, individual students will in fact move back and forth along the continuum depending on knowledge, skills, and context. Additionally, how and when students will enter and continue along the continuum will depend on a host of factors. The adapted model reinforces the notion that how students engage with education abroad will be influenced by students' academic studies, experiences, and characteristics of particular relevance to studying abroad (previous international travel, proficiency in more than one language, identity awareness, flexibility and adaptability, willingness to challenge one's assumptions, etc.). Thus, a student who has already experienced being an outsider for a sustained period of time may experience being an outsider abroad differently from a student who has always been a part of a majority; the former is aided by adaptation skills. Or students conditioned to associate education abroad with travel, no matter their financial means, may need support to understand that remaining on-site provides advantages, such as getting to know place and people more deeply than would be possible with frequent travel away. On the other hand, students focused on amplifying their academic studies will approach education abroad through that lens.

Importantly, both models emphasize the importance of linking learning outcomes to institutional context. Both also suggest that no single experience will enable students to make connections among their various curricular and cocurricular experiences. Rather, students need opportunities to make connections among experiences over time (Newell, 2001; Pascarella & Terenzini, 1991). Further, learning outcomes must be differentiated according to when education abroad takes place, for how long, and in which format (Engle, 2013).

Application of the Education Abroad Student Development Model

To revisit students X and Y, both made decisions about what to major in, with whom to socialize, and whether to study abroad, all of which were influenced by their previous experiences and backgrounds. Student X sought out courses and extracurricular activities to help prepare for study abroad in a particular country and abroad engaged in a collaborative research project with a local student. Studying abroad helps X strengthen X's academic studies, but X also stumbles. Though X is conditioned to associate with diverse other students, X nonetheless is ill-equipped to understand how X's positionality (Cook et al., 2005) as an outsider with "textbook" knowledge might impact the collaboration with a local partner. While X clearly exercises agency, which is a sign of developing capacity to learn, the teamwork with the local student is negatively affected by X's inability to acknowledge the limits of X's knowledge. X does not seem to regard the local student as a potential teacher. Following the semester abroad, X further develops technical skills during an internship. Back on campus, a faculty member then encourages X to take courses to continue to develop X's research project, and X tutors off campus. X is clearly goal oriented, and this suggests capacity to self-assess (Magolda, 2007). There is little evidence, however, that X's classes at home or abroad have taught X self-reflection. Further, neither the program director, who rebuked X for placing blame on the partner, nor the faculty adviser at home appear to prompt X to engage in self-reflection. Only the education abroad adviser prompts the reflection that results in an apology to the program director. Underdeveloped reflection skills hinder X's ability to take others' perspectives into account, and to become more self-aware. Yet both are critical to intercultural development and global learning (Kahn, 2018). The disciplinary training of most faculty members, however, has not prepared them to teach reflection and perspective taking, despite research that suggests that empathy and perspective taking outweigh knowledge in intercultural encounters (Pettigrew, 2008). Thus, while X's friendships suggest X is comfortable with cross-cultural encounters, X struggles when working with the local student. Fortunately, new scholarship suggests ways to incorporate intercultural development into disciplinary teaching (Lee, 2017).

Y, as well as Y's home institution, also faces challenges to maximize the learning outcomes of Y's education abroad experience. As a new business major and, potentially, a future professional working in the private sector, the ability to work in multicultural/multilingual/international teams will be essential. Y's confidence in and comfort with navigating unfamiliar environments grew abroad, and this will be important for Y's personal and professional future. However, similar to X, Y's education has not cultivated self-reflection and intercultural development. Nor does it appear that while in Italy the course helped Y to anticipate how lessons from the experience might be relevant to future private sector (and other social) contexts. Perhaps Y's posteducation abroad studies will help Y further develop the intercultural skills that seem to have been a goal of the three-week course, rather than, in essence, leaving the brief exploration of intercultural concepts as a footnote to Y's education. Hopefully, future short-term courses will be more intentional in clarifying linkages to institutional context and suggesting transferability of lessons.

In short, in both Y's and X's cases, the home institutions have work to do to make education abroad a more meaningful and impactful part of undergraduate education. The discussion now moves to how the various chapters take up this theme.

Book Organization and Chapter Summaries

Education Abroad and the Undergraduate Experience is organized into three parts: "Critical Perspectives on Education Abroad and Its Integration Into Undergraduate Education," "Supporting Student Learning Along the Educational Continuum," and "Partnerships in Education Abroad Integration." Preceding these distinct parts is an introductory chapter on the development of U.S. education abroad. Anthony C. Ogden and Elizabeth Brewer trace the beginnings of education abroad as an activity at the margins of undergraduate education and largely restricted to privileged students to today, when it is widely understood as a high-impact practice relevant to the education of all students, regardless of socioeconomic background and disciplinary focus.

Part One begins with chapter 2, in which John P. Haupt and Anthony C. Ogden discuss education abroad as a high-impact educational practice. After introducing concepts developed by the Association of American Colleges & Universities, they draw on research to make the case for education abroad's recognition as a high-impact practice. They conclude by recommending that education abroad professionals strengthen campus networks to ensure that students engage in multiple high-impact practices and draw connections between and among them.

In chapter 3, Elizabeth Brewer, Giselda Beaudin, and Michael Woolf use the lens of spatial theory to argue for curriculum integration's rethinking. When too narrowly conceived, education abroad curriculum integration, by focusing on course matching, can mask the importance of experiential and situated learning to education abroad, and prevent students from experiencing the disruptions necessary for transformative learning. They suggest reconceiving education abroad curriculum integration as enhancing and enriching learning at home by integrating new ideas from abroad.

Drawing on postcolonial theory and the literature on subjectivity, in chapter 4 Roger Adkins and Bryan Messerly discuss neocolonial tendencies in U.S. education abroad. These have their origin in early conceptualizations of education abroad's purpose as the improvement of the individual (student). Together with education abroad's commodification, this positions hosts abroad (residents, institutions, organizations, environments) as accessories in narratives of student (and sending institutions'/organizations') development rather than as reciprocal partners. Adkins and Messerly argue that the decolonization of education abroad will require sustained commitment and self-reflexive practice on the part of education abroad professionals, their colleagues, and their institutions, and that the process will be iterative and aspirational.

Part Two begins with Rosalind Latiner Raby's discussion in chapter 5 of adult learners, who are often neglected in education abroad discussions and research. Focusing on adult learners attending community colleges, Raby uses evidence to counter prevailing perceptions that adult learners do not want to study abroad, and argues for eliminating obstacles to their participation, including such perceptions. The adult learners she quotes help convey the need to accommodate adult learners' preferences and realities when designing and promoting education abroad in order to broaden access.

The focus of chapter 6 is American students' dearth of geographic imagination, and its impact on students' abilities to navigate the ambilocation and physical spaces encountered when studying abroad. Consonant with themes discussed in chapter 4, Darren Kelly and Anthony Gristwood argue that a colonialist legacy contributes to conceptions of education abroad as adventure to imagined pasts. This is compounded by neoliberal models that emphasize self-actualization and reduce education abroad to a commodity. When realities do not match expectations, the cognitive and emotional disruptions students experience can cause them to retreat to physical and virtual comfort zones. Concepts and pedagogies from the discipline of geography, however, applied to program design and pedagogy and incorporated into predeparture educational activities can mitigate this effect by teaching students to engage critically and reflexively with their host environments.

Chapter 7 returns to the theme of students' preparedness to study abroad. To foster their growth and development, it is important to understand who they are and what their needs are. Tailoring supports is especially important as students diversify and face a more complex world. Contributor Paige E. Butler suggests that foundational student development theories provide important insight into stages of cognitive and psychological development. More recent theories lend insight into students' social and emotional development. Additionally, emerging adulthood theory helps to illuminate generational shifts and expectations that can impact students when studying abroad. The chapter includes examples of application of theory to practice.

Following on the themes of chapter 7, in chapter 8 Katherine N. Yngve focuses on how formative assessment can lead to improved learning outcomes of education abroad. Yngve challenges educators to cease focusing on program design to achieve complex outcomes. Instead, formative assessment can differentiate learning needs and processes among students at different developmental stages and/or of different ethnicities, genders, or majors. Effective instruction related to education abroad aligns learning goals (and curriculum design and delivery) with assessment methods, uses SMART (specific, measurable, attainable, realistic, and time-bound) learning objectives to guide it, measures learning students care about, and shares responsibility for education abroad assessment.

In chapter 9, Victor Savicki and Michele V. Price focus on reflection's contribution to learning. Reflection is key to translating experience into learning and can be learned; with practice, it improves. The contributors draw on constructivism to emphasize that students will give different meanings to events based on their prior experiences, on experiential learning theory to discuss the importance of generating alternative interpretations of events, and on transformative learning theory to discuss how reflection on disorienting experiences can help students challenge their assumptions. Examples of written reflections of students studying abroad illustrate the chapter.

Finally, in chapter 10, Bruce La Brack and Anthony C. Ogden critique contemporary predeparture orientation and reentry training, which tends to bookend education abroad. Instead, they advance the idea of ongoing orientation programming that emphasizes the continuity of learning pre-, during, and postprogram. The argument is not new; indeed, La Brack advanced it in a seminal article published in 1993. The University of Pacific's groundbreaking pre– and post–education abroad cross-cultural training courses are offered as an early, but still relatively rare, theoretically grounded model for ongoing orientation. Other models considered include courses based at single institutions, and a curriculum available virtually to students anywhere.

The chapters in Part Three discuss the critical role stakeholders beyond the education abroad office play in integrating education abroad into the educational continuum. In chapter 11, Anne M. D'Angelo and Mary Pang argue that education abroad, by placing students in environments outside their comfort zones, helps students develop the "soft" skills (confidence, flexibility, adaptability) employers want as they look to hire graduates with the capacity for lifelong learning. However, while some studies find that employers understand this connection, others indicate that hiring managers rarely prioritize education abroad. International educators can partner with career offices to help students both understand education abroad's value and convey this value when seeking employment.

In chapter 12, Joan Gillespie places the discussion of education abroad integration in the broader context of internationalization to argue the relevance of faculty. Although today education abroad professionals are often largely responsible for administrative aspects of education abroad, faculty remain engaged through their teaching, research, and service. Further, professional development activities can help strengthen this engagement. Learning theories and a global learning framework ground the chapter's discussion of faculty members' contributions to education abroad as teachers, and the chapter is illustrated with examples of practice.

Chapter 13 discusses the role of local partners, an underexamined topic in education abroad. Introducing a local partner engagement process model, Julie M. Ficarra posits that *local partners*, a term she argues is preferable to *hosts*, are both teachers and learners, whether voluntarily or involuntarily. Further, their motivations to engage with U.S. students impact both them and the students. The model considers how experiences of harmony and disharmony with students influence how local partners make sense of themselves and the students. Drawing on service-learning research and a study of local partners in Costa Rica, Ficarra concludes that the evaluation of education abroad must extend to local partners' roles and experiences.

In chapter 14, Kris Holloway, Lisa Chieffo, Rich Kurtzman, and Anthony C. Ogden propose that the partnership between colleges and universities and external provider organizations facilitating education abroad become more relational. Partnerships between international education organizations and higher education institutions have a long history. However, when the partnership is transactional, much is lost. Relational partnerships, in contrast, can benefit institutions and organizations by tapping into each other's expertise and resources; the resulting synergies benefit student learning. Specific recommendations are provided.

The volume concludes with chapter 15, which includes 10 short essays on the future of education abroad. Three themes span the essays. First, the why, how, and what of education abroad matters more than numbers, and scholarship is critical to elucidating their interplay. Second, education abroad has to become both more inclusive and interconnected with students' other learning. Third, only through partnerships with actors beyond the education office will education abroad contribute to students' preparation for careers and social responsibility.

References

American Council on Education. (n.d.). *CIGE model for comprehensive internationalization.* Available from http://www.acenet.edu/news-room/Pages/Center-for-Internationalization-and-Global-Engagement.aspx

Astin, A. W. (1984). Student involvement: A developmental theory for higher education. *Journal of College Student Personnel, 25*(4), 297–308.

Cook, I., et al. (2005). Positionality/situated knowledge. In D. Sibley, P. Jackson, D. Atkinson, & N. Washbourne (Eds.), *Cultural geography: A critical dictionary of key concepts* (pp. 16–26). London, UK: I.B. Taurus.

Dewey, J. (1938). *Experience and education.* New York, NY: Macmillan.

Engle, L. (2013, April 3). *What do we know now and where do we go from here?* Opening Plenary Talk, The Forum on Education Abroad Conference, Chicago, IL.

Farrugia, C., & Sanger, J. (2017). *Gaining an employment edge: The impact of study abroad on 21st century skills & career prospects in the United States.* New York, NY: Institute for International Education. Available from file:///C:/Users/brewere/AppData/Local/Temp/Gaining%20an%20Employment%20Edge%20-%20The%20Impact%20of%20Study%20Abroad-1.pdf

Kahn, H. (2018, Winter). Vulnerabilities in global classrooms. *Peer Review* 13–15. Available from https://drive.google.com/drive/u/0/folders/1ReRV7JVvZINz53b G1Hq97UBYfAJe5T7V?ogsrc=32

Kolb, D. (1984). *Experiential learning: Experience as the source of learning and development.* Englewood Cliffs, NJ: Prentice Hall.

La Brack, B. (1993). The missing linkage: The process of integrating orientation and reentry. In R. Michael Paige (Ed.). *Education for the intercultural experience* (pp. 241–279). Yarmouth, ME: Intercultural Press.

Lee, A. (2017). *Teaching interculturally: A framework for integrating disciplinary knowledge and intercultural development.* Sterling, VA: Stylus.

Magolda, M. B. (2007). Self-authorship: The foundation for twenty-first-century education. *New Directions in Teaching and Learning, 2007*(109), 69–83.

Newell, W. H. (2001). Powerful pedagogies. In B. L. Smith & J. McCann (Eds.), *Reinventing ourselves: Interdisciplinary education, collaborative learning and experimentation in higher education* (pp. 196–211). Bolton, MA: Anker Press.

Pascarella, E. T., & Terenzini, P. T. (1991). *How college affects students: Findings and insights from twenty years of research.* San Francisco, CA: Jossey-Bass.

Pettigrew, T. F. (2008). Future directions for intergroup contact theory and research. *International Journal of Intercultural Relations, 32*(3), 187–199.

Westerberg, C., & Wickersham, C. (2015). More than community-based learning: Practicing the liberal arts. In E. Chamlee-Wright (Ed.), *Liberal learning and the art of self-governances* (pp. 71–90). New York, NY: Routledge.

I

U.S. EDUCATION ABROAD

Historical Perspectives, Emerging Trends, and Changing Narratives

Anthony C. Ogden and Elizabeth Brewer

Over time, education abroad has gradually moved from the margins of undergraduate education where only the most privileged students participated, toward becoming a recognized and increasingly valued educational practice that resonates with students of all backgrounds and disciplines. This chapter provides a concise overview of this development, beginning with a brief discussion of the growth and expansion of U.S. education abroad programming, followed by an outline of the distinct periods and notable milestones in its evolution since the nineteenth century. Because U.S. education abroad programming has grown and evolved, the chapter reflects on the changing rationale for why U.S. institutions have invested in education abroad and the key political, economic, cultural and social, and academic drivers that have shaped its direction and scope. The chapter concludes with a forward-looking perspective of the major issues and challenges ahead for the further development and evolution of education abroad programming and practice.

Brief Overview of the Growth and Expansion of U.S. Education Abroad

Education abroad participation is increasingly understood as an essential feature of higher education and along with international student enrollment is often cited as evidence of an institution's commitment to internationalization. Worldwide, there has been unprecedented growth in the number of students traveling abroad for academic study; according to United Nations

Educational and Cultural Organization (UNESCO), the number of internationally mobile students now exceeds over 4.6 million annually and is expected to continue growing (Institute for International Education, 2018). The United States has long been considered the premiere destination for higher education in the world. Far surpassing that of other host nations, the enrollment of international students in the United States now tops 1,000,000 (Farrugia & Bhandari, 2017). By comparison, only about 46,000 U.S. students studied abroad to obtain degrees from foreign institutions (Institute for International Education, 2018). The outbound movement of U.S. students abroad as part of their home degrees, however, has experienced steady growth in recent decades and has become the mainstay for student mobility from the United States. In 2015–2016, 329,339 U.S. students received academic credit for education abroad, which is up dramatically from the mere 84,403 students in 1994–1995. Despite the growth, the number indicates that only 10% of all U.S. undergraduate students (15% for bachelor's degree students) will study abroad before they graduate (Farrugia & Bhandari, 2017).

With more than 25 years of sustained enrollment growth, the once traditional junior year abroad (JYA) is largely a phenomenon of the past, and its decline signals a shift in the perceived value of education abroad in regard to the educational continuum. The JYA once formed a critical bridge between students' general education requirements as first- and second-year students with their more specialized studies in the third and final years. In fact, those who participate in full academic year programs abroad today account for just 2.3% of the total today, while 63% of students chose programs of less than eight weeks in duration and most often during the summer months (Farrugia & Bhandari, 2017). The popularity of shorter durations may suggest that students and their home institutions see a more diminished role for education abroad in fulfilling a significant portion of a student's education. As discussed in chapter 2, this may also point to why students are increasingly encouraged to engage in multiple high-impact practices, in addition to education abroad.

Whereas international students are primarily drawn to the United States to earn degrees (de Wit, 2008), U.S. students have long been motivated by the idea of seeing the world and experiencing other cultures. U.S. students have been encouraged to learn languages in context, experience world cultures firsthand, develop marketable skills for career enhancement, and expand their worldviews. As international perspectives have increasingly been embedded into the undergraduate curricula, however, students are increasingly being encouraged to leverage education abroad to either supplement or complement their academic studies. While once the majority of students studied the social sciences, humanities, and foreign languages, students who study engineering, business and management, mathematics, and computer science now collectively account for 44% of the total study abroad population In fact, over 60% of the total enrollment represents just three disciplines: science, technology, engineering, and mathematics (25%); business and management (21%); and the social sciences (17%). It can be argued that U.S. students today can study virtually any subject in most any part of the world and for nearly any length of time.

The growth and expansion of education abroad over the years has also led to the diversification of the primary modes of student mobility. The most popular modes today include *reciprocal student exchanges, consortia programming, provider programs,* and *faculty-directed programs.* Reciprocal student exchange programs have a long history in U.S. higher education, reaching back to 1909 when the Association for the International Interchange of Students was formed to promote exchanges of students among England, Canada, and the United States (Hoffa, 2007). Bilateral and multilateral exchanges continue to offer a relatively affordable way for students to spend a semester or academic year abroad. Also well regarded are interinstitutional consortia programs, or those programs wherein institutions "share one or more education abroad programs within a membership group in order to provide greater access, quality control, and/or cost efficiency in education abroad programs to students" (Peterson et al., 2007). Today, consortia are relatively commonplace with region-specific consortia such as the Kentucky Institute for International Studies (KIIS) and nationwide consortia such as the Institute for the International Education of Students (IES Abroad) and the Council on International Educational Exchange (CIEE), both of which work with over 200 public and private U.S. colleges and universities. Similar to consortia, there has been a proliferation of for-profit and nonprofit organizations that offer education abroad programs and services to students. Often referred to as "providers," these organizations offer a wide range of programs, from island programming to direct enrollment. Many institutions selectively include provider programs in their portfolios of education abroad options. A rapidly growing mode of student mobility in the United States today are faculty-directed programs, with home-campus faculty accompanying cohorts of students abroad and teaching home institution courses. Although these programs are typically discipline specific, short term, and offered during the summer months (Chieffo & Spaeth, 2017), variations are emerging (e.g., semester-length faculty-directed programs, residential courses that have an embedded international travel component). Faculty-directed programs allow faculty to experiment pedagogically and to broaden their international knowledge and experience while giving students an intensive learning experience around a particular topic.

Just as the modes of student mobility have expanded over time, so too have the variety of program experience types. While once *study abroad* was the catchall term for outbound mobility, the term *education abroad* is increasingly preferred as a broader category to better encompass the distinct experience types of outbound study that have emerged over time. These in turn serve different purposes within the educational continuum. Today, *study abroad* more often refers specifically to taking courses abroad that will count toward the home school degree. Depending on student choice and institutional culture and policy, courses may count toward general education requirements and electives or toward majors and minors. Other common experience types include *undergraduate research abroad, global service-learning,* and *international internships*. Undergraduate research abroad programming allows students to conduct supervised research in their target disciplines. Global service-learning has long been an interest of U.S. students, reaching back to the latter half of the nineteenth century when American students began to pursue overseas missionary and volunteer service programs (Hoffa, 2007). Today, global service-learning programs generally offer structured service-learning in host communities for academic credit. Similarly, international internships have proliferated in response to growing student demand to develop internationally oriented skills and knowledge to potentially enhance their effectiveness in navigating the globalizing workforce (Farrugia & Bhandari, 2017). Moreover, there are a number of other emerging experience types, such as teach abroad programs that allow students to fulfill student teaching requirements abroad. Students in the health-care professions are increasingly conducting rotations and clerkships abroad in local healthcare contexts that fulfill academic requirements back at home. Global entrepreneurship programs are also emerging as a means to enable students to pursue an entrepreneurial initiative in an international context.

While much attention has been given to tracking overall enrollment growth and the expansion of new modes of student mobility and experience types, there has also been consistent attention placed on understanding the education abroad participant profile and on developing strategies to ensure broader student access and inclusion. For years, the typical education abroad student profile has been a White female majoring in the humanities, social sciences, or business, and studying in Europe. Female students account for roughly 66.6% of the total education abroad enrollment (Farrugia & Bhandari, 2017), a percentage that has scarcely changed over decades, despite efforts to increase male participation. The fact that female students account for only 57% of the total enrollment in U.S. degree-granting institutions (National Center for Education Statistics [NCES], n.d.-a) illustrates just how disproportionate these enrollment patterns actually are. Similarly,

White students represented 72.9% of education abroad participants, while accounting for only 57.6% of U.S. undergraduate enrollment (Farrugia & Bhandari, 2017; NCES, n.d.-b). Beyond race, ethnicity, and gender, attention has begun to focus on other populations that have traditionally been underrepresented in education abroad programming, namely students from low socioeconomic backgrounds, first-generation students, learning or physically disabled students, community college students, student athletes, veterans, transfer students, and students whose gender identities do not fit traditional categorization. Despite this expanded focus and related efforts to develop strategies to boost participation of underrepresented populations, the general student profile has only modestly changed over the decades.

Overview of the Evolution of Education Abroad Programming in the United States

International student and scholar mobility has been an important element of U.S. higher education since the nineteenth century (de Wit & Rumbley, 2008). The flow of students and scholars into the United States has a long history reaching back to the sons of the early English colonial governors and other administrators. The earliest forms of outbound student mobility from the United States usually resembled the European Grand Tour of the seventeenth and eighteenth centuries, through which elite Americans traveled abroad to make acquaintances with important families and prepare themselves for eventual leadership roles back at home. From this influential beginning, a high degree of asymmetry in student flows has existed, with many more degree-seeking foreign students coming to the United States than American students studying abroad. As enrollment has grown over time and as mobility patterns have shifted, distinct periods and notable milestones in the evolution of U.S. education abroad programming have emerged.

Early Beginnings, 1910s–1930s

According to Hoffa (2007), the earliest forms of U.S. education involved grand tours for cultural enlightenment, graduate study, and missionary activities. Formal education abroad programming began in the 1870s when faculty at Indiana University encouraged students to enroll in summer courses taught in Europe. Nondegree institutes for international students began to be established in Europe in 1910, some of which continue to this day. The U.S. liberal education tradition of training citizens rather than specialists helped justify overseas study, although as an add-on to the home degree. With the influx of international students onto U.S. campuses post–World War I, the internationalization of U.S. colleges and universities gained momentum. In turn, faculty and administrators who had benefited from enrollment in international institutes initiated the credit-bearing JYA for language acquisition and country-specific learning, as well as issue-focused study tours that crossed borders. Although the number of such programs was small, a precedent had been set for approaching education abroad as combining serious academic study with out-of-classroom cultural engagement. Disruption of the home school educational continuum was avoided by having home school faculty accompany and supervise the students and their studies and arranging for selected instruction by host country nationals.

Post-WWII Internationalization, 1940s–1950s

The period immediately following World War II followed a similar pattern to the period following World War I, with an influx of international students into U.S. colleges and universities, and an outflow of U.S. students, particularly to Europe. As after WWI, education abroad was linked to a desire to develop peaceful relationships with other countries. The scale of student mobility, however, was considerably larger, and new organizations were needed to help manage it. The Institute of International Education (IIE), established in 1919, continued to support international students in coming to the United States and to conduct applied research and policy analysis. To support the outward flow of American students, the Council on Student Travel was founded in 1947 to assist agencies taking U.S. students abroad. By the mid-1950s, it was also bringing international students to the United States and convening stakeholders for international education strategy and policy discussions. A 1967 name change to CIEE would reflect this broader commitment (CIEE, n.d.). In 1948, efforts on the part of colleges and universities, government agencies, and private organizations led to the establishment of the National Association of Foreign Student Advisers (NAFSA: Association of International Educators, n.d.). With an initial mandate to train college and university personnel to assist and advise international students, the term *"Affairs"* replaced *"Advisers"* in 1964 to reflect the diversity of actors and efforts within and beyond campuses supporting international students. A reinterpretation of NAFSA's funding on the part of the U.S. State Department in 1976 allowed NAFSA to include study abroad in its scope of activities.

Beginning after 1945, a number of U.S. federal government initiatives had indirect impacts on education abroad. The 1946 Fulbright Act, which funded inbound-outbound graduate student and faculty mobility, impacted campuses by normalizing educational exchange. If the Fulbright

Act deliberately decoupled foreign policy from educational exchange, the 1958 National Defense Education Act (NDEA), passed in response to the Soviet Union's early superiority in the space race and the launch of the Sputnik satellite, saw education as a matter of national security. Funding addressed weakness in U.S. education, including in basic education, science and math, and modern foreign languages (U.S. House of Representatives, n.d.). Matching funding from the Ford Foundation led to the establishment of over 100 Areas Studies Centers by 1972, when funds could also support undergraduate programs (Hoffa, 2007). The emphasis on language acquisition and country knowledge was consistent with earlier education abroad content, although the national security rationale was new. It would take nearly three decades to consistently link education abroad to other areas of college curricula. However, student loan programs that began with the NDEA and expanded in the 1960s would eventually legally require that federal financial aid be made available to help meet the costs of studying abroad.

New Development, 1960s–1980s

From the 1960s, education abroad was characterized by semester- and year-long programming facilitated by bilateral exchange agreements, state and nonprofit organization consortia, and faculty-directed programs. It was expected that studying abroad would directly connect to disciplinary studies. Further, what happened outside of the classroom, while earlier recognized as adding value to students' educations, was not thought worthy of academic credit. Education abroad was not yet influenced by experiential learning theory, nor were methods developed to assess out-of-classroom learning. Nonetheless, cross-cultural education was increasingly associated with credit-bearing education abroad, such that Bruce La Brack, a pioneer in recognizing and valuing this aspect of learning abroad, began offering credit-bearing post–study abroad courses to help students make sense of their cultural experience. His work helped lead to the emphasis on intercultural learning that took hold in the first decades of the twenty-first century. Eventually, he added a preparatory course and shifted from country-specific cultural training to a more generalized approach (La Brack, 2016).

As internationalization took hold on U.S. campuses and education abroad programming and participation rates grew, so did concerns about the education abroad experience. Was education abroad contributing to student learning, or diverting students' attention because of the lack of control over their extracurricular endeavors? Conferences were convened, reports issued, and in the late 1980s, the first major study of student learning abroad was undertaken, focusing on language acquisition, knowledge of host cultures and attitudes toward them and the home country, the development of what might today be called an international mind-set, and career development (Carlson, Burn, Useem, & Yacchimowicz, 1990). Program design and the demographics of participants were also gaining attention.

Rapid Expansion, 1990s

The 1990s saw attempts to diversify the education abroad population, what students studied abroad, and where they studied. Additionally, for-profit organizations emerged to facilitate education abroad, and attention to the professional development of education abroad practitioners grew. Participation rates doubled over the decade as education abroad options diversified, and it became clear that federal student loans could help support education abroad.

By 1990, it was clear that the students most likely to study abroad were White middle-class students, even as the undergraduate student population was diversifying in terms of race and ethnicity, income, and field of study. The 1990 CIEE conference focused on this topic and helped lead to IIE collecting data on ethnicity. Its first such report covering the 1993–1994 academic year found that 83.8% of participants were White (Stallman, Woodruff, Kasravi, & Comp, 2010). Concerns about finances, racism abroad, fit with academic program, and family support raised by students at the time would continue to prevent participation in education abroad from mirroring participation in higher education into the next decades, as would new concerns related to social identities around gender, disability, and mental health. Study abroad consortia, colleges and universities, and international education organizations responded with better data collection and diversity initiatives. Nonetheless, education abroad would continue to be dominated by White women from better educated and better financed families.

Already in the 1970s, education abroad organizations such as the Institute for European Studies (now widely known as IES Abroad) and Arcadia University's Center for Education Abroad (formerly Beaver College) had created oversight groups of education abroad practitioners to help guide their work (Sideli, 2010). In so doing, they provided professional development for the practitioners. NAFSA's now defunct Section on the Education Abroad of Students, not yet eligible for federal support, had nonetheless initiated professional development for practitioners through a grant from the Carnegie Foundation in 1974. A five-day training for 50 practitioners resulted in publication of a sourcebook on education abroad. Such publications would continue and become more specialized as needs for guidance emerged around such topics as safety and security.

As education abroad gained traction in higher education, calls for better information on its merits grew. In 1990, Ernest Boyer argued that a scholarship of teaching and learning was necessary within higher education. His call meshed well with the conversations and concerns about education abroad that had emerged in the prior decade, and that helped lead to the establishment of *Frontiers: Interdisciplinary Journal of Study Abroad* in 1995. A double-blind, peer-reviewed journal currently owned and managed by The Forum on Education Abroad (The Forum), *Frontiers* today is an open-access, online journal that "communicates the latest research on education abroad within a multi-disciplinary forum to reflect on critical issues and concerns for academics and professional practitioners" (Frontiers, n.d.). With a purview beyond education abroad, *Journal of Studies in International Education*, founded two years later in 1997, and published on behalf of the European Association of International Educators and of the Association for Studies in International Education, has both helped raise the bar for scholarship on education abroad and helped link education abroad to larger issues around the internationalization of higher education.

International education scholars such as John Hudzik (2016) have rightly raised concerns about the quality of scholarship around education abroad, pointing out the lack of training in research methods on the part of many producing the literature. Nonetheless, the relationship between scholarship and education abroad learning outcomes is better understood, as is the need for greater professionalism of those facilitating education abroad, whether as advisers or in other roles. This would lead to a rise in specialized graduate training programs in the next decade.

Standards and Compliance, 2000s–2010s

In July 2001, The Forum was incorporated as a stand-alone organization, whose institutional, organizational, consortial, and agency members would be committed to improving education abroad programming and practice. An inaugural annual meeting in 2002 attracted over 150 members; 10 years later, over 1,100 would attend. By 2005, The Forum would be recognized as the standards development organization for education abroad by both the U.S. Department of Justice and the Federal Trade Commission. The Forum's Standards of Good Practice for Education Abroad are widely used by education abroad practitioners, while workshops and a certification program provide guidance on how to implement the standards in institutions of higher education and organizations facilitating education abroad (The Forum, n.d.). The establishment of The Forum helped cement the idea that education abroad practitioners should possess and continue to develop expertise related to education abroad. Institutions of higher education took note, creating graduate degree and certificate programs focused on both scholarship and practice in international education and in education abroad more specifically.

Questions about who studies abroad and who is excluded led to two different trends: attention to curriculum integration and portfolio diversification. At the same time, an effort would take place at the federal level to expand funding for education abroad, comprehensive internationalization would begin to emerge as an alternative to disparate international education activities, and the nascent assessment movement in U.S. higher education would begin to envelop education abroad. Programming would expand to include more niche options, and intercultural learning would emerge as the dominant desired outcome of U.S. education abroad, as sessions on intercultural learning proliferated at conferences, and articles and books were published on the topic. When the U.S. Congress failed to fund the Senator Paul Simon Study Abroad Foundation Act of 2007 (H.R. 1469 and S. 991), legislation intended to increase study abroad participation to one million undergraduates by 2016–2017, IIE stepped in with Generation Study Abroad in 2014. In 2011–2012, the baseline year for the initiative, 283,332 students enrolled in U.S. undergraduate colleges and universities would study abroad, representing less than 10% of the total U.S. undergraduate population (IIE, n.d.). At this pace of growth, achieving 1 million abroad within two years was unrealistic without concerted action. IIE set a more modest goal of 600,000 by the end of the decade (IIE, n.d.) and called on institutions and organizations to set and report annually on their goals for growth and diversification of the education abroad population. Generation Study Abroad argues that international experience is necessary for career development in today's workplace, has produced reports to demonstrate the link, and suggests that alternatives to credit-bearing experiences can increase access by reducing cost. This raises questions for campuses about risk management, quality, and connections to the educational continuum.

Expanding Rationales for Education Abroad

As this historical overview suggests, education abroad programming has grown and evolved over the years and, not surprisingly, so too have the broader rationales for why institutions are investing in such initiatives (Ogden, 2017a). Whether the popularity of education abroad programming is being driven by changing student interests and demands, or whether institutional leadership and increasing faculty engagement are guiding the direction and scope of programming, the fundamental rationale for education abroad programming has expanded over time. Although much attention has focused on the increasing number of participants and increasingly on participant demographics, there has also been a consistent discussion of why and for what purpose education abroad programming is being leveraged. There are now arguably four broad rationales driving education abroad programming in the United States today:

1. Language acquisition and cultural knowledge
2. Intercultural competency development
3. Discipline-specific learning
4. Community-based learning

For decades, institutions leveraged education abroad programming to enhance student learning in the areas of *language acquisition* and *cultural knowledge*. Developing proficiency in a foreign language was once a major consideration for students in choosing to study abroad (Kinginger, 2009). This is less often the case today. Indeed, the majority of established education abroad programs no longer impose a language prerequisite. While foreign language learning remains a central and viable rationale for developing and promoting education abroad, it is no longer the leading rationale for doing so. In fact, foreign language majors now represent fewer than 7% of U.S. education abroad students (Farrugia & Bhandari, 2017).

Developing *intercultural competency* has also been a long-held and widely regarded rationale driving education abroad. With the development of the Intercultural Development Inventory and other measures of intercultural competence, much attention and effort of late has been given to assessing the extent to which education abroad participation, or some programming elements therein, leads to measurable gains in this area (Savicki, 2008). Related outcomes measures focus on the development of global citizenship, intercultural sensitivity, global competence and knowledge, and so on. The overall assumption is that education abroad programming can be strategically leveraged to support the development of global-ready graduates who are able to work effectively in international and intercultural settings. However, it is also noted that these kinds of complex learning outcomes may not result from education abroad participation alone, but instead may require multiple, interlinked learning opportunities (Twombly, Salisbury, Tumanut, & Klute, 2012).

As education program participation has increased over the years, particularly in short-term programming (less than eight weeks), the rationales for education abroad have expanded to include an emphasis on *discipline-specific learning*. Innovative models for faculty-directed programming have allowed more faculty members to design education abroad programs with the primary purpose of engaging their students in the study of their disciplines in a broader international context. It is one thing to study art history in a U.S. classroom, for example, but quite another to see the artwork firsthand and to interact with members of the communities that produced it. An increasing number of faculty members recognize the importance of graduating students who understand the international dimensions of their chosen disciplines and the need to establish and nurture global networks to support future careers. Faculty-directed education abroad programs have provided a growing number of faculty members with an ideal means through which they can jump-start discipline-specific international learning among their students, which in turn has arguably spurred greater momentum with curriculum integration efforts throughout higher education.

In much the same way, short-term education abroad programs have presented a means through which to involve students in other forms of *community-based learning*, such as international internships, global service-learning, and undergraduate research. Also emerging are programs that engage students in teaching opportunities, global health, and international entrepreneurship. Campus units that may have once been removed from education abroad programming, such as career centers, community engagement/service-learning centers, and undergraduate research offices, are increasingly active partners in promoting the broad value of education abroad. They are also helping to ensure that education abroad provides students with an array of opportunities to develop career readiness skills and civic engagement skills and to establish international research networks.

In short, the rationales for education abroad programming have expanded over the years from long-held loyalties to semester-length and full-year programs designed primarily for language acquisition, country-specific knowledge, and intercultural competency development to include short-term programs driven by expanded rationales such as discipline-specific learning and community-based learning. All four remain viable and important even though their popularity may vary across institutions and demographic populations and be influenced by the pervasive drive to link undergraduate education to career development and professional readiness. What is certain, however, is that the rationale for education abroad, whatever the perspective, is continually being reframed by the ever-shifting drivers or forces that shape higher education.

Drivers Shaping Education Abroad

When considering the expanding rationales for education abroad, it is important to also examine the primary drivers or those key influencers that have determined the direction and scope of education abroad. Such drivers have generally been presented in four broad areas: *political, economic, cultural/social,* and *academic* (Altbach & Knight, 2006; de Wit, 2008; Knight, 2008). Considered together, these drivers provide a useful framework for further understanding the general dynamics of international higher education and specifically how education abroad programming in the United States has been shaped over time and what major issues today may be influencing future directions of tomorrow.

Political

Political drivers generally relate to issues of foreign policy, national security, peace and mutual understanding, and so on (Altbach & Knight, 2006; de Wit, 2008; Knight, 2008). International competition, for example, has long been an important factor in the U.S. government's rationale for promoting international education (de Wit & Rumbley, 2008). As mentioned earlier, the educational and foreign policy crisis sparked by the Soviet launch of the Sputnik satellite led to the NDEA of 1958 and the establishment of Title VI programming, which has been used to promote language study and encourage U.S. students to pursue study and research abroad in areas deemed strategically important to national interest. The federal government has since continued to prioritize international education initiatives that promise to develop national capacity with respect to understanding foreign cultures, strengthening U.S. economic competitiveness, and enhancing international cooperation and security. Other major federal initiatives in recent years have included, for example, the development of the 2006 National Security Language Initiative aimed to expand the number of students studying critical needs languages, the 2010 launch of the 100,000 Strong Initiative to dramatically increase the number of U.S. students studying in China, and the 2012 Obama-Singh 21st Century Knowledge Initiative to further strengthen partnerships between American and Indian institutions of higher education.

International educators have long echoed this political driver in federal advocacy efforts, arguing that education abroad programming in particular supports a broad public good with respect to national security, economic competitiveness, and cultural understanding. In fact, the ill-fated Senator Paul Simon Study Abroad Act (S. 991 & H.R. 1469), first introduced in

2007, came out of the Commission on the Abraham Lincoln Study Abroad Fellowship Program, which was in response to the influential 2003 NAFSA call to action *Securing America's Future: Global Education for a Global Age* (NAFSA, 2003). Consistent throughout these advocacy efforts has been the fourfold promise to leverage international education to, first, significantly enhance the global competitiveness and international knowledge base of the United States; second, enhance foreign policy capacity by expanding the pool of individuals with foreign language skills and cultural knowledge; third, ensure that an increasing number of students study in destinations such as China and the Middle East; and, fourth, create greater cultural understanding.

The current political environment in the United States suggests that this long-standing political driver may now be shifting away from accepting international education as a public good in support of national interests to one that presupposes international education as a private good for the sole benefit of those individuals who participate. For example, recent federal budget proposals have called for substantial funding cuts to the U.S. Department of State, suggesting a potentially diminished value of cultural-exchange programming via the Bureau of Educational and Cultural Affairs and student scholarship programs, such as the Gilman and Boren Scholarships. If indeed the federal budget is any indication of a substantial change in national priorities, and thereby a shift from viewing international education as a public good to a private one, then the political driver shaping education abroad may necessitate a dramatic shift in how international educators advocate for and promote the value of education abroad.

Economic

Economic drivers generally relate to issues of economic growth and competitiveness, national education demands, the labor market and workforce development, and so on (Altbach & Knight, 2006; de Wit, 2008; Knight, 2008). Within the context of U.S. higher education, economic drivers have focused primarily on the impact made by international students on the U.S. economy, especially as competition among countries for international students has increased. According to NAFSA (2017), the 1,043,839 international students studying at U.S. colleges and universities contributed $36.9 billion and supported more than 400,000 jobs to the U.S. economy during the 2015–2016 academic year, thereby demonstrating that higher education is a major export tied to U.S. economic growth worthy of further investment. International educators often rely on this claim, stating frequently that international education is vital to strengthening economies and societies both in the United States and around the world. This perspective helped lead to the passage of the American Competitiveness in the 21st Century Act during the Clinton Administration in 2000.

The importance of educating U.S. students to work effectively in the global economy has also been leveraged as an economic driver. Perhaps one of the more recent and compelling government-sponsored initiatives concerning the internationalization of U.S. higher education is the aforementioned Senator Paul Simon Study Abroad Act. Although never authorized, the Simon Act sought to significantly enhance the global competitiveness and international knowledge base of the United States by dramatically increasing the number and diversity of students studying abroad. It was argued that investing in education abroad significantly expands and diversifies the talent pool of individuals available for recruitment by U.S. foreign affairs agencies, legislative branch agencies, and nongovernmental organizations involved in foreign affairs activities.

In recent years, however, the national economic drivers for education abroad are being overshadowed by the growing undercurrent within U.S. higher education that appears to prioritize the notion that one pursues higher education primarily for the purposes of career readiness and employability. Because of this, the value of education abroad is in turn being increasingly scrutinized by students (and their parents) on terms of its value in regard to enhancing long-term career prospects. Consequently, international educators have begun to shift attention to investigating the relationship between education abroad participation and career readiness (Farrugia & Sanger, 2017; Potts, 2015; Tillman, 2014). Promotion and outreach strategies for education abroad have already begun to move away from language that emphasizes travel to expanded marketing strategies that suggest that education abroad can be effectively leveraged to realize long-term career goals and prosperity. For example, this perspective very explicitly underscores the rationale behind IIE's Generation Study Abroad initiative, launched in 2014, to double and diversify the number of U.S. students studying abroad (IIE, 2018).

Cultural/Social

The next driver relates to cultural and social considerations that have shaped education abroad programming (Altbach & Knight, 2006; de Wit, 2008; Knight, 2008). Cultural considerations have generally focused on the role that higher education can play in furthering students' intercultural understanding and competency development. In recent years, however, the concept of global citizenship has emerged in much of the language that used to prioritize the internationalization of higher education. In its 2017 edition of *Mapping Internationalization on U.S. Campuses*, the American Council on Education reported that approximately half (49%) of U.S. institutions now specifically refer to internationalization or related activities in their mission statements (Helms & Brajkovic, 2017). Global citizenship features prominently in much of this language. Although global citizenship remains a highly contested concept that scholars continue to discuss and debate from a variety of theoretical and philosophical perspectives, many institutions state that graduating global citizens has become central to their missions and that education abroad programming is a key methodology for achieving this outcome (Doerr, 2013; Hartman & Kiely, 2014; Morais & Ogden, 2010). Consequently, there has been considerable attention to assessing and documenting the extent to which students make measurable gains in global citizenship through education abroad participation (Deardorff & Ararasatnam-Smith, 2017; Lewin, 2009). In fact, a number of instruments have been developed in recent years in an attempt to assess global learning and citizenship, including the Global Perspective Inventory (Braskamp, Braskamp, & Merrill, 2009), the Global Citizenship Scale (Morais & Ogden, 2010), and the Global Competence Aptitude Assessment (Hunter, White, & Godbey, 2006).

Social considerations focus on the extent to which institutions, and thereby their faculty and students, develop sustainable networks, partnerships, and activities with communities at local, national, regional, and international levels. As noted earlier, combining international education and community-based programming has long been an interest of U.S. students (Hoffa, 2007; Ogden & Hartman, 2019). According to the National Survey of Student Engagement (2008), for example, 52% of all incoming U.S. college and university freshmen today indicate an interest in community-based learning. Not surprisingly, more institutions today are responding to this increasing interest by using community-based learning approaches, both domestically and abroad, as a means to engage students in service and support their growth as critical and conscious citizens, which include credit-bearing, education abroad programs that feature some component of deliberate community partnership or engagement. Additional approaches have included global service-learning, international internships, and undergraduate research. Many of these institutions are also now seeking the Carnegie Community Engagement classification as a way to have their commitment recognized (Driscoll, 2006). So popular has this classification been that the Carnegie Foundation is now exploring a structure and process for an international classification.

Related to cultural/social considerations, a major driver shaping education abroad programming has unquestionably been the increased emphasis on health, safety, security, and risk management. In recent years, this has been one of the more significant, and likely most challenging, drivers shaping education abroad programming, particularly in regard to ensuring student safety and security, minimizing institutional risk exposure, and complying with federal reporting requirements (Rhodes, 2014). In response to this heightened attention to global health, safety and security, education abroad practitioners have had to take extraordinary measures to manage potential risk. To list only a few, this has included developing crisis management protocols for handling emergencies, including natural and political disasters; implementing strict protocols for health insurance and evacuation coverage; executing comprehensive evaluation and review measures for programming; and developing enhanced systems for tracking student enrollment. While education abroad programming continues to be shaped by cultural/social drivers, a primary focus today is on allowing this to continue but within a broad safety net of educating students to minimize and manage risk, and assurances that the health, safety, security, and risk management protocols are in place.

Academic

Academic drivers generally relate to the extent to which institutions prioritize the international dimensions of their teaching, research, and service (Altbach & Knight, 2006; de Wit, 2008; Knight, 2008). Within the United States, this has most commonly been gauged by the extent to which institutions recruit international students to their campuses and support U.S. students participating in education abroad. Related aspects of comprehensive internationalization have also been influential factors, namely faculty research and engagement, international collaborations, internationalization of the curriculum, and so on. Perhaps most central to academic drivers inasmuch as they impact education abroad programming are increasingly important issues relating to (a) international rankings, (b) student success, and (c) curriculum integration.

While world university rankings have existed for some decades, there has been a huge increase in the attention paid to rankings in recent years. Numerous world university rankings now exist, but the most notable are *Times Higher Education, QS World University Rankings,* and *Academic Ranking of World Universities* by Shanghai Jiao Tong University. U.S. institutions have come to value and even trumpet their standings in international rankings and comparisons. In addition to leveraging rankings to appeal to prospective international students and scholars, U.S. institutions are capitalizing on their "brand-name recognition" to establish international partnerships and linkages with peer institutions, which generally lead to memoranda of understanding around research collaboration, technology transfer, and student and faculty exchange. Because world university rankings, and increasingly domestic rankings, assess various indicators of comprehensive internationalization, education abroad participation rates have an increasingly important role to play.

In recent years, there has been an increased focus within U.S. higher education on retention and university degree completion rates, commonly referred to as *student success*. Often cited as the motivation for this increased focus is the fact that in 2012 the United States ranked 17 out of 26 countries in degree attainment for undergraduate students (Organisation for Economic Co-operation and Development [OECD], 2014), which is particularly troubling when compared to the fact that the United States was ranked second in 1995 (Haupt, Ogden, & Rubin, 2018). Given the implications of student success indicators on institutional rankings, public funding, accreditation standards, and public perception, higher education leaders are exploring new strategies to bolster degree completion rates (Kelly & Schneider, 2012). Thus, attention has begun to turn to education abroad, a noted high-impact educational practice (Kuh, 2008), and the extent to which participation can positively affect graduation rates (Kilgo, Ezell Sheets, & Pascarella, 2015). Counter to common perception, preliminary evidence suggests that education abroad participation does not slow time to degree, rather it increases the odds of graduating in four, five, and six years (Hamir, 2011; O'Rear, Sutton, & Rubin, 2012; Xu, de Silva, Neufeldt, & Dane, 2013). Moreover, racial minorities who participate in education abroad appear to have significantly higher four-, five-, and six-year graduation rates than racial minorities who do not participate (Malmgren & Galvin, 2008; Rubin, Sutton, Sutton & Rubin, 2010; O'Rear, Rhodes, & Raby, 2014). This is especially important because racial minorities have traditionally been at risk for higher rates of attrition.

In much the same way education abroad is leveraged to enhance international rankings and graduation rates, education abroad programming, through curriculum integration initiatives, is being used as a means to further internationalize the undergraduate curriculum. Although students often come to education abroad with their sights set on where they want to go, likening it more to international travel than an investment in their education, curriculum integration initiatives reorient the focus to what one can learn and achieve through international study. Efforts to internationalize the curriculum can take many forms, such as the utilization of new technologies, expansion of instructional pedagogies, and comprehensive curricula review. The central purpose of curriculum integration efforts, however, has been to complement the curriculum with discipline-specific education abroad programming that enables students to pursue a more international orientation to their studies in ways different from or complementary to what they can do on their home campuses. In other words, the more international programming is embedded into the curriculum, in alignment with accreditation standards and expectations, the more the curriculum at the home institution drives the direction and flow of education abroad participation.

Future Pathways in Education Abroad

More and more colleges and universities are integrating education abroad programming into the undergraduate curriculum and setting it as an expectation for more students. It is not surprising, then, to see annual incremental increases in participation rates, although the rate of increase has slowed somewhat in recent years. As trends continue to emerge and as the major rationales for education abroad expand and evolve, those students who may have at one time not pursued international opportunities may be better situated today to avail themselves of education abroad programming that better aligns with their personal, educational, and career interests. Moreover, the primary political, economic, cultural and social, and academic drivers for education abroad will continue to shape the directions for where programming and practice are headed. Looking to the future, the education abroad profession will not be without certain challenges as well as its own set of unique opportunities. The following are likely five of the more critical issues ahead for the future of U.S. education abroad.

Articulating the Value

As the United States seems to be moving in a direction of creating more boundaries and breaking down long-standing alliances, it may become more challenging to talk with students about why they should study abroad (Ogden, 2017a). It may become harder to continue prioritizing the importance of engaging openly and respectfully with other cultures and people. Learning foreign languages and developing intercultural competence will likely remain important, but only insofar as doing so enhances prospects for employability. Rather, articulating the value of education abroad may be more aptly couched in terms of investing in one's education and career readiness. Related to this is the need for education abroad professionals to utilize language that is consistent with higher education. If indeed the purpose of education abroad is about academic learning, for example, then language that prioritizes international travel and tourism should be avoided. And just as students do not "sign up" for college, they should not be signing up for education abroad. Instead, they apply, are admitted, and are enrolled. Phrases like "Where do you want to go?" and "Bring a friend" imply that education abroad is about travel and that academic fit does not matter. Faculty members do not "lead" a trip, but rather "direct" a program.

Shifting Emphasis

Alas, some students still come to education abroad with their sights set on where they want to go, likening it more to international travel than as an investment in their education. While students may be swayed by the allure of visiting specific locations or by other personal curiosities, it is important that education abroad professionals and other key stakeholders maintain an emphasis on education and learning and supporting students to leverage education abroad strategically for targeted personal, educational, and career goals. As explained earlier, curriculum integration initiatives have fortunately advanced in recent years (Brewer & Cunningham, 2009; Woodruff & Henry, 2012). A major component of curriculum integration has been to develop resources to assist students in program selection and faculty and staff with advising and guiding students interested in pursuing education abroad within their disciplines. An intended outcome is for education abroad programming to be viewed primarily as an academic endeavor that is integral to undergraduate education. Thereby, the focus shifts away from language that emphasizes destinations, trips, and travel to the more appropriate language of discipline-specific education. The value of education abroad in the future will likely be tied to the extent to which programming is embedded meaningfully and strategically into the undergraduate curriculum.

Diversification

As previously mentioned, the contemporary education abroad participant remains White; female; majoring in the humanities, social sciences, or business; and studying in Europe (Farrugia & Bhandari, 2017). Yet, as the U.S. population becomes increasingly diverse, there has been a dramatic shift in the makeup of campus populations and in terms of not only race, ethnicity, and gender but also religion, sexual orientation, socioeconomic status, age, and so on. In order to further integrate international education programming into the mainstream American undergraduate experience, it will be increasingly important that professionals identify and remove barriers and provide sustained support to a greater diversity of students. This may require looking differently at the use of financial aid and scholarships (Salisbury, Umbach, Paulsen, & Pascarella, 2009), developing a more responsive portfolio of program offerings, and strengthening networks throughout our campuses to encourage the participation of and support for the unique needs of different student populations. Unless the current enrollment trends are reversed, certain student populations in U.S. higher education may risk falling farther behind in developing the essential knowledge and skills for today's global society, and education abroad programming, as we know it, will linger on the educational periphery as a private good for select populations.

Utilization of Technology

The use of technology is revolutionizing higher education in the United States and directly impacting the nature of international student mobility. Social networking sites and communication media such as Facebook, Twitter, YouTube, Instagram, and Skype, to name just a few, have begun to change how education abroad programming is marketed and promoted and how we communicate with students and other key stakeholders. Moreover, the emergence of new forms of distance learning, massive online open courses, and virtual classrooms has introduced new instructional technologies that will likely alter how students learn and engage in international education. New database and programming software is similarly advancing enrollment management processes, scholarship management, and financial mechanisms. Thus, as social networks, instructional technologies, and programming software evolve, so too must the education abroad profession. It is increasingly important that education abroad professionals and other key stakeholders monitor the impact of new technologies and, as appropriate, leverage new approaches to advance education abroad programming and student learning.

Use of Research

It is no longer acceptable to make assertions of the value and benefit of education abroad without offering specific evidence to support such claims. It will be ever more important in the years ahead that education abroad professionals be grounded in research, evidence, and assessment as scholar-practitioners of international education (Streitwieser & Ogden, 2016). Through advanced graduate education and training, education abroad professionals must be comfortable with accessing, understanding, and applying existing research to inform best practices and shape new directions in education abroad programming and practice. It will be similarly important to be adept with basic statistics and with leveraging data and empirical evidence when advocating for institutional resources and support from senior institutional leadership. While education abroad professionals may not necessarily need to maintain active research agendas, it will, however, be increasingly important to challenge untested claims and casual assumptions and remain open to engaging in opportunities to partner with international education scholars to advance research that aims to provide a clearer understanding of the totality of the education abroad experience.

Conclusion

As education abroad programming continues to develop and secure a prominent position within the undergraduate curriculum, its potential for enhancing the educational continuum has become undeniable. Whereas once education abroad participation was considered an exceptional experience for only the most privileged students, many in U.S. higher education have over time come to regard education abroad programming as a high-impact educational practice that has value and educative potential for all students. This chapter has sought to provide a foundational overview of the development of U.S. education abroad, highlighting important historical milestones, the changing rationales and key drivers that have shaped its direction and scope, and some potential issues and challenges that may lie ahead. Other chapters in this volume will build on this brief foundation to focus, often critically, on important and specific aspects of contemporary education abroad programming and practice with the intention of both challenging and demonstrating the value of further leveraging education abroad programming to support the learning and development of all students, today and tomorrow.

References

Altbach, P., & Knight, J. (2006). The internationalization of higher education: Motivations and realities. *In NEA almanac of higher education* (pp. 27–36). Washington, DC: National Education Association.

Boyer, E. L. (1990). *Scholarship reconsidered: Priorities of the professoriate*. Princeton, NJ: Carnegie Foundation for the Advancement of Teaching.

Braskamp, L., Braskamp, D. C., & Merrill, K. C. (2009). Assessing progress in global learning and development of students with education abroad experiences. *Frontiers: The Interdisciplinary Journal of Study Abroad, 18*, 101–118.

Brewer, E., & Cunningham, K. (Eds.). (2009). *Integrating study abroad into the curriculum: Theory and practice across the disciplines*. Sterling, VA: Stylus.

Carlson, J. S., Burn, B. B., Useem, J., & Yacchimowicz, D. (1990). *Study abroad: The experience of American undergraduates*. Westport, CT: Greenwood Press.

Chieffo, L., & Spaeth, K. (Eds.). (2017). *The guide to successful short-term programs abroad* (3rd ed.). Washington, DC: NAFSA: Association of International Educators.

Council on International Educational Exchange (CIEE). (n.d.). *History. What we stand for.* Available from https://www.ciee.org/about/what-we-stand-for/history

Deardorff, D. K., & Ararasatnam-Smith, L. (2017). *Intercultural competence in international higher education: International approaches, assessment, application.* New York, NY: Taylor & Francis.

de Wit, H. (2008). The internationalization of higher education in a global context. In H. de Wit, P. Agarwal, M. Elmady Said, M. T. Sehoole, & M. Sirozi (Eds.), *The dynamics of international student circulation in a global context* (pp. 1–14). Rotterdam, The Netherlands: Sense Press.

de Wit, H., & Rumbley, L. (2008). The role of American Higher education in international student circulation. In H. de Wit, P. Agarwal, M. Elmady Said, M. T. Sehoole, & M. Sirozi (Eds.), *The dynamics of international student circulation in a global context* (pp. 199–231). Rotterdam, The Netherlands: Sense Press.

Doerr, N. (2013). Do 'global citizens' need the parochial cultural others? Discourse of immersion in study abroad and learning-by-doing. *Compare: A Journal of Comparative and International Education, 43*(2), 224–243.

Driscoll, A. (2006). *The benchmarking potential of the new Carnegie Classification: Community engagement.* Available from https://compact.org/resource-posts/the-benchmarking-potential-of-the-new-carnegie-classification-community-engagement/

Farrugia, C. A., & Bhandari, R. (2017). *Open Doors 2017 report on international educational exchange.* New York, NY: Institute of International Education.

Farrugia, C. A., & Sanger, J. (2017). *Gaining an employment edge: The impact of study abroad on 21st century skills and career prospects in the United States.* Institute of International Education. Available from https://www.iie.org/employability

The Forum on Education Abroad. (n.d.). *Forum history.* https://forumea.org/about-us/mission/history/

Frontiers. (n.d.). *About.* Available from https://frontiersjournal.org/about/

Hamir, H. B. (2011). *Go abroad and graduate on-time: Study abroad participation, degree completion, and time-to-degree* (doctoral Dissertation). University of Nebraska–Lincoln. Available from http://world.utexas.edu/forms/abroad/barclay-dissertation.pdf

Hartman, E., & Kiely, R. (2013). A critical global citizenship. In P. M. Green & M. Johnson (Eds.), *Crossing boundaries: Tension and transformation in international service-learning.* Sterling, VA: Stylus.

Haupt, J., Ogden, A., & Rubin, D. (2018). Toward a common research model: Leveraging education abroad participation to enhance college graduation rates. *Journal of Studies in International Education, 22*(2), 91–107.

Helms, R., & Brajkovic, L. (2017). *Mapping internationalization on U.S. campuses, 2017 Edition.* American Council on Education. Available from http://www.acenet.edu/news-room/Documents/Mapping-Internationalization-2017.pdf

Hoffa, W. (2007). *A history of U.S. study abroad: Beginnings to 1965.* Carlisle, PA: The Forum on Education Abroad.

Hudzik, J. K. (2016). Internationalization practitioners and scholarship: Dichotomies and crosswalks. In B. Streitwieser & A. C. Ogden (Eds.), *International higher education's scholar-practitioners: Bridging research and practice* (pp. 39–54). Oxford, UK: Symposium.

Hunter, B., White, G., & Godbey, G. (2006). What does it mean to be globally competent? *Journal of Studies in International Education, 10*(3), 267–285.

Institute of International Education (IIE). (n.d.). *Baseline. IIE Generation Abroad.* Available from https://www.iie.org/en/Programs/Generation-Study-Abroad/About/Our-Baseline

Institute for International Education (IIE). (2018). *Research & insights: Project atlas.* Available from https://www.iie.org/Research-and-Insights/Project-Atlas

Kelly, A. P., & Schneider, M. (2012). *Getting to graduation: The completion agenda in higher education.* Baltimore, MD: Johns Hopkins University Press.

Kilgo, C., Ezell Sheets, J. & Pascarella, E. (2015). The link between high-impact practices and student learning: Some longitudinal evidence. *Higher Education, 69*, 509–525.

Kinginger, C. (2009). *Language learning and study abroad: A critical reading of research.* New York, NY: Palgrave Macmillan.

Knight, J. (2008). Internationalization: Key concepts and elements. In M. Graebel, L. Purser, B. Wächter, & L. Wilson (Eds.), *Internationalisation of European higher education* (A 1.1, pp. 1–21). Brussels, Belgium: European University Association and Academic Cooperation Association.

Kuh, G.D. (2008). *High-impact educational practices: What they are, who has access to them, and why they matter.* Washington, DC: Association of American Colleges & Universities.

La Brack, B. (2016). The interplay and co-evolution of theory and practice in preparing students for international education experiences: A retrospective analysis. In B. Streitwieser & A. C. Ogden (Eds.), *International higher education's scholar-practitioners: Bridging research and practice* (pp. 169–181). Oxford, UK: Symposium.

Lewin, R. (Ed.). (2009). *The handbook of practice and research in study abroad: Higher education and the quest for global citizenship.* New York, NY: Routledge.

Malmgren, J., & Galvin, J. (2008). Effects of study abroad participation on student graduation rates: A study of three incoming freshmen cohorts at the University of Minnesota, Twin Cities. *NACADA Journal, 28*(1), 29–42.

Morais, D., & Ogden, A. (2010). Initial development and validation of the Global Citizenship Scale. *Journal of Studies in International Education, 20*(10), 1–22.

NAFSA: Association of International Educators. (n.d.). *The history of NAFSA: Association of International Educators.* Available from http://www.nafsa.org/About_Us/About_NAFSA/History/The_History_of_NAFSA__Association_of_International_Educators/

NAFSA: Association of International Educators. (2003). *Securing America's future: Global education for a global age: Report of the Strategic Task Force on Education*

Abroad. Available from http://www.nafsa.org/uploadedFiles/NAFSA_Home/Resource_Library_Assets/Public_Policy/securing_america_s_future.pdf

NAFSA: Association of International Educators. (2017). *NAFSA international student economic value tool.* Available from http://www.nafsa.org/Policy_and_Advocacy/Policy_Resources/Policy_Trends_and_Data/NAFSA_International_Student_Economic_Value_Tool/

National Center for Education Statistics (NCES). (n.d.-a). *Total fall enrollment in degree-granting postsecondary institutions, by attendance status, sex of student, and control of institution: Selected years, 1947 through 2026.* Available from https://nces.ed.gov/programs/digest/d16/tables/dt16_303.10.asp

National Center for Education Statistics (NCES). (n.d.-b). *Total fall enrollment in degree-granting postsecondary institutions, by level of enrollment, sex, attendance status, and race/ethnicity of student: Selected years, 1976 through 2015.* Available from https://nces.ed.gov/programs/digest/d16/tables/dt16_306.10.asp

National Survey of Student Engagement (NSSE). (2008). *Experiences that matter: Enhancing student learning and success.* Bloomington: Indiana University Center for Postsecondary Research. Available from http://nsse.indiana.edu/NSSE_2007_Annual_Report/index.cfm

Ogden, A. (2017a, September/October). The value proposition of education abroad. *International Educator.* Available from https://www.nafsa.org/ProfessionalResources/Publications/International_Educator/International_Educator_September_October_2017/

Ogden, A. (2017b). What we know and need to know about short-term, education abroad: A concise review of the literature. In L. Chieffo & C. Spaeth (Eds.), *NAFSA's guide to successful short-term programs abroad* (3rd ed. pp. 7–30). Washington DC: NAFSA: Association of International Educators.

Ogden, A., & Hartman, E. (2019). To hell and back with good intentions: Global service learning in the shadow of Ivan Illich. In A. Paczynska & S. Hirsch (Eds.), *Conflict zone, comfort zone: Ethics, pedagogy, and effecting change in field-based courses* (pp. 221–241). Athens, OH: Ohio University Press.

Ogden, A., Soneson, H., & Weting, P. (2010). The diversification of geographic locations. In B. Hoffa & S. DePaul (Eds.), *A history of U.S. study abroad: 1965 to the present.* Carlisle, PA: The Forum on Education Abroad.

Organisation for Economic Co-operation and Development (OEDC). (2014). *Education at a glance 2014: OECD indicators.* Available from http://www.oecd.org/edu/Education-at-a-Glance-2014.pdf

O'Rear, I., Sutton, R. L., & Rubin, D. L. (2012). *The effect of study abroad on college completion in a state university system.* Available from http://glossari.uga.edu/wpcontent/uploads/downloads/2012/01/GLOSSARI-Grad-Rate-Logistic-Regressions-040111.pdf

Peterson, C., Engle, L., Kenney, L., Kreutzer, K., Nolting, W., & Ogden, A. (2007). *Education abroad glossary.* Carlisle, PA: The Forum on Education Abroad.

Potts, D. (2015, April 6). Understanding the early career benefits of learning abroad programs. *Journal of Studies in International Education, 19*(5), 441–459.

Rhodes, G. (2014). Risk management planning for education abroad: Issues, challenges, and resources. In M. Hernandez, M. Wiedenhoeft, & D. Wick (Eds.), *NAFSA's guide to education abroad for advisers and administrators* (4th ed., pp. 159–174). Washington, DC: NAFSA: Association of International Educators.

Rubin, D., Sutton, R. C., O'Rear, I., Rhodes, G., & Raby R. L. (2014, Fall). Opening the doors of education abroad to enhance academic success for lower achieving students. *IEE Networker* (pp. 38–41). Available from http://www.nxtbook.com/naylor/IIEB/IIEB0214/index.php?startid=38

Salisbury, M. H., Umbach, P. D., Paulsen, M. B., & Pascarella, E. T. (2009). Going global: Understanding the choice process of the intent to study abroad. *Research in Higher Education, 50*(2), 119–143.

Savicki, V. (Ed.). (2008). *Intercultural competence and transformation: Theory, research, and application in international education.* Sterling, VA: Stylus.

Sideli, K. (2010). The professionalization of the field of education abroad. In W. W. Hoffa & S. C. DePaul (Eds.), *A history of U.S. study abroad: 1965–present* (pp. 369–416). A special publication of *Frontiers: The Interdisciplinary Journal of Study Abroad.*

Stallman, E., Woodruff, G. A., Kasravi, J., & Comp, D. (2010). The diversification of the student profile. In W. W. Hoffa & S. C. DePaul (Eds.), *A history of U.S. study abroad: 1965–present* (pp. 115–160). A special publication of *Frontiers: The Interdisciplinary Journal of Study Abroad.*

Streitwieser, B., & Ogden, A. (Eds.). (2016). *International education's scholar-practitioners: Bridging reflection and practice.* Oxford, UK: Symposium.

Sutton, R. C., & Rubin, D. L. (2010, May). *Documenting the academic impact of study abroad: Final report of the GLOSSARI project.* Paper presented at the annual conference of NAFSA: Association of International Educators, Kansas City, MO.

Tillman, M. (2014). *Supporting education abroad & student career development.* Stamford, CT: American Institute for Foreign Study Publications. Available from http://www.aifsabroad.com/advisors/pdf/Tillman_Best_Practices.pdf

Twombly, S., Salisbury, M., Tumanut, S., & Klute, P. (2012). Study abroad in a new global century: Renewing the promise, refining the purpose. *ASHE Higher Education Report, 38*(4), 1–152. Hoboken, NJ: Wiley.

United Nations Educational, Scientific and Cultural Organization (UNESCO). (2017). Education. Outbound internationally mobile students by host region. Available from http://data.uis.unesco.org/

U.S. House of Representatives. (n.d.). *National Defense Education Act.* Available from http://history.house.gov/HouseRecord/Detail/15032436195

Woodruff, G., & Henry, H. (2012). *Curriculum integration of education abroad.* Washington, DC: NAFSA: Association of International Educators. Available from http://www.nafsa.org/epubs

Xu, M., de Silva, C. R., Neufeldt, E., & Dane, J. (2013). The impact of study abroad on academic success: An analysis of first-time students entering Old Dominion University, Virginia, 2000–2004. *Frontiers: The Interdisciplinary Journal of Study Abroad, 23*, 90–103.

PART ONE

CRITICAL PERSPECTIVES ON EDUCATION ABROAD AND ITS INTEGRATION INTO UNDERGRADUATE EDUCATION

2

EDUCATION ABROAD AS A HIGH-IMPACT PRACTICE

Linking Research and Practice to the Educational Continuum

John P. Haupt and Anthony C. Ogden

For nearly a decade, education abroad (EA) has been promoted as a high-impact practice (HIP) with the potential to promote deep and transformative learning in students (Kuh, 2008; Kuh, O'Donnell, & Reed, 2013). Supporting these claims is compelling research that has demonstrated a positive impact of EA participation on student learning and academic success (O'Rear, Sutton, & Rubin, 2012; Vande Berg, Connor-Linton, Paige, 2009; Williams, 2005). However, this research has generally examined EA participation in isolation of other experiences students have with HIPs. Examining EA in isolation of other HIPs deviates from the initial intent with which HIPs were first introduced by the Association of American Colleges & Universities (AAC&U) in 2007. In fact, AAC&U envisioned students participating in multiple HIPs throughout their collegiate careers to increase the likelihood of student success. Building on AAC&U's conceptualization of HIPs as interconnected experiences that promote student success, this chapter positions EA as a HIP on the educational continuum so as to advance a more complex understanding of the impact EA has on student success and to connect the learning that occurs through EA participation to other learning experiences students have during their collegiate careers. Therefore, this chapter introduces AAC&U's concept of student success and the role that HIPs play in its promotion. It then explains why EA is considered a HIP and provides evidence that supports this assertion. Finally, the chapter introduces a conceptual model that scholars can use to better isolate the impact of EA in order to understand its influence on student learning and development as well as to encourage practitioners to link EA programming with other HIPs as a means to amplify student learning and development.

High-Impact Practices and Student Success

In 2007, AAC&U released a report titled *College Learning for the New Global Century* in which it called for colleges and universities to make a concerted effort to better prepare students for the complex and dynamic challenges of the twenty-first century. AAC&U identified the following essential student learning outcomes: (a) knowledge of human cultures and the physical and natural world, (b) intellectual and practical skills, (c) personal and social responsibility, and (d) integrative learning. AAC&U suggests that students who achieve these outcomes can be characterized as having developed multidisciplinary knowledge and advanced training and skills that will allow them to be personally and socially responsible members of society who possess the ability to solve new and complex problems. These learning outcomes provide a framework to measure colleges' and universities' success in preparing students for life in the twenty-first century. AAC&U proposed that when defining student success, it is necessary to look beyond commonly used measures, such as retention and degree completion, to examine how students' cumulative collegiate experiences prepare them to be productive and responsible members of society.

In addition to declaring the need for reframing student learning outcomes and the notion of student success, AAC&U identified 10 specific HIPs that have the potential to lead to this more reframed view of student success:

1. First-year seminars and experiences
2. Common intellectual experiences
3. Learning communities
4. Writing-intensive courses
5. Collaborative assignments and projects
6. Undergraduate research
7. Diversity or global learning
8. Service-learning or community-based learning
9. Internships
10. Capstone courses and projects

AAC&U contends that when made available to students, these HIPs provide opportunities for intellectual and social engagement throughout students' collegiate careers. Participation in more than one of these HIPs increases the likelihood that the intended learning outcomes are achieved by enhancing and reinforcing learning over an extended period of time.

Shortly after the 2007 AAC&U report, Kuh (2008) elaborated on the relationship among HIPs, student engagement, and student success. Kuh argued that when students participate in "well-done" HIPs, a correlation exists between participation and higher levels of retention and future engagement on campus. Kuh states that a plausible reason for this correlation is due to five distinct features of HIPs. First, HIPs are time-intensive activities that require students to put forth a significant amount of effort to complete what is perceived as a meaningful task. Second, while engaged in HIPs, students are provided with the opportunity to interact meaningfully with faculty and peers over extended periods of time. Third, HIPs provide students with opportunities to engage with others from diverse backgrounds. Fourth, students who participate in HIPs receive feedback in a variety of forms, which allows them to reflect on their experiences. Finally, HIPs allow students to apply what they are learning or have previously learned in a variety of settings, both on and off campus. Thus, a "well-done" HIP will be structured so that students have the chance to meaningfully interact with their peers, faculty, and diverse others while applying learned knowledge in a variety of experiences outside the classroom, and as a result of participation in these experiences, students will be more likely to remain engaged, achieve academic success, and be prepared for ongoing learning and decision-making postgraduation.

Education Abroad as a High-Impact Practice

Given the five HIP features, it is not surprising that both Kuh (2008) and AAC&U (2007) identified EA as a HIP within the category of diversity and global learning. It is easy to imagine how a "well-done" EA program could be structured in a way to possess all five HIP features. Take, for example, a short-term faculty-directed program to Germany during which students take courses in the academic area of supply chain management and they have the opportunity to engage with representatives from international corporations to learn how supply chain management works in international settings. In such a program, students spend extended periods of time with their peers and their faculty members learning discipline-specific content within their major field of study, which students value because they are able to see how what they are learning applies to their future careers. Students are also immediately able to apply what they are learning in real-world contexts, while simultaneously interacting with individuals from cultures different from their own. These interactions in real-world settings provide students with the opportunity to experience differences and reflect on the underlying causes of those differences. It is through a combination of these program features that deep and transformative learning can occur, and students have the chance to acquire the knowledge and skills necessary to effectively engage with the world around them (Brownell & Swaner, 2010; Kuh, 2008; Kuh et al., 2013).

This assertion of EA as a HIP has been widely supported, and researchers have been actively trying to establish a clear relationship between EA participation and student success. Building upon AAC&U's learning outcomes, numerous studies have investigated the relationship between EA participation and personal and social responsibility gains in students. For example, studies have shown that EA participation has positive direct and measurable impact on intercultural competency development and the development of global awareness (Braskamp, Braskamp, & Merrill, 2009; Dwyer, 2004; Engle & Engle, 2004; Mulvaney, 2017; Paige, Fry, Stallman, Josic, & Jon, 2009; Stebleton, Soria, & Cherney, 2013; Vande Berg et al., 2009; Williams, 2005). Others have investigated the extent to which EA alumni pursue community engagement activity, locally and globally (DeGraaf, Slagter, Larsen, & Ditta, 2013; Murphy, Sahakyan, Yong-Yi, & Magnan, 2014; Mulvaney, 2017; Paige et al., 2009). Such studies have indeed shown that EA alumni generally tend to be more locally and globally engaged throughout their lives compared to those who do not study abroad.

In addition to investigating personal and social responsibility gains, others have investigated intellectual and practical skills development in EA participants. Such studies have focused primarily on the development of employability traits in students after studying abroad (European Commission, 2014; Farrugia & Sanger, 2017; Franklin, 2010; Institute for the International Education of Students [IES], 2016; Van Mol, 2017). Researchers have analyzed the impact EA has on the development of skills that employers identify as important in potential hires, such as communication skills, adaptability, problem-solving skills, self-awareness, and teamwork (Farrugia & Sanger, 2017; IES, 2016). The results of self-reported gains from these studies have shown that overall students believed EA participation had a positive impact on skill development (European Commission, 2014; Farrugia & Sanger, 2017; Franklin, 2010; IES, 2016). When a pre- and posttest design measured the direct outcomes of EA on skill development, results showed that statistically significant gains occurred (European Commission, 2014).

Research has also begun to compare the impact of EA with the impact of other HIPs on a variety of AAC&U's learning outcomes. Kilgo, Ezell Sheets, and Pascarella (2015), using data from the Wabash National Study of Liberal Arts Education, analyzed the impact of 10 HIPs on the development of intellectual and practical skills and personal and social responsibility in students. The analysis consisted of outcome measures for critical thinking, moral reasoning, inclination to lifelong learning, intercultural competency, and socially responsible leadership. Results showed participation in undergraduate research and active and collaborative learning were consistently strong predictors of significant, positive gains in almost all outcome measures. Participation in EA, internships, service-learning, and capstone courses showed both positive and negative impacts on the selected outcome measures. EA had a significant, positive impact on both intercultural competency development and socially responsible leadership. However, the analysis showed a nonsignificant negative correlation between EA participation and critical thinking and EA participation and moral reasoning. Lastly, participation in first-year seminars, an academic learning community, and writing-intensive courses had no significant impact on gains in each outcome measure.

Although Kilgo and colleagues (2015) provide EA researchers with greater insight into the impact of EA compared to other HIPs, the study grouped all EA program types and experience types into one. For example, the study did not investigate the difference between a student who studied abroad at an international institution and a student who participated in undergraduate research abroad. In fact, students who participate in undergraduate research abroad are essentially "doubling up," or engaging in more than one HIP simultaneously. The same could be said for students who participate in service-learning abroad, internships abroad, or incorporate their experiences abroad into a capstone. However, students who study abroad at a university in another country may also be engaging in HIPs that fly under the radar. The learning outcomes will need to be teased out postexperience, as, it can be argued, is true of other HIPs. Thus, future research will need to make distinctions between EA programs and experience types in order to fully understand the impact of EA on student learning and development.

Beyond investigating the impact of EA on AAC&U's four learning outcomes, an increasingly active area of inquiry is focused on the relationship between EA participation and persistence toward graduation (Hamir, 2011; Haupt, Ogden, & Rubin, 2018; Malmgren & Galvin, 2008; O'Rear et al., 2012; Raby, Rhodes, & Biscarra, 2013; University Planning, Institutional Research, and Accountability, 2009; Xu, de Silva, Neufeldt, & Dane, 2013). Thus far, results from analyses of bachelor's degree–granting institutions have shown that when comparing EA participants and nonparticipants (a) the percentage of EA participants graduating in four, five, or six years[1] is significantly greater than the percentage of nonparticipants who graduated within these time frames (Hamir, 2011; Malmgren & Galvin, 2008; O'Rear et al., 2012; University Planning, Institutional Research, and Accountability, 2009; Xu et al., 2013); (b) EA participation increases the odds of graduating in four, five, or six years (Hamir, 2011; O'Rear et al., 2012; University Planning, Institutional Research, and Accountability, 2009; Xu et al., 2013); and (c) non-White students who participate in EA have significantly higher four, five, and six-year graduation rates than non-White students who do not participate (Malmgren & Galvin, 2008; O'Rear et al., 2012). Similar results were found in the investigation of the impact of EA participation on community college students (Raby et al., 2013). As noted by AAC&U, measuring student success in terms of retention and degree completion is considered partial at best; however, this area of research is beginning to suggest a clear relationship between EA participation and retention and persistence to graduation.

A Conceptual Model to Better Understand and Isolate the Impact of Education Abroad

Despite the compelling evidence that suggests a positive relationship among EA participation, student learning, and academic success, the existing research has consistent limitations that raise concerns about the validity and generalizability of this research (Twombly, Salisbury, Tumanut, & Klute, 2012). For example, numerous studies draw on single institutions (Hamir, 2011; Mulvaney, 2017; Murphy et al., 2014); there is a reliance on cross-sectional research design instead of a longitudinal design including a pretest, posttest, and delayed posttest (Paige et al., 2009); rarely is there an attempt to control for confounding variables or self-selection bias in participants (DeGraaf et al., 2013; Vande Berg et al., 2009); there is no examination of the differential effects of program type and experience type (i.e., Mulvaney, 2017; Williams, 2005); and there is a limited use of mixed-methods research design (O'Rear et al., 2012; Salisbury, An, & Pascarella, 2013; Williams, 2005).[2] If this area of research is to eventually generate a reliable understanding of the complex relationships among EA participation, student learning, and academic success, researchers may need to adopt existing conceptual frameworks used in other areas of higher education research to understand the effects of collegiate experiences, including HIPs, on student development and success (Astin, 1993; Pascarella & Terenzini, 2005). However, research from Salisbury and colleagues (2013) and Kilgo and colleagues (2015), discussed in the following paragraphs, has demonstrated the applicability of established conceptual models that arguably overcome some of the methodological limitations identified previously.

The conceptual model used by both Salisbury and colleagues (2013) and Kilgo and colleagues (2015) to analyze the impact of EA on student success derives from three decades of college impact research (Pascarella & Terenzini, 2005). This model (Figure 2.1) suggests that when measuring for a correlation between a college experience and student success, it is necessary to use a longitudinal research design that accounts for three other groups of influences on students (Astin, 1993; Kilgo et al., 2015; Pascarella, 1985; Pascarella & Terenzini, 2005; Salisbury et al., 2013). The first is *precollege traits*, which researchers need to account for to control for self-selection bias and for confounding variables that might have a direct influence on the outcome of the analysis. Precollege traits generally include student background characteristics, such as race, gender, socioeconomic status, and SAT and ACT scores, and experiences students bring to college, such as involvement in volunteer activities or sports. The second influence is the *institution type,* which accounts for the differential effects based on the context of the home institution (e.g., liberal arts college versus public institution). The third influence is other *collegiate experiences*. These experiences can include academic major, involvement in a fraternity or sorority, and participation in other HIPs. Such experiences can have a direct impact on student success (Kilgo et al., 2015; Pascarella & Terenzini, 2005).[3]

Salisbury and colleagues (2013) and Kilgo and colleagues (2015) have effectively demonstrated the applicability of this conceptual model, but there arguably remain important limitations. Given the increasing variations in EA programming, it is important to account for differences in program features, experience types, and program types. Such variation may have differential

Figure 2.1. Conceptual model to isolate the impact of EA on student success.

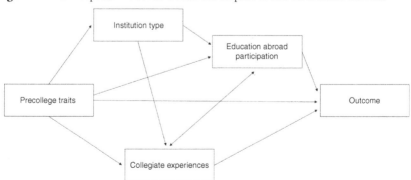

Note. A simplified version of the model presented in Salisbury and colleagues (2013).

effects on student outcomes. For example, some studies have looked at how differences in program length, location, and certain program features, such as living with a host family or in a student residence hall (Dwyer, 2004a; Vande Berg et al., 2009), impact learning outcomes. Few studies have looked at the impact of differential experience types, such as study abroad in comparison with (or in combination with) conducting research abroad, interning abroad, or engaging in service-learning abroad. Moreover, there has been only minimal research that has compared program type, such as the differences in student learning outcomes among faculty-directed programs, exchange programs, and provider programs. Thus, future research should also account for variations in programming and attempt to determine if these variations significantly impact the degree to which students achieve the desired outcomes being measured (Figure 2.2).

Salisbury and colleagues (2013) and Kilgo and colleagues (2015) rely solely on quantitative analysis to draw conclusions about the impact of EA participation. Although extremely important for generalizing about and isolating EA's impact, relying solely on quantitative analysis limits the understanding of the student experience abroad and the context in which positive gains occur. Qualitative analysis allows researchers to better understand the complexities of the EA experience beyond the causal relationship among variables that a quantitative analysis provides (Engle, 2013; Tierney & Clemens, 2011; Williams, 2009). Additionally, qualitative analysis provides researchers with a mechanism to better understand why some students do not make gains or make gains to a lesser extent than others through participation in an EA program. For example, qualitative analysis can provide insight into the

Figure 2.2. Adapted conceptual model to account for variation in EA programming.

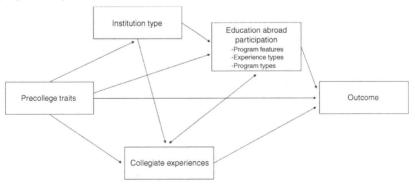

Note. This conceptual model is adapted from the model presented in Salisbury and colleagues (2013). The model was adapted to account for the variation that exists in EA programming and the impact that this variation might have on student learning outcomes.

motivations and intentions of students who study abroad and the impact this might have on desired outcomes. If a student approaches EA primarily as an escape from life at home or as an adventure abroad, this might cause the student to have a very different outcome from one who sees EA as adding value to studies. Moreover, a student might go abroad only to focus on discipline-specific field research and may be prepared to learn a lot from that, but this student might not know how to engage with host nationals in a meaningful way. In this scenario, the student might not achieve the desired learning outcomes for intercultural competency development. Therefore, researchers may find advantages in adopting a mixed-methodological design or conducting follow-up qualitative studies to fully understand the differing effect that EA has on student participants. Further, if in fact intercultural competency is a desired learning outcome, programs need to be designed to this end, and faculty need to be equipped to facilitate such learning, even if the primary program objective is disciplinary learning.

Mapping the Collegiate Environment: Connecting Education Abroad to Other High-Impact Practices

To understand the full potential of EA as a HIP, it will be necessary to develop methods to connect the learning that occurs through EA with other experiences students have on and off campus that can lead to student learning outcomes (Kuh, 2008; Pascarella & Terenzini, 2005). Kuh (2008) points out that participating in one HIP increases a student's engagement on campus and the likelihood that a student will participate in other HIPs. In fact, recent results from the National Survey of Student Engagement (NSSE; 2017) shows that over 60% of seniors at U.S. universities participate in two or more HIPs during their time in college (see Table 2.1).

TABLE 2.1
Total Number of HIPs Experienced by U.S. Seniors

# of Experiences	None	One	Two	Three	Four	Five	Six	Two or more
% of Overall Participation	15	25	22	18	12	6	1	60

Note. Data presented in this table show only the overall percentage of seniors who participate in one or more HIP. Data are not broken down by student characteristics or institution type. For a more detailed breakdown by different student groups see the NSSE (2017) full report.

Based on the premise that students tend to participate in more than one HIP, Kuh (2008) stressed the importance of developing purposeful pathways and the role such pathways play in helping students achieve success. According to Kuh, pathways are intentionally designed bridges in programming that allow students to make associations to knowledge and skills they have learned in the past to experiences they will encounter in the future. In other words, students must be intentionally guided to build upon the learning that occurs through participation in HIPs (Borrego, 2006; Wawrzynski & Baldwin, 2014). For this to occur, campus units must collaborate and develop partnerships with the goal of helping students achieve desired learning outcomes. Borrego (2006) identified this pathway process as *mapping the learning environment*. The mapping process can happen at all levels of the institution and requires the campus community to identify where both formal and informal learning take place. When this is done, all members of the campus community, administration, faculty, and staff can participate in educating students to help them acquire new knowledge and skills and to help reinforce and extend previously learned knowledge and skills.

EA professionals are well positioned to facilitate this mapping process and integrate EA into the educational continuum. EA professionals are able to activate and develop campus partnerships that can support students to build on their learning abroad and to do so in a more interconnected way. The development of these partnerships needs to occur to help integrate learning both prior to and after studying abroad. EA professionals must be able to demonstrate how EA programming can enhance and extend learning and opportunities that are already occurring for a student on campus. For example, on many campuses today, students have the opportunity to participate in leadership development programs. These programs seek to help students identify and develop their personal leadership styles, learn about the challenges facing leaders, and create methods to solve these challenges (Chesnut & Tran-Johnson, 2013). EA programs that similarly focus on leadership development can further extend this learning by engaging students in an examination of how leadership styles vary across international and intercultural contexts. A presents students the chance to encounter new viewpoints on leadership and further expand their understanding of what is required for effective leadership in international contexts. For students to be made aware of this connection, EA professionals and those who run leadership programs on campus must collaborate to inform students how the experiences are interconnected and valuable. Raising awareness in students can occur through goal-setting activities prior to students going abroad, through assignments and activities while students are abroad, and through reflection activities after students return to campus. This intentionality and collaboration between partners allows students to make connections between the two learning experiences and enhance overall learning outcomes.

Similarly, partnerships need to be developed that will facilitate opportunities to extend the learning that occurs abroad upon return to campus. EA professionals can help students make these connections by informing them of relevant opportunities available before, during, and after their EA programs. For example, students who participated in global service-learning programming may value learning about similar opportunities upon their return to campus. Often, students are unaware of parallel opportunities in their local communities. Although occurring in different contexts, such opportunities provide a chance for students to enhance and extend their learning by being able to make comparisons between what they experienced abroad and what they experience in their own communities.

In addition to guiding students to available opportunities on campus, EA professionals might collaborate with campus partners to incorporate students' experiences abroad into activities on campus; this helps students make the connections between their learning abroad and at home. Similar to how connections can be made between previous on-campus experiences and EA, campus partners might develop activities that allow students to reflect on how their experiences and the learning that occurred abroad are related to the activities in which they participate on campus. Using service-learning as an example, if students return to campus and participate in a course with a service-learning component, faculty can encourage and allow students to compare their experiences abroad with experiences in their local communities. They can also encourage students to think about how solutions used abroad could be applied in a local context and what impact this might have. Opportunities like this provide students with the chance to make meaningful connections between their experiences abroad and their lives at home. Thus, EA professionals must engage with campus partners to provide these reflective opportunities for returnees, as they are instrumental in helping students make these connections between their experiences abroad and their experiences on campus.

Conclusion

Since the publication of both AAC&U's (2007) and Kuh's (2008) reports, HIPs have been promoted on campuses as activities with the potential to better engage students and lead to enhanced student success, in turn helping to equip graduates to address the complex, ever-changing situations they will encounter throughout their lives. EA provides a unique learning opportunity for students to interact with faculty, peers, and others from different cultures while applying their new experiences and learning to real-world settings. Although EA provides this unique opportunity, questions remain about the extent to which EA impacts student success. As this chapter highlights, EA researchers need to better understand how to effectively leverage EA program participation to maximize student learning and success (Kilgo et al., 2015). It is not enough to only isolate the impact of EA through more sophisticated research designs. Instead, it is necessary to better understand how the educational continuum can be leveraged to strengthen EA learning outcomes and how EA can be leveraged to enhance student learning and development along the educational continuum. In other words, the impact of EA and the learning that occurs while a student is abroad must be connected to other experiences and embedded in the greater educational continuum. EA professionals must serve not only to help students develop new knowledge and skills through EA programming but also to support students in building upon and reinforcing learning that occurs abroad throughout students' lives. For this to happen, EA professionals need to develop a network of partnerships across campus to map where learning occurs and develop purposeful pathways to help students draw connections between and among experiences. EA must not be understood in isolation from the other student experiences but instead be understood as an interrelated experience among many that advance and propel students along in their education.

Notes

1. For four-year postsecondary institutions in the United States, graduation within four, five, and six years is an accepted standard for calculating graduation rates.
2. For a more detailed analysis of these limitations see Brownell and Swaner (2010), Edelstein (2014), and Salisbury and colleagues (2013).
3. The statistical analysis used in this conceptual model is beyond the scope of this chapter. For detailed information on the statistical analysis see Kilgo and colleagues (2015), Padgett, Salisbury, An, and Pascarella (2010), and Salisbury and colleagues (2013).

References

Association of American Colleges & Universities (AAC&U). (2007). *College learning for the new global century: A report from the National Leadership Council for Liberal Education and America's Promise.* Washington, DC: Author.

Astin, A. W. (1993). *What matters in college? Four critical years revisited.* San Francisco, CA: Jossey Bass.

Borrego, S. (2006). Mapping the learning environment. In R. P. Keeling (Ed.), *Learning reconsidered 2: A practical guide to implementing a campus-wide focus on the student experience* (pp. 11–16). Washington, DC: NASPA.

Braskamp, L. A., Braskamp, D. C., & Merrill, K. C. (2009). Assessing progress in global learning and development of students with education abroad experiences. *Frontiers: The Interdisciplinary Journal of Study Abroad, 13,* 101–118.

Brownell, J. E., & Swaner, L. E. (2010). *Five high-impact practices: Research on learning outcomes, completion, and quality.* Washington, DC: Association of American Colleges & Universities.

Chesnut, R., & Tran-Johnson, J. (2013). Impact of a student leadership development program. *American Journal of Pharmaceutical Education, 77*(10), 225.

DeGraaf, D., Slagter, C., Larsen, K., & Ditta, E. (2013). The long-term personal and professional impacts of participating in a study abroad program. *Frontiers: The Interdisciplinary Journal of Study Abroad, 23,* 42–59.

Dwyer, M. (2004). More is better: The impact of study abroad program duration. *Frontiers: The Interdisciplinary Journal of Study Abroad, 10,* 151–164.

Edelstein, R. (2014). Globalization and student learning: A literature review and call for greater conceptual rigor and cross-institutional studies. *CSHE Research and Occasional Paper Series, 14*(6). Available from https://cshe.berkeley.edu/sites/default/files/publications/rops.cshe_.6.14.edelstein.internationallearning.4.24.2014.pdf

Engle, L. (2013). The rewards of qualitative assessment appropriate to study abroad. *Frontiers: The Interdisciplinary Journal of Study Abroad, 22,* 111–126.

Engle, L., & Engle, J. (2004). Assessing language acquisition and intercultural sensitivity development in relation to study abroad program design. *Frontiers: The Interdisciplinary Journal of Study Abroad, 10,* 219–236.

European Commission. (2014, September). *The ERASMUS impact study: Effects of mobility on the skills and employability of students and the internationalisation of higher education institutions.* Available from http://ec.europa.eu/dgs/education_culture/repository/education/library/study/2014/erasmus-impact_en.pdf

Farrugia, C., & Sanger, J. (2017, October). *Gaining an employment edge: The impact of study abroad on 21st century skills & career prospects in the United States, 2013–2016.* Available from https://www.iie.org/Research-and-Insights/Publications/Gaining-an-Employment-Edge---The-Impact-of-Study-Abroad

Franklin, K. (2010). Long-term career impact and professional applicability of the study abroad experience. *Frontiers: The Interdisciplinary Journal of Study Abroad, 19,* 169–191.

Hamir, H. B. (2011). *Go abroad and graduate on-time: Study abroad participation, degree completion, and time-to-degree* (doctoral dissertation). University of Nebraska–Lincoln. Available from http://world.utexas.edu/forms/abroad/barclay-dissertation.pdf

Haupt, J., Ogden, A., & Rubin, D. (2018). Toward a common research model: Leveraging education abroad participation to enhance college graduation rates. *Journal of Studies in International Education, 22*(2), 91–107.

Institute for the International Education of Students (IES). (2016). *Career outcomes of study abroad students: Survey of IES abroad alumni 2012–2015.* Available from https://www.iesabroad.org/system/files/resources/career_outcomes_of_study_abroad_students.pdf

Kilgo, C. A., Ezell Sheets, J. K., & Pascarella, E. T. (2015). The link between high-impact practices and student learning: Some longitudinal evidence. *Higher Education, 69*, 509–525.

Kuh, G. D. (2008). *High-impact educational practices: What they are, who has access to them, and why they matter.* Washington, DC: Association of American Colleges & Universities.

Kuh, G. D., O'Donnell, K., & Reed, S. (2013). *Ensuring quality and taking high-impact practices to scale.* Washington, DC: Association of American Colleges & Universities.

Malmgren, J., & Galvin, J. (2008). Effects of study abroad participation on student graduation rates: A study of three incoming freshmen cohorts at the University of Minnesota, Twin Cities. *NACADA Journal, 28*(1), 29–42.

Mulvaney, K. (2017). The long-term impact of study abroad on honors program alumni. *Frontiers: The Interdisciplinary Journal of Study Abroad, 29*(1), 46–67.

Murphy, D., Sahakyan, N., Yong-Yi, D., & Magnan, S. S. (2014). The impact of study abroad on the global engagement of university graduates. *Frontiers: The Interdisciplinary Journal of Study Abroad, 22*, 1–19.

National Survey of Student Engagement (NSSE). (2017). *NSSE 2017 high-impact practices: U.S. summary percentages by student characteristics.* Available from http://nsse.indiana.edu/2017_institutional_report/pdf/HIPTables/HIP.pdf

O'Rear, I., Sutton, R. L., & Rubin, D. L. (2012). *The effect of study abroad on college completion in a state university system.* Available from http://glossari.uga.edu/wpcontent/uploads/downloads/2012/01/GLOSSARI-Grad-Rate-Logistic-Regressions-040111.pdf

Padgett, R. D., Salisbury, M. H., An, B. P., & Pascarella, E. T. (2010). Required, practical, or unnecessary? An examination and demonstration of propensity score matching using longitudinal secondary data. *New Directions for Institutional Research, S2*, 29–42.

Paige, R. M., Fry, G., Stallman, E. M., Josic, J., & Jon, J. (2009). Study abroad for global engagement: The long-term impact of mobility experiences. *Intercultural Education, 20*, S29–S44.

Pascarella, E. T. (1985). College environmental influences on learning and cognitive development: A critical review and synthesis. In J. Smart (Ed.), *Higher education: Handbook of theory and research* (Vol. 1, pp. 1–64). New York, NY: Agathon.

Pascarella, E. T., & Terenzini, P. T. (2005). *How college affects students: A third decade of research* (Vol. 2). San Francisco, CA: Jossey-Bass.

Raby, R. L., Rhodes, G. M., & Biscarra, A. (2013). Community college study abroad: Implications for student success. *Community College Journal of Research and Practice, 38*(2–3), 174–183.

Salisbury, M. H., An, B. P., & Pascarella, E. T. (2013). The effect of study abroad on intercultural competence among undergraduate college students. *Journal of Student Affairs Research and Practice, 50*(1), 1–20.

Stebleton, M. J., Soria, K. M., & Cherney, B. T. (2013). The high impact of education abroad: College students' engagement in international experiences and the development of intercultural competencies. *Frontiers: The Interdisciplinary Journal of Study Abroad, 22*, 1–24.

Tierney, W. G., & Clemens, R. F. (2011). Qualitative research and public policy: The challenges of relevance and trustworthiness. In J. C. Smart & M. B. Paulsen (Eds.), *Higher education: Handbook of theory and research* (Vol. 26, pp. 56–83). New York, NY: Springer.

Twombly, S. B., Salisbury, M. H., Tumanut, S. D., & Klute, P. (2012). Study abroad in a new global century—renewing the promise, refining the purpose. *ASHE Higher Education Report, 38*(4), 1–52.

University Planning, Institutional Research, and Accountability. (2009, May). *Plans, participation, and outcomes: Overseas study at Indiana University Bloomington.* Available from http://overseas.iu.edu/docs/UIRR_Overseas_Study.pdf

Vande Berg, M., Connor-Linton, J., & Paige R. M. (2009). The Georgetown Consortium Project: Interventions for student learning abroad. *Frontiers: The Interdisciplinary Journal of Study Abroad, 18*, 1–75.

Van Mol, C. (2017). Do employers value international study and internships? A comparative analysis of 31 countries. *Geoforum, 78*, 52–60.

Wawrzynski, M., & Baldwin, R. (2014). Promoting high-impact student learning: Connecting key components of the collegiate experience. *New Directions for Higher Education, 165*, 51–62.

Williams, T. R. (2005). Exploring the impact of study abroad on students' intercultural communication skills: Adaptability and sensitivity. *Journal of Studies in International Education, 9*(4), 356–371.

Williams, T. R. (2009). The reflective model of intercultural competency: A multidimensional, qualitative approach to study abroad assessment. *Frontiers: The Interdisciplinary Journal of Study Abroad, 18*, 289–306.

Xu, M., de Silva, C. R., Neufeldt, E., & Dane, J. (2013). The impact of study abroad on academic success: An analysis of first-time students entering Old Dominion University, Virginia, 2000–2004. *Frontiers: The Interdisciplinary Journal of Study Abroad, 23*, 90–103.

3

CURRICULUM INTEGRATION

Opportunities for Continuity and Disruption Along the Educational Continuum

Elizabeth Brewer, Giselda Beaudin, and Michael Woolf

Right Reverend Host. "I'm afraid you've got a bad Egg, Mr. Jones!"
The Curate. "Oh no, my Lord, I assure you! Parts of it are excellent!

—George du Maurier (1895)

At a not only basic but also critically important level, curriculum integration in education abroad refers to institutional approaches "designed to fully integrate study abroad options into the college experience and academic curricula for students in all majors" (Parcells & Woodruff, 2016). In so doing, it helps ensure continuity along the educational continuum. Further, when courses taken abroad are integrated seamlessly into home school degree programs, education abroad moves away from the periphery of the academic agenda.

Curriculum integration then, like the proverbial curate's egg, is demonstrably a good thing—in parts. For all of its advantages, there is a danger that education abroad curriculum integration, and the course equivalencies it looks for, can undermine one of the central purposes of education abroad, namely disrupting students' habits, assumptions, and behaviors so that they gain new perspectives and arrive at new ways of understanding themselves, their studies, and their relationship to the world. If education abroad is thus to be a transformative learning experience (Brewer & Cunningham, 2009), then perhaps our understanding of curriculum integration needs to be expanded to become both an opportunity for continuity along the educational continuum and an opportunity for disrupting the continuum. This will require attention not only to what students learn but also to how they learn, particularly in contexts abroad that present both new opportunities and challenges. Importantly, attention also needs to be paid to what students bring with them to their undergraduate education, including education abroad, and their aspirations for the future. Further, if a central purpose of undergraduate education is to equip students to apply "knowledge, skills, and responsibilities to new settings and complex problems" (Association of American Colleges & Universities [AAC&U], n.d.a), perhaps education abroad curriculum integration should focus more on the challenge of the new, rather than establishing course equivalencies.

Education Abroad Curriculum Integration: What It Is, Why It Is Necessary, and What It Has Achieved

Curriculum integration is not new. As noted in a history of the development of study abroad in the United States (Hoffa, 2007), the foundation for integrating education abroad into home school degrees lies in the development of a modular credit system for higher education in the nineteenth century. This made it possible to divide students' studies into countable units and to substitute courses taken at other institutions in the United States and abroad for courses normally taken at the home institution. As seen in chapter 1, U.S. colleges and universities began to experiment with credit-bearing education abroad programs after World War I, with programs proliferating after World War II as higher education recognized the need to internationalize. Foreign language study and area studies were deemed of particular importance, and academic rigor was expected as preparation for careers and citizenship. Thus, one of the first major studies of education abroad (Carlson, Burn, Useem, & Yachimowicz, 1990) emphasized the importance of integrating education abroad into U.S. undergraduate studies. Recommendations included giving students greater access to information about education abroad opportunities, equipping faculty and advisers to inform students about courses that could count toward their degrees, making education abroad an option in all degree programs, and reducing students' alienation upon return by modifying courses to help them incorporate their learning abroad. Mechanisms for integrating studies abroad into home school degrees were uneven. Indeed, a 1992 handbook on curriculum internationalization (Pickert & Turlington, 1992) made note of Kalamazoo College's exceptional leadership in this regard. Kalamazoo made education abroad possible regardless of major, accommodated it in the academic calendar, and supported participation with financial aid.

Within a decade, the much larger University of Minnesota would demonstrate similar leadership. Initially a pilot project focused on increasing education abroad in technology fields; its curriculum integration model (University of Minnesota, n.d.) quickly grew into an institution-wide effort to internationalize undergraduate education and, to this end, increase education abroad participation. A hallmark of the project was outreach to academic units from the Learning Abroad Center aimed at identifying education abroad opportunities appropriate to the learning goals and curricula of the academic units. "Curriculum integration" soon became "colleague integration" as faculty and education abroad professionals partnered in the process. This led to "an eventual progression to 'Campus Internationalization,' where the campus culture shifts as more units take responsibility for study abroad advising and program development, and the conversations broaden to be more inclusive of internationalizing the curricula as a whole" (Woodruff, 2009, p. 3).

In 2004, a conference on the model convened. Conference proceedings were published (Anderson, 2005), and the initiative quickly spread to other institutions. This was due both to the national attention received (the nascent The Forum on Education Abroad was a cosponsor) and the model's transportability (Vande Berg, 2005). It is thus now commonplace for education abroad offices to adhere to the following guidelines:

1. Collaborate with academic units and registrars' offices to identify courses offered abroad that can count toward major, minor, or general education requirements.
2. Work with financial aid offices and senior leadership to establish policies that make education abroad affordable for both students and their home institutions.
3. Develop partnerships with universities abroad as well as with education abroad organizations for curriculum integration purposes.
4. Produce outreach materials to make clear the possibility of education abroad for all students, without delaying graduation.

Matching courses at home with those abroad, the core practice in education abroad curriculum integration, was not in itself a radical departure from historical practice. However, widespread and systematic implementation dramatically changed disciplinary representation in education abroad. Science, technology, engineering, and mathematics (STEM) and business, for example, feature much more prominently now than was true before the curriculum integration movement took hold. In addition, as curriculum integration became an accepted best practice, international education organizations in the United States embraced the concept. The American Council on Education's Center for International and Global Engagement includes *curriculum integration* in the mobility section of its model for comprehensive internationalization (American Council on Education, n.d.), The Forum on Education Abroad defines the term in its glossary (The Forum on Education Abroad, n.d.a) and discusses the concept in its standards (The Forum on Education Abroad, n.d.b), and NAFSA: Association of International Educators publishes a list of resources on the topic (NAFSA, 2016). Although much less commonly looked to by education abroad professionals, the AAC&U has issued a number of publications and developed rubrics useful for curricular and cocurricular design and assessment. More than one, including a rubric for integrative learning, are pertinent to education abroad curriculum integration (AAC&U, n.d.d). These should be consulted more widely by education abroad stakeholders.

Ultimately, the process of curriculum integration creates benchmarks that enforce domestic educational norms and offer easily comprehended and unchallenging ways of acting and thinking. It becomes the mechanism through which colleges and universities create or select courses abroad that most resemble those that they already teach. This is, ostensibly, reasonable; education abroad becomes integral (Woodruff, 2009). When U.S. institutions operate their own programs or work with international educational organizations abroad, they anticipate and demand standards or benchmarks that align, broadly, with domestic practice. This is also, in part, the rationale for faculty-led programs abroad: The foreign is mediated through the academic perspectives of home. Mediation—via faculty-led programs, program providers, or, increasingly, universities abroad that create curricula tailored to education abroad students—becomes a tool for making education abroad a part of undergraduate education. Today, education abroad curriculum integration is a widely accepted and expected practice in U.S. higher education. Beyond making education abroad broadly possible across disciplines, it affirms that what is studied abroad is as serious and academically valid as that which is studied at home.

Curriculum Integration Limitations

All learning is situated within a geographical, political, and historical context. In education abroad, however, location is an explicit part of the learning agenda: Interactions between the subject studied and the host environment are embedded within the pedagogy. This involves, in one way or another, multidisciplinary perspectives and learning experiences that are unlikely to be the norm domestically. Students abroad are far more likely to encounter unfamiliar approaches to curriculum and teaching strategies through the education abroad program, at the university in which they are enrolled, or informally in encounters with locals who become "teachers." These experiences encourage changes in perspective. Best practice for education abroad customarily includes some form of experiential engagement with the host country, culture, and/or environment: action research, basic ethnography, site visits, internships, service-learning, or other forms of teaching that make specialist demands on faculty and that locate the curriculum within a distinct geographical and historical context. Courses taken abroad frequently transcend the boundaries of traditional disciplines and the opportunities to draw connections between classroom and experiential learning abound. Students abroad become temporary residents in a world elsewhere that is both geographical and intellectual space, separated from the parochial comforts of home literally and metaphorically and dislocated from the security of the familiar.

The very nature of education abroad offers learning environments that are potentially creative, innovative, and particularly relevant to student experience in a world in which "all fixed, fast-frozen relations, with their train of ancient and venerable prejudices and opinions, are swept away, all new-formed ones become antiquated before they can ossify. All that is solid melts into air" (Marx & Engels, 1848/1888, p. 16). There is much that students can learn through education abroad, not least to engage with messy, complex, interconnected but divergent worlds. The enormous potential of education abroad exists, however, in tension with the need to conform to the requirements and expectations of U.S. higher education.

In general, higher education is not renowned for innovation or radical reform, restrained as it is by departmental interests, the tenure process, course scheduling, and so on. It is a conservative environment and values continuity and tradition. U.S. higher education is no exception. To illustrate, at the undergraduate level academic credit is measured by the mechanistic, if convenient, number of hours a student spends in the classroom. Other, more sophisticated, measures exist in the world and are periodically debated: workload, student outputs, and competencies. However, despite these discussions, most U.S. institutions have resisted any significant changes to the use of contact hours as the basic unit of learning.

To understand the tenacity of conservative impulses within U.S. higher education, it is worth considering the concepts of striated and optic space, developed by Deleuze and Guattari. *Striated space* is space that has been delineated and marked for certain uses (Deleuze & Guattari, 1987). *Optic space* is best described with the image of a shoreline: Imagine walking along a beach where the waves are breaking. Although the water and wind are constantly moving around you, you have a clear path to follow, a straight line toward a goal on the horizon. This is optic space: the space created when we follow our line of sight forward to a point on the horizon. Striated and optic spaces are not in and of themselves either positive or negative—both can be used purposefully and productively, but they can also be used as mechanisms of control and constraint.

Within U.S. higher education are examples of both striated and optic spaces. Most institutions are still largely organized in silos: There are individual offices, separate academic departments, and distinct academic fields. The siloed structure of academia is an example of a striated space. It is possible and indeed quite common for siloed structures to have overlaps, as in a Venn diagram of sets and subsets. In higher education, there are degree programs that involve faculty from multiple departments, or offices that sit within larger institutional divisions. However, in a siloed structure, even when there is overlap, the boundaries are still rigid, as is their placement, size, and purpose.

Optic spaces are also prevalent within U.S. higher education. Most degree programs, for example, are designed as optic spaces: The student moves along a linear path through progressively specialized content until mastery (i.e., the degree) is achieved. Most syllabi follow a linear fashion, with a series of assignments designed to channel a student toward intended learning outcomes. Striated and optic spaces thus serve clear purposes: They help organize the institution and provide students (and faculty) with goals and maps for progress. However, the fixed nature of siloed structures can result in hierarchies and inequities when power becomes anchored into those structures and is then fixed in place (Foucault, 1975/1995). When this occurs, power can become tied to a particular person, title, space, or office. An example might be a higher administrator who feels empowered to make decisions without consultation because of the administrator's role or title. Similarly, optic spaces can limit possibilities when students (or institutions themselves) become wedded to a delineated path. Ultimately, striated and optic spaces are not inherently negative or positive, but due to their fixed natures, they tend to limit change and encourage conservative impulses.

Since the legitimacy of U.S. education abroad depends substantially on the extent to which it meets the standards of U.S. higher education, and conservative structures and impulses are the norm within U.S. higher education, there is a tendency to interpret curriculum integration narrowly despite the fact that education abroad is inherently disruptive: Students cross frontiers and boundaries to engage with the critically unfamiliar.

Unfortunately, crudely applied curriculum integration can restrict curricular innovation and opportunities for transformative learning. Domesticating the disturbing disruptions and dislocations that may lurk in foreign lands and on alien shores constrains the learning potential of education abroad by containing and reconstructing the unfamiliar within the comforting boundaries of hearth and home. The need to "fit" the foreign within domestic parameters may ultimately limit the potential for innovation and disruption.

Imagine a music major whose home institution focuses on European musical traditions. The student studies abroad in Japan and learns about Japanese musical traditions. If education, the process of learning, is viewed as a striated space, it is easy to understand the anxiety that might be provoked in this situation, as well as the potential logistical challenges. The student may replace the European tradition with the new silo of Japanese music or create a hierarchy that places Japanese music above or below European traditions. The student may see the home institution faculty as limited in understanding or experience, or may return to the home institution demanding course-work that the home institution is not poised to offer. Meanwhile, the home institution department may not allow the Japanese music courses to fulfill requirements in the major, sending the message that studying abroad is not valuable to music majors. Or, if more students study abroad, and the home institution department grants major credit for the courses they took abroad, the department may face declining course enrollments, or feel that students have missed crucial content normally taught at home. Broadly speaking, tra-ditional disciplines and conventional ways of defining areas of knowledge are potentially subverted in education abroad. A realignment of learning boundaries may then conflict with the interests of academic departments, which have an investment in protecting themselves and the discreet nature of their disciplines.

Furthermore, many of the learning outcomes associated with education abroad (resilience, maturity, independence, intercultural competence, civic engagement, critical thinking, etc.) are complex to define and assess. While there are some tested ways to measure them, there are still substantial gaps in our knowledge and disagreements about how best and when to assess these kinds of outcomes (Savicki & Brewer, 2015; Yngve, chapter 8, this volume). In a striated and optic view of education, this is a problem. If learning cannot be assessed, its value for education cannot be proven, and it becomes impossible to demonstrate that students have reached the horizon at the end of the optic path. This encourages a reliance on classroom learning, which is easier to grasp and to measure. Thus, the traditional model of curriculum integration focuses on classroom learning and by extension implies that classroom learning is more important than learning that occurs outside the classroom. Integrative learning theory, however, shows us that both are important. Instead of focusing entirely on classroom content and outcomes, we should create structures that help students to draw connections between classroom content and experiential learning (AAC&U, n.d.b; Newell, 1999, 2010). Curriculum integration may actually discourage these connections by providing students (and faculty/staff) with a narrow understanding of learning abroad. This can limit student agency and ownership of learning to the process of identifying course equivalencies, even as student self-reports overwhelmingly reference what they learned outside the classroom, not within it. Further, students' responses to opportunities largely determine the extent to which they learn. This is why student agency, learning theories, and experiential, integrative, and transformative pedagogies are so important to achieving the potential that education abroad can contribute to undergraduate education. If education abroad can change learners' perspectives (the goal of transformative learning), it will have done a great deal in fostering lifelong learning skills development.

Much writing on curriculum integration talks about it as multidisciplinary, interdisciplinary, or transdisciplinary inquiry around a problem or an issue (Drake, 2007; McBrien & Brandt, 1997); further, it may also involve reflection on the learning process (Beane, 1997). Curriculum integration can be emblemized by project-based learning (Worcester Polytechnic Institute, n.d.), which is also termed *problem-centered learning* (AAC&U, n.d.c). Yet, within education abroad, curriculum integration has too often become a rote exercise in course-matching. To make a meaningful contribution to undergraduate education, education abroad cannot serve as a mechanism for reproducing the conventions of mainstream higher education in another location. Rather, it needs to be liberated from traditions of academic conservatism. Education abroad ought to unpack the baggage of convention and disturb and disrupt not only the students but also their teachers. This is its real promise.

Rethinking Curriculum Integration

To move the discussion of curriculum integration beyond course matching, education abroad must both be placed in the educational continuum, and become a disruptive force within that continuum. Students' educations before they study abroad need to advance their abilities to self-author while abroad, and to equip them to engage with and learn from dissonance. While abroad students need to experience and begin to process dissonance, and post–study abroad, coursework and other activities should help them address questions raised during study abroad.

This is even more important in the contemporary context of education abroad. In the increasingly rare instances that students study abroad for an academic year, study abroad constitutes just one-fourth of a typical undergraduate education in the United States. A semester is one eighth, while short-term study abroad occupies far less time, space, and credits. Education abroad does not exist in a vacuum. It is preceded and followed by curricular and noncurricular learning opportunities, and these need to move beyond orientation and reentry activities organized by education abroad offices or faculty leading short-term programs. What happens before and after is critical to enhancing the impact of education abroad. Expectations for education abroad's contributions and connections to pre– and post–education abroad learning should be higher. Students need to be given opportunities to own their education abroad. This can include helping them cultivate intention and find connectivity at the time of application, and asking them to think forward to connections post–study abroad. It can also encompass experiential learning opportunities, whether embedded in courses, research projects, or field studies. Further, as was already evident in 1990 (Carlson et al., 1990), students need opportunities upon return to incorporate their learning abroad into their studies (see case studies in Brewer & Cunningham, 2009, for examples of practice). In the current model, the home campus curriculum most likely does not change in order to accommodate or integrate students learning abroad. However, if experiential learning and intercultural learning are critical to successful learning abroad, the courses students take before going abroad should prepare them for these kinds of learning. Further, given the importance of reflection in making meaning of experience and turning experience into learning (chapter 9, this volume), the curriculum post–study abroad should include opportunities to reflect on their experiences and integrate them into their ongoing studies (Twombly, Salisbury, Tumanut, & Klute, 2012).

Within the constructed spaces of education abroad, international educators have academic and intellectual responsibilities: to develop, maintain, and review valid learning objectives; to create an ethos in which creative and innovative teaching is the norm; to challenge students to explore and analyze learning environments with commitment and curiosity; to disrupt and disturb students' assumptions through the conjunction of new ideas in new places.

Deleuze and Guattari's (1987) concept of smooth and haptic space, as opposed to striated and optic space, relates to these goals and helps resolve the tensions between narrow and expanded understandings of curriculum integration. *Smooth space* is space that is completely unmarked, uncategorized, and therefore open to all possibilities. The ocean works as a

place both in structured and unstructured contexts is critical for the holistic learning that is particularly well suited to education abroad contexts. It is also critical, however, to help students understand that studying abroad will be disruptive at times, and that such disruption is part of a critical learning process. Attention to developing metacognitive skills before, during, and upon return will help students navigate disruption, make sense of it, and empower them to connect their learning abroad with other educational endeavors; this is the promise of integrative learning. Post–education abroad practices that combine reflection with action research are developing at a number of institutions. This engages students in high-impact practice while also generating research findings and projects that can benefit the institution and prospective education abroad students.

Second, gather evidence of what, how, and where students are learning abroad. Use the evidence to improve practice, and to educate the campus. Chapter 8 in this volume discusses use of formative assessment to improve learning outcomes, and to align curriculum design and delivery with differentiated learning needs and goals. Here we stress the importance of sharing the assessment work. For example, analysis of students' reflective writing offers insights into individual learning processes abroad. This in turn can provide direction for both education abroad professionals and other faculty and staff for taking steps to improve student learning abroad and integrate that learning into the educational continuum. Furthermore, when students are encouraged to present aspects of their learning abroad publicly, this creates an additional opportunity for reflection and connection making. In turn, the audience is alerted to the rich learning potential that can result from education abroad's integration into undergraduate education, and to the fact that learning processes beyond the campus may also be simultaneously powerful, disruptive, messy, and confusing.

Third, discussions of education abroad need to be embedded into campus conversations about teaching and learning. Some institutions are using frameworks (intercultural learning, global learning, integrative learning, civic engagement) to establish agendas for the professional development of faculty and staff, and guide curriculum and cocurriculum development. Further, such frameworks can also be used for assessment purposes. AAC&U's VALUE rubrics (n.d.d) provide models that can be adapted to institutional/organizational mission and practice. As pointed out in chapter 2, education abroad is but one high-impact practice. The more it is interconnected with other elements of students' learning and development along the educational continuum, the more it will have value.

The process of connection is not a simple matter. Instead, it requires a nuanced awareness of the degree to which curriculum integration is both an opportunity to embed education abroad in the institution and, simultaneously, to broaden the curriculum beyond the parochial. Curriculum integration should not mean the slavish reproduction of domestic standards abroad. Rather, it should embrace the notion of enhancement and enrichment through the integration of new ideas and new locations with the power of learning at home. Integration and enhancement are not in contradiction; they connect to each other in our collective aspiration for high-impact education abroad. In short, we learn most at the conjunction of that which we know and that which disrupts that knowledge.

References

American Council on Education. (n.d.). *CIGE model for comprehensive internationalization.* Available from http://www.acenet.edu/news-room/Pages/CIGE-Model-for-Comprehensive-Internationalization.aspx

Anderson, L. (Ed.). (2005). *Internationalizing undergraduate education: Integrating study abroad into the curriculum.* Minneapolis: Board of Regents of the University of Minnesota.

Association of American Colleges & Universities (AAC&U). (n.d.a). *Essential learning outcomes.* Available from https://www.aacu.org/leap/essential-learning-outcomes

Association of American Colleges & Universities (AAC&U). (n.d.b). *Integrative and applied learning VALUE rubric.* Available from https://www.aacu.org/value/rubrics/integrative-learning

Association of American Colleges & Universities (AAC&U) (n.d.c). *Transparency and problem-centered learning.* Available from https://www.aacu.org/problem centeredlearning

Association of American Colleges & Universities (AAC&U) (n.d.d). *VALUE rubric development project.* Available from https://www.aacu.org/value/rubrics

Beane, J. (1997). *Curriculum integration.* New York, NY: Teachers College Press.

Brewer, E., & Cunningham, K. (2009). *Integrating study abroad into the curriculum: Theory and practice across the disciplines.* Sterling, VA: Stylus.

Carlson, J. S., Burn, B. B., Useem, J., & Yachimowicz, D. (1990). *Study abroad: The experience of American undergraduates.* Westport, CT: Greenwood Press.

Deleuze, G., & Guattari F. (1987). *A thousand plateaus: Capitalism and schizophrenia.* (B. Massumi, Trans.). Minneapolis: University of Minnesota Press. (Original work published 1980)

Drake, S. M. (2007). *Creating standards-based integrated curriculum: Content, standards, assessment, and instruction.* Thousand Oaks, CA: Corwin Press.

Du Maurier, G. (1895, November 9). "True humility" [Cartoon]. *Punch.* Available from https://punch.photoshelter.com/image/I0000vVolHOJX5FQ

Engle, L. (2015). The rewards of qualitative assessment appropriate to study abroad. *Frontiers: The Interdisciplinary Journal of Study Abroad, 20,* 111–126.

The Forum on Education Abroad. (n.d.a). *Glossary*. Available from https://forumea .org/resources/glossary/

The Forum on Education Abroad. (n.d.b). *Resources/standards of good practice*. Available from https://forumea.org/resources/standards-of-good-practice/

Foucault, M. (1995). *Discipline and punish: The birth of the prison* (A. Sheridan, Trans.). New York, NY: Vintage Books. (Original work published 1975) Available from https://www.michigan.gov/documents/mde/Integration_Research_ document_ADA_v2-2017_556112_7.pdf

Hoffa, W. W. (2007). *A history of US study abroad: Beginnings to 1965*. Carlisle, PA: The Forum on Education Abroad.

Marx, K., & Engels, F. (1888). *Manifesto of the communist party* (S. Moores, Trans.). London, UK: William Reeves. (Original work published 1848.)

McBrien, J. L., & Brandt, R. S. (1997). *The language of learning: A guide to education terms*. Alexandria, VA: Association for Supervision and Curriculum Development.

Newell, W. H. (1999). The promise of integrative learning. *About Campus, 4*(2), 17–23.

Newell, W. H. (2010). Educating for a complex world: Integrative learning and interdisciplinary studies. *Liberal Education, 96*(4), 6–11.

Parcells, C., & Woodruff, G. (2016, August 4). *Curriculum integration: Best practices*. Washington, DC: NAFSA: Association of International Educators. Available from https://www.nafsa.org/Professional_Resources/Browse_by_Interest/Education_ Abroad/Network_Resources/Education_Abroad/Curriculum_Integration__Best_ Practices/

Pickert, S., & Turlington, B. (1992). *Internationalizing the undergraduate curriculum: A handbook for campus leaders*. Washington, DC: American Council on Education.

Savicki, V., & Brewer, E. (Eds.). (2015). *Assessing study abroad: Theories, tools, and practice*. Sterling, VA: Stylus.

Twombly, S. B., Salisbury, M. H., Tumanut, S. D., & Klute, P. (2012). Study abroad in a new global century—renewing the promise, refining the purpose. *ASHE Higher Education Report, 38*(4), 1–52.

University of Minnesota. (n.d.). *University of Minnesota model of curriculum integration*. Available from https://umabroad.umn.edu/professionals/curriculumintegration/ general/minnesotamodel

Vande Berg, M. (2005). An outsider's inside perspective: The transportability of the University of Minnesota's curriculum integration initiative. In L. C. Anderson (Ed.). *Internationalizing undergraduate education: Integrating study abroad into the curriculum* (pp. 38–40). Minneapolis: University of Minnesota.

Woodruff, G. A. (2009). *Curriculum integration: Where we have been and where we are going*. Internationalizing the Curriculum and Campus Paper Series. Minneapolis: University of Minnesota.

Worcester Polytechnic Institute. (n.d.). *Project-based learning at WPI*. Available from http://wp.wpi.edu/projectbasedlearning/proven-pedagogy/project-based-learning-at-wpi/

4

TOWARD DECOLONIZING EDUCATION ABROAD

Moving Beyond the Self/Other Dichotomy

Roger Adkins and Bryan Messerly

Much of the history of U.S. education abroad has at its heart a focus on the improvement of the individual. From its deep roots in the Grand Tour of early modern Europe to contemporary recruitment efforts that promise life-changing experiences, its core value is self-improvement and enrichment, perhaps with the underlying assumption that the individual will use that experience to contribute to the home society upon return. Too often this focus on the individual produces neocolonial practices and encounters that exploit local people and cultures for the consumption of privileged visitors. Other countries and cultures are reduced to classrooms or laboratories, or are essentialized to provide an authentic experience. Even many well-intentioned practices (home-stays, bilateral exchanges) may still involve neocolonial relationships when program designers do not account for economic and cultural power differences.

The patterns of participation in U.S. education abroad also frequently reinforce inequity and uphold stereotypes as student participation remains overwhelmingly White and middle class. While these problems may manifest differently in programming designed for students at various stages of their education, students throughout the educational continuum are susceptible to neocolonial thinking and practices. For example, a student who is well versed in theories of power and inequality, has studied the local culture, and is beginning to make connections among courses may be just as susceptible to taking for granted the local community's availability for her research as would a peer traveling abroad for the first time through a short-term group program. Neocolonial attitudes and approaches are also not limited to interactions between relatively wealthy U.S. students and individuals from postcolonial countries. Much education abroad programming that occurs in Western Europe offers students superficial engagement with the host countries, essentializes local cultures, and packages an experience for students to consume. Furthermore, the neocolonial impulses are not unique to U.S. education abroad programming and can be at work in both the education abroad programming of other nations and the general contexts in which intercultural interactions occur beyond the scope of education abroad.

This chapter explores inherited neocolonial approaches and outcomes and contemplates a comprehensive approach to decolonize education abroad. It traces the contours of the historical context for U.S. education abroad and the origins of neocolonial approaches, explores how both consumerist individualism and binary constructions of subjectivity contribute to neocolonial attitudes, enumerates some of the problematic practices current in education abroad, and suggests alternative approaches to create programs that are less neocolonial in character.

What Does It Mean to Decolonize?

The ethos of decolonizing stands in stark contrast to common neocolonial practices in education abroad, such as the failure to involve local voices in discussions in faculty-led and other group programming; the pressure U.S. institutional partners place on exchange partner institutions to offer in English courses that align with curricular integration goals at home; and the ways in which U.S. organizations can wield prestige and financial power to influence local communities, such that student accommodations, service projects, and other arrangements become more palatable to U.S. students and their families at home. The consequences of such practices are dire and include both direct effects on local communities and an ongoing failure in the mission to educate participants about culture, power, and politics.

Consider a few examples. First, existing power and economic imbalances in local communities are exacerbated when the wealthiest are contracted for student accommodations (or, worse, the contract goes to a hotel corporation based in another country). Second, students in a faculty-led program spend six weeks using visits to historic sites and museum exhibitions to learn about the local cultural context without hearing from local commentators, expert or otherwise. The students leave with some of their biases or misinformed notions about the local site reinforced, and without having come face-to-face with either cultural difference or their own relative privilege as short-term visitors having a casual encounter with an entire way of life. Third, to attract U.S. students, a university abroad launches an entirely separate curricular program, instructed in English, in anticipation of the demands of U.S. students and their home institutions, inadvertently creating a comfortable bubble. The U.S. participants will not be challenged to navigate educational differences, nor to engage more than superficially with the local culture. Neither will they address critical questions about their own identities in relation to those of local residents.

To decolonize education abroad programming, then, is to eliminate approaches that are one sided, ethnocentric, touristic, uncritical, oversimplifying of cultural complexity, and operating within the savior complex (particularly in community-based learning programs). Instead, approaches are respectful, reciprocal, critically self-reflexive, involve building long-term relationships, and seek to understand and interact holistically with local institutions and cultures and individual hosts—in all their profound complexities.

The notion of decolonizing education abroad stems from postcolonial theory that deconstructs notions of European exceptionalism (Blaut, 1993) and presents general and/or discipline-based methodologies for decolonizing work (Smith, 2002). In addition, efforts to decolonize education abroad build on scholarship about decolonizing pedagogies. Contemporary sources range from Freire (1972) and hooks (1994, 2003) to theorists of asset pedagogies (Cazden & Leggett, 1976; Garcia, 1993; Ladson-Billings, 1994; McCarty & Zepeda, 1995; Moll & Gonzalez, 1994; Smitherman, 1977) and, more recently, culturally sustaining pedagogies (CSPs), particularly as described in Paris and Alim (2017). CSP is a collection of pedagogical approaches that seek to decenter privileged identities and systems of privilege (such as, in the United States, Whiteness, cisheteronormativity, the dominance of Judeo-Christian values), and to sustain, in pluralistic and inclusive classrooms, the rich linguistic and cultural assets that diverse peoples employ. In the work of such radical theorists of pedagogy, efforts to decolonize education abroad find inspiration for decentering the privileged traveler and rethinking the composition of the learning communities in education abroad contexts.

Within education abroad, specifically, scholar-practitioners have addressed the problematic nature of a neocolonial approach, defined how neocolonial education abroad participants think and behave (Ogden, 2007), and discussed the ways in which programs themselves encourage a neocolonial approach (Ramírez, 2013; Sharpe, 2015). Others focus on the troublesome (neocolonial) nature of the idea of global citizenship (Zemach-Bersin, 2007) and of the nation as the foundational concept of international education (Gristwood & Woolf, 2014), or examine the hidden curriculum observable in how institutions frame education abroad within the contexts of mission and values statements and assemble program portfolios (Ficarra, 2017). Other work gestures toward the approaches that will be needed to decolonize education abroad, whether by directing attention to the effects of programs on local communities (Wood & Schroeder, 2017) or radically rethinking what partnership with local partners means (Gardner & Krabill, 2017). Although these studies have drawn attention to the problems presented by neocolonial approaches and indicated some of the ways to begin the work of decolonizing, none have yet sought to connect the historical context in which education abroad emerged to the politics of subjectivity in Western societies. This chapter will address this connection.

The scope of decolonizing education abroad involves all aspects of the work of advisers, administrators, and faculty program directors, including program conception and planning, academic content design and delivery, participant recruitment and selection processes, program finance practices, and modes of interacting with local people (whether partners or not) and their cultural and natural environments. Importantly, decolonizing education abroad is not a distinct goal to be completed but rather an aspirational approach, rooted in ongoing self-reflection, assessment, and revision. Educators who engage with the ongoing work of decolonizing acknowledge the neocolonialism haunting education abroad practices, care about the ways in which their work may perpetuate inequities, and are compelled by moral imperative.

Grand Tourists, Heroes, Citizen Diplomats: Education Abroad's Historical Roots

An exploration of the historical antecedents of education abroad reveals some of the assumptions and challenges that education abroad professionals face if they are committed to more equitable encounters among students, scholars, and local communities. The language that educators use to talk about young people's experiences abroad and the assumptions that they make about the purpose of the endeavor have changed to match an evolving understanding of world affairs, but the foundational rationale for education abroad has remained surprisingly durable: self-discovery and self-improvement of the individual, gaining local knowledge, the utility of intercultural competence, strengthening ties abroad, and exploiting local resources. This is partly why, despite good intentions in the field and greater awareness, education abroad continues to suffer from exploitative tendencies.

Grand Tourists

Students today would probably relate to the experiences and expectations of ancient forebears who went on voyages of self-discovery. As William Hoffa (2007) notes, "Many early cultures sent their young leaders on journeys of initiation and discovery, believing that their experiences in the realms of the unknown would provide them with the maturity, confidence, understanding and skills needed for the survival of the tribe" (p. 1). While education abroad is no longer explicitly pitched as a rite of initiation, students still expect life-changing experiences that also advantage them by giving them tangible skills.

Heroes

In *The Hero With a Thousand Faces,* Joseph Campbell (1949/2008) identifies the pattern of journeying outward to make inner discoveries as one of the great motifs of early mythology. Such journeying also underlies students' and educators' assumptions about the modern experience. In story after story, the physical dislocation that a hero faces during a quest leads to the intellectual and spiritual dislocation necessary for self-discovery and broader insights into the human condition. Heroes are also typically aided in their quests by altruistic, benevolent local interlocutors who appear at just the right time to assist them. Education abroad professionals would do well to help students be wary of seeing local community members as such helpers and instead see them as persons with motivations equally complex as their own. While students and educators today may not think in terms of questing and local helpers, they share the foundational assumption that education abroad disrupts the educational continuum, allowing for unique kinds of growth and self-discovery by way of interaction with local residents and sites.

Citizen Diplomats

Much of the early history of U.S. education abroad is colored by the experience of global conflict and a more assertive role of the United States in the world. Thus, in 1922, University of Delaware President Walter Hullihen approved the establishment of one of the pioneering junior-year programs, because he saw the United States' growing influence. Additionally, in the wake of the Great War, he hoped that such a program would "pave a way toward greater international understanding and goodwill" (Hoffa, 2007, p. 72) and give Delaware graduates an advantage in government and business. Similarly, New York University Dean of Arts and Sciences James Edwin Lough envisioned a faculty-led world issues program that would circumnavigate the globe over a semester to prepare students to be globally minded leaders and "citizen diplomats" engaged in a reciprocal exchange of ideas with the people they encountered (Hoffa, 2007, p. 88). In both cases, a mixture of a naïve altruism (tinged with notions of U.S. influence) and an effort to give students a unique advantage drove education abroad programming.

Perhaps the largest-scale and most well-known education abroad endeavor in the United States, the Fulbright Program, established by the U.S. Congress in 1946, also has at its core a goal of increasing mutual understanding between Americans and people of other countries. Indeed, writing about the history of the program, Senator J. William Fulbright, who introduced the bill establishing the program, noted:

> The Fulbright Program aims to bring a little more knowledge, a little more reason, and a little more compassion into world affairs and thereby to increase the chance that nations will learn at last to live in peace and friendship. (Bureau of Educational and Cultural Affairs, n.d.)

Organized on a binational basis, the program exchanges students and faculty between the United States and countries around the world. While the program continues to aim toward Senator Fulbright's goal of building mutual understanding, it is also an important element of U.S. soft power.[1]

All of this is not to diminish the importance of the altruistic goals of education abroad, but rather to argue that these have always been intertwined with self-interest—for nations, universities, faculty, and students.

The Neocolonial Mind-Set

The trouble with operative assumptions about colonialism is that they tend to imagine it taking place in a sepia-toned past, when Western powers were peopled with individuals less informed about cultural differences and not yet keen to the idea of a global society. The colonial is contained and hermetically sealed off from the more enlightened and cooperative present. Indeed, education abroad is often proffered as an antidote to the colonizer's view of the world, promoting deeply meaningful intercultural interaction, and honoring the unique contributions and inherent value of each culture by encouraging students (and others) to cross international (and other) boundaries and learn with and from each other.

In spite of laudable intentions, (neo)colonial practices not only abound in the education abroad field but also influence the experiences of students and their interlocutors at every phase of the educational continuum. Given pressures to help programs make their numbers, administrators and faculty alike often resort to marketing language and techniques that sell education abroad by highlighting programs' touristic elements and the sights that participants will be able to Instagram back to their envious social networks. Such tactics set student expectations and frame education abroad as a consumer activity. After marketing exotic or authentic educational sites, administrators and faculty then encourage students to use their local sites as laboratories, approaching the local culture and people with a traditional ethnographic lens. Further, if students study abroad in groups, they often form homogenous enclaves that fail to facilitate anything other than a stilted interaction with local residents.

In the worst cases, programs fail to help students be self-critical and reflexive. This (inadvertently) leaves intact students' instincts toward constantly measuring the local culture against the home culture. Instead of meaningfully engaging and contributing to the local community, such programs focus only on the experience of the participants, with the local community at the service of the students. Inattention to reciprocity can negatively impact the local environment or siphon scarce resources away from the local population. Even when programs intentionally prioritize reciprocity and self-critical reflection, students may still mistake superficial appropriation of elements of the local culture with cultural competency. In other cases, students will focus on the elements of the local culture that reinforce stereotypes of authenticity. Worse still, local partners may seek to present a culture *they* believe the program and the students want, promoting a static, nostalgic, even anachronistic version of various cultural details. At a broader level, the trend in higher education to push students to solve the world's major problems can give rise to a savior complex among students and faculty that confuses acting on behalf of local people with true collaboration and partnership.

Enlightenment Underpinnings

In many ways, the good intentions behind education abroad programming share a direct continuity with projects of the colonial era, whose humanitarian motives follow from the Enlightenment's ideological underpinnings—most notably, the Self/Other distinction inherited from Descartes and others (Lacan, 1977). The Self, ideologically situated in a privileged position, looks upon Others as needing assistance. Like colonizers, international educators believe their work will profoundly improve the world. This can lead to a failure (purposeful or not) to take full measure of the uneven distribution of the benefits and costs of education abroad. Moreover, education abroad programming helps force disparate peoples and their experiences into an already hegemonic configuration of Self/Other subjectivity.

Commodification

U.S. education abroad tends to treat a Western style of education as a commodity. Alienated from any particular cultural context, it can be mobilized for consumption in any location by anyone. Thus, what initially appears to be a project focused on experiencing cultural situatedness ends up instead replicating Western education worldwide, using the same cookie-cutter models. It shares certain marketing strategies with tourism and ecotourism industries and operates within a globalized industry of education in which there have been clear winners and losers, in terms of imports and exports, market shares and brain drain. Furthermore, as noted before, education abroad often operates along with aid programs and other international projects as a form of soft power, disseminating certain values and propagating Western understandings of human subjectivity in neocolonial contexts.

Education Abroad as Investment

Tellingly, practitioners routinely describe education abroad as an investment when speaking with prospective students and their families. The metaphor is appealing: Education abroad requires a large, up-front expenditure of resources in the hopes of obtaining both concrete and esoteric benefits that slowly pay out over a student's lifetime. The good faith of the investor is required—good faith also led to the speculation that funded colonization projects and their promised returns. If Westerners tend to see colonialism today as nakedly opportunistic and exploitative, colonizers also believed that they were engaging in a humanitarian project that broke sharply with less informed ways of engaging with the Other from the medieval and early modern periods.

Toward Intersubjectivity: Untangling Oppositional Conceptions of Identity

The persistence of this particular form of engagement with the Other across major historic and cultural changes lies in part with the Western formulation of subjectivity. How Westerners understand themselves *as* themselves is predicated on a hierarchical binary distinction of Self and Other. This self-centered experiential logic, in turn, permeates the cultural, socioeconomic, religious, juridical, and other modes of social organization and interaction with the world. There is a rich literature on subjectivity in Western contexts, with many disparate themes, approaches, and explanations (Allen, 2009; Althusser, 1998; Diseger, 1994; Duncan, 1993; Foster, 1982; Friedman, 1991; Johnston, 2008; Strassburg, 2000; Žižek, 2000). Lacanian psychoanalytic understanding is one of the most influential and provides a useful model for explaining the power of the neocolonial impulse.

To Lacan, subjectivity is *discursive;* we become ourselves through the entire web of utterances, gestures, interactions, and nuances in and through which meaning is communicated by human beings. Subjectivity is always negatively construed: We can understand ourselves only by way of opposition from the Other. Gender difference was the primary metonym for this formulation: Man signifies not-Woman, and exists outside of itself in a negative relationship with the concept of Woman. To be male is to not be female. Woman is thus the Other (with the capital *O*) that, by way of subjection (oppression and loss of voice), makes the identity of male possible. Identities of the Self (the dominant subject position) are *symptomatic* and rely on negation from a particular Other that is subjected to a power imbalance (Žižek, 1990).

The symptomatic nature of subjectivity is just the beginning, however. The subject also has a *melancholic attachment* to its lack (the fact that its identity is contingent on the Other). This attachment means that subjectivity as we know it—being a person capable of participating in the particular form of sociality that "we" experience in Western cultures—is necessarily fractured and contingent. It needs the Other to remain the Other (i.e., to remain subjugated), if the Self's supposedly fixed identity is to make sense (Sarup, 1993).

Furthermore, in any fully elaborated relationship between Self and Other, another force is at work. *Anamorphosis* is the misrecognition of an object—of the Other—in such a way that the very material (lived) reality of the object is distorted and the subjective gaze is "inscribed into its objective features" (Žižek, 2000, p. 659). That is, the Self requires the Other to become, to some extent, what the identity of the Self *needs* the Other to be—meaning that systems of subjugation (colonialism, sexism) have real, material effects on the lives and experiences of those marked as Other. (Consider, as an example, the social enforcement of arbitrary standards of femininity faced by women in the United States.) Thus, colonized peoples are irrevocably changed by the relationship of colonialism; they become the colonized required by the colonizer identity. Anamorphosis also occurs in education abroad contexts; local residents are inscribed (by students, faculty, administrators, themselves) with the identities needed for the students to be explorers, cultural learners, and volunteers. Of course, none of this means that those cast as Other do not have agency. Whether women, the colonized, or Others encountered in education abroad, members of subjugated groups may actively resist the ways in which hierarchical systems position them. Indeed, they may seek to enact resistant and counterhegemonic identities of their own.

The theoretical approach discussed here considers the overdetermining, large-scale forces that shape contemporary social dynamics. However, as illustrated in Table 4.1, it is also a powerful tool for investigating the inequities and injustices of these dynamics, and for beginning to theorize and practice new ways of interacting with other(s) that might work against such detrimental forces as anamorphosis.

TABLE 4.1
Decolonizing Subjectivity

	Subjectivity as it is usually understood in Western contexts	*Intersubjectivity*
Operating modality	Neocolonial	Decolonizing
The "self" is . . .	Individual, unitary, whole, the not-Other	Divided, complex, necessarily partial, one of many others
	Negatively defined in opposition to the Other	Defined in dynamic interactions with many others
Common modalities of experience	Individualistic	Communitarian
	I am unique and everyone else is not-me.	*I am one of many who share similarities and differences.*
Common modalities of relationship	Transactional	Cooperative
	I use my personal resources to obtain what I need and want, trading wealth for goods and services.	*We use our shared and personal resources to advance shared objectives.*
Cross-cultural encounters are . . .	Moments in which the Self encounters the Other	Moments in which multiple, differential selves encounter one another
	Primarily narrated from the perspective of the Self	Conarrated from multiple, shifting points of view
Education abroad programs employing this sort of subjectivity . . .	Focus on using the experience and the resources of the site to enhance the intellectual, personal, and professional gains of the individual study abroad participants	Focus on defining shared objectives and working toward mutual benefits for both the study abroad participants and the local community participants

Note. This table is intended to illustrate the general differences between these two approaches to understanding a privileged observer's relationship to others in the world. Of course, this presentation in columns and rows is a simplification of what are, in reality, complicated and less binary modes of thinking.

Theories of subjectivity are helpful in pointing to the need for a new formulation of the subject that is not entirely dependent on the (subjugation of the) Other. Increasingly, progressive scholars working with subjectivity theory are directly or indirectly gesturing toward intersubjectivity (Chow, 1993; Dreger, 2005; Haraway, 1991), though there are varying ideas about what such a new way of relating to others might look like in practice. Žižek, for example, notes that subject position is not being abandoned altogether, but rather the particular sense of the Self that is predicated upon the Other. The responsibility for defining one's own identity then falls back to the (speaking, acting) subject self (Žižek, 1990). It is therefore not a lack or gap that defines subjects, but rather the overlaps, moments of contiguity, and a fundamental acceptance of the existence of many quite mutable, transitory, and unknowable differences between the two—an acceptance of the necessary ontological inconsistency of all subject positions. In other words, we can understand ourselves as having multiple, competing identities in interaction with the multiple, competing identities of those with whom we engage.

Intersubjective identities are contingent upon but no longer externalized in the identities of others. To mitigate self-centered use of the Other for our own purposes—whether in education abroad or in any cultural encounters—we must understand and situate ourselves within a complex web of relationalities. Part of the work here is to acknowledge and assume responsibility for the ways in which our own identities have been historically dependent on the subjugation of others. In short, what is needed is decolonization.

Toward a Comprehensive Approach to Decolonizing Education Abroad

A comprehensive approach to decolonizing education abroad requires intentionality and engagement from administrators, faculty, and students to reduce the distinction between Self and Other and to form cooperative and mutually beneficial relationships with local communities. The following principles, while not exhaustive, can serve as a guide for decolonizing education abroad efforts. As illustrated in Table 4.2, the principles fall into three general categories: planning and recruiting, collaborating with local partners and communities, and employing decolonizing pedagogies that enhance students' awareness of their own positionalities and connect the education abroad experience to other parts of the educational continuum.

TABLE 4.2

Strategies for Decolonizing Education Abroad

Category	Intervention	Impact
Planning and recruiting	Work with local businesses and organizations when possible.	Program supports the local community and builds lasting relationships.
	Consider sustainability and minimize impact on local resources.	Program uses fewer resources and competes less with local population for scarce resources.
	Choose interactive or collaborative program elements.	Students learn from hosts and share their own experiences with hosts; both students and hosts gain more nuanced and complex understandings of each other's cultures.
	Offer range of program types.	Students have support necessary to have a mutually positive interaction with host culture.
	Avoid consumeristic advertising and promote mutual impact of the program.	Students have a clearer idea of the program and are less focused on having the "experience of a lifetime."
	Employ best practices for equitable recruiting, with targeted outreach to underrepresented populations, as well as ways to increase access to program participation.	Program participation is diversified, allowing for richer conversations among group participants or individual participants enrolled in an array of exchanges and direct-enrollment programs.
Collaborating with local partners and communities	Share ownership of programs.	Whether the model is exchange, direct enrollment, "island" programs, faculty led, or otherwise, both the home institution's and local host's values and priorities are considered, and both have input into program design, modeling for the students positive intercultural collaboration.

	Be intentional when selecting local partners.	Institutions select partners that are interested in mutually beneficial collaboration, consider the impact each partner will have on the other, and educate students on the partner institution's role in the host society.
	Plan for reciprocity.	Both communities have opportunities to learn from each other beyond providing the education abroad experience for the students.
Employing decolonizing pedagogies	Enhance on-campus and arrival orientations.	Regardless of program type, orientation programming or preprogram readings or assignments should push students to think intentionally and reflexively about their own identities, stereotypes, and the role of culture in daily life.
	Consider prerequisites or recommended courses prior to education abroad.	As much as we recognize that courses and majors may require some preparatory coursework, we should also recognize that basic background coursework will help students be prepared to make sense of their experience abroad and better able to contextualize the cultures they encounter.
	Offer return programming or coursework.	Students will benefit from venues in which they can continue to process their experience abroad and discuss with others ways they might apply what they learned to future coursework and career plans.
	Foster pedagogies of global learning on home campuses.	Education abroad experiences become a feature within the overall educational continuum, rather than a departure from it, and students' learning about global challenges and contexts is enhanced, thereby preparing them to be better equipped to engage fully while abroad and to use their learning while abroad as part of their overall collegiate experience.

Planning and Recruiting

Resource use. Administrators and faculty planning programs can head off negative impacts by supporting the local economy through use of local service providers and researching the environmental and resource implications of the program's presence. This may result in limiting participation numbers or dividing participants among multiple sites to distribute the impact. Long-term consequences of choices should be considered, as well as impacts of the larger constellation of programs operating in the local site.

Pedagogy. How program elements (assignments, activities, and site visits) promote exploration of the local culture should be considered in relation to learning outcomes such as intercultural understanding. Interactive and collaborative activities benefiting both members of the local communities and program participants place student participants and their local interlocutors on more equal footing, give the latter more agency in the cultural interaction, and help all move beyond stereotypes. For example, education abroad students can be prepared to share aspects of their own culture any time they ask their hosts about theirs.

Program portfolio. When establishing a portfolio of programs, education abroad professionals must consider how the portfolio will serve the diversity of their student populations. While students with significant intercultural coursework are likely prepared for a direct exchange with a university abroad, early-career students with little travel experience may need more formalized intervention to process the experience before, during, and/or after the abroad period.

Honoring local curricula. It is important to offer students course options that fulfill home school requirements. However, imposing home curricula on international partners is not advised; the validity of partner institutions' educational approaches should be acknowledged and understood as adding value. This becomes particularly important with exchange and direct enrollment partners; when home departments imply that courses abroad are inferior to home courses (and therefore do not meet home requirements) this undermines the partnerships—and education abroad.

Program promotion. Advertising efforts influence student perceptions. As discussed previously, selling education abroad as an investment, adventure, or experience of a lifetime suggests the student protagonist will strike out into the world to encounter the exotic Other. Images can be problematic, suggesting conquest (the triumphant student on a mountaintop or overlooking a city) or discovery (students wearing keffiyeh while riding camels or surrounded by children who represent the Other). Predeparture workshops for students and faculty on taking compelling, culturally sensitive photos can help, as well as discussions of using social media to share critical thinking about experiences rather than reinforcing cultural stereotypes. This in turn can supply images and text for marketing purposes that do not support the Self/ Other dichotomy.

Inclusive excellence. Program design must address access. (Who feels welcome? Who can afford it—financially, disciplinarily?) An inclusive and equitable approach to recruitment, student selection, and financial support can enable more underrepresented students to participate in education abroad, bringing to the experience differing backgrounds, perspectives, and understandings of privilege. Equity and inclusion particularly matter in group-based programs, where relative homogeneity may bolster Self/Other thinking in regard to local community members. Although attention to equity and inclusion will not remove obstacles to positive interactions abroad—and students from underrepresented backgrounds are not necessarily better-informed participants—more diverse participation brings a wider array of perspectives and complicates students' notions of identity and belonging.

Collaborating With Local Partners and Communities

Shared ownership. Rather than maintaining a narrow definition of *partners* and seeing local community members as a means to an end, education abroad organizations and offices, as much as possible, should seek to share ownership of programs with their local partners. This requires engaging them not only in logistical discussions but also in questions related to curriculum, instruction, and planning of activities. Long-term, mutually beneficial relationships with partners and local communities help ensure rich intercultural interactions for all and model a mutual respect for both the local and home cultures. Long-term thinking also encourages consideration of each other's priorities and interests in seeking to maintain the health of the partnership. *Exchange agreements,* by definition, include a degree of reciprocity, but all programming can benefit from additional measures of bilaterality. Ideally, local community members can visit the students' home campus or community, or, at the least, local students can be invited to participate in program activities.

Partner choice. Choices regarding local partnerships must be intentional. Institutional fit is important in exchanges, but what is also important is how choice of partner will influence students' perceptions of local culture. Institutional similarities, for example, in presenting students with the familiar, can be comforting. This, however, can result in distorted views of the local culture and cocoon students rather than disrupt them. Yet disruption is key to shifts in perspective and other learning processes. Similarly, students will be pushed to reconsider their role in the world more by social justice–oriented partners than travel-oriented ones.

Employing Decolonizing Pedagogies

Resisting cultural simplification. Perhaps the most challenging of the three areas lies in preparing students for their experiences and then continuing to support them as they critically respond to experiences during and after being abroad. Orientations, which for many reasons tend to focus on practicalities of going abroad, can be reframed to help students become more self-critical of their own roles. Acknowledging that exotic places live primarily in the imagination and asking students to avoid judging the local culture will help them sidestep neocolonial pitfalls as visitors and observers, and encourage students instead to approach program locations and cultures on equal terms with their own. Such reframing can help students to begin to recognize local cultures realistically as dynamic, complex, syncretic, and made up of diverse individuals.

Infusing the decolonizing ethos into the educational continuum. However, orientation is insufficient. More effectively, preparation will begin in students' campus coursework. Programs that start on campus or ask students to complete preprogram reading or assignments can establish an initial frame for the experience abroad. Exchange programs with formal mechanisms that match outbound students with counterparts resident on their campuses can encourage students to contemplate what living in a new culture will mean. Once students are abroad, self-reflection folded into program assignments and activities can move students beyond their initial stereotypes and assumptions to reflect critically on their own identities. Ultimately, this should help them acknowledge their own complex experiences of privilege and oppression without adopting an attitude of either superiority or uncritical alliance with others who are oppressed. Finally, return programming (e.g., venues to present the learning from abroad) and courses that encourage reflection can help students continue to process what they learned abroad, arrive at more nuanced conclusions, and develop tools to share their experiences with the broader campus community. Senior theses and capstone projects can enable students to build on their experiences abroad and apply a decolonizing approach to such work. Ideally, the education abroad experience nestles (un)comfortably within a home-campus curriculum that bolsters global learning at all stages of the educational continuum, from first-term seminars to senior projects.

Conclusion

Any discussion of decolonizing education abroad must acknowledge the challenges of putting ideas into practice and the sheer difficulty of adopting a decolonizing approach. Involving partners abroad fully in program design, planning, and curricula multiplies the number of cooks in the kitchen and increases the odds that disagreements—even impasses—will arise. In addition, education abroad professionals work within a Western business and professional culture and a context of Western jurisprudence. These largely determine expected standards, best practices, and deliverables. Students (and their parents) may expect education abroad to be a seamlessly connected segment of their Western-style college learning, and to adhere closely to the norms of that context. The pressures that resist decolonization come from all directions. Only with a serious commitment to the ethos of decolonization can modest headway be made. Thus, practitioners must do their best to follow decolonizing approaches while addressing concerns that this approach engenders as they arise. They must try to shape expectations on their campuses (or within their organizations) and among students and their families. This may feel like swimming upstream, but inspiration is to be found in small successes. Indeed, the entire project of decolonizing education abroad is one that requires a long-term commitment to change and plays out in stops and starts, and that is certainly worthwhile.

Educators have a responsibility to examine and address neocolonial tendencies and colonial legacies in academic programming on and off campus. These affect every aspect of education and bolster largely uncritical assumptions about the good that higher learning does to foster peace and encourage intercultural understanding. As argued throughout this chapter, high-minded goals are not without merit, but the real effects of education abroad are much less clearly beneficial, and the benefits that do exist are not evenly distributed. Taken-for-granted understandings of individual subjectivity largely help to obfuscate education abroad's problematic effects; employing a more intersubjective and decolonizing approach, however, can begin to dismantle the machinery that continuously reinforces neocolonial patterns of relating and interacting. As more international (and other) educators strive to employ decolonizing approaches in programs and curricula, researchers can begin to assess their outcomes. In the meantime, it is imperative that practitioners, faculty, and institutions undertake the decolonizing project. For it is only in approaching local community members abroad, not as accessories in our own narratives of self-improvement, but as collaborators in the project of true intercultural exchange, that we can begin to achieve the full promise of education abroad.

Note

1. As a binational program, Fulbright receives funding from many of the partner governments around the world—in the case of some countries, more funding comes from the partner government—but overall, the congressional appropriation is the largest source of funding for the program.

References

Allen, A. (2009). Discourse, power, and subjectivation: The Foucault/Habermas debate reconsidered. *The Philosophical Forum, 40*, 1–28.

Althusser, L. (1998). Ideology and ideological state apparatuses. In J. Storey (Ed.), *Cultural theory and popular culture: A reader* (2nd ed., pp. 153–164). Athens: University of Georgia Press.

Blaut, J. M. (1993.) *The colonizer's model of the world: Geographical diffusionism and eurocentric history*. New York, NY: Guilford Press.

Bureau of Educational and Cultural Affairs. (n.d.). *J. William Fulbright quotes*. Available from https://eca.state.gov/fulbright/about-fulbright/history/j-william-fulbright/j-william-fulbright-quotes

Campbell, J. (2008). *A hero with a thousand faces* (3rd ed.). Novano, CA: New World Library. (Original work published 1949)

Cazden, C., & Leggett, E. (1976). *Culturally responsive education: A discussion of LAU remedies II*. Prepared for the U.S. Department of Health, Education, and Welfare. Washington, DC: U.S. National Institute of Education.

Chow, R. (1993). *Writing diaspora: Tactics of intervention in contemporary cultural studies*. Bloomington: Indiana University Press.

Diseger, P. (1994). Performativity trouble: Postmodern feminism and essential subjects. *Political Research Quarterly, 47*, 655–673.

Dreger, A. D. (2005). *One of us: Conjoined twins and the future of normal*. Cambridge, MA: Harvard University Press.

Duncan, J. (1993). Sites of representation: Place, time and the discourse of the Other. In J. Duncan & D. Ley (Eds.), *Place/culture/representation* (pp. 39–56). London, UK: Routledge.

Ficarra, J. M. (2017). Curating cartographies of knowledge: Reading institutional study abroad portfolio as text. *Frontiers: The Interdisciplinary Journal of Study Abroad, 29*(1), 1–14.

Foster, S. W. (1982). The exotic as a symbolic system. *Dialectical Anthropology, 7*, 21–30.

Freire, P. (1972). *Pedagogy of the oppressed*. New York, NY: Herder and Herder.

Friedman, M. (1991). The social self and the partiality debates. In C. Card (Ed.), *Feminist ethics* (pp. 161–179). Lawrence, KS: University of Kansas Press.

Garcia, E. (1993). Language, culture, and education. *Review of Research in Education, 19*, 51–98.

Gardner, B., & Krabill, R. (2017). *Against the romance of study abroad. Africa is a country: Not the continent with 54 countries*. Available from from https://africasacountry.com/2017/07/against-the-romance-of-study-abroad/

Gristwood, A., & Woolf, M. (Eds.). (2014). Woven by memory: The idea of nation in education abroad. *CAPA Occasional Publications, 3*. Boston, MA: CAPA International Education.

Haraway, D. (1991). *Simians, cyborgs, and women: The reinvention of nature*. New York, NY: Routledge.

Hoffa, W. (2007). *A history of US study abroad: Beginnings to 1965.* Carlisle, PA: The Forum on Education Abroad.

hooks, b. (1994). *Teaching to transgress: Education as the practice of freedom.* New York, NY: Routledge.

hooks, b. (2003). *Teaching community: A pedagogy of hope.* New York, NY: Routledge.

Johnston, A. (2008). Žižek's ontology: A transcendental materialist theory of subjectivity. J. M. Edie (Ed.), *Northwestern University studies in phenomenology and existential philosophy* (series). Evanston, IL: Northwestern University Press.

Lacan, J. (1977). *Ecrits, a selection* (A. Sheridan, Trans.). London, UK: Tavistock.

Ladson-Billings, G. (1994). *The dreamkeepers: Successful teachers of African American children.* San Francisco, CA: Jossey-Bass.

McCarty, T. L., & Zepeda, O. (1995). Indigenous language education and literacy: Introduction to the theme issue. *The Bilingual Research Journal, 19*(1), 1–4.

Moll, L., & Gonzalez, N. (1994). Lessons from research with language minority children. *Journal of Reading Behavior, 26*(4), 23–41.

Ogden, A. (2007). The view from the veranda: Understanding today's colonial student. *Frontiers: The Interdisciplinary Journal of Study Abroad, 15,* 35–55.

Paris, D., & Alim, H. S. (Eds.). (2017). *Culturally sustaining pedagogies: Teaching and learning for justice in a changing world.* New York, NY: Teachers College Press.

Ramírez, G. B. (2013). Learning abroad or just going abroad? International education in opposite sides of the border. *The Qualitative Report, 18*(62), 1–11. Available from http://www.nova.edu/ssss/QR/QR18/ramirez62.pdf

Sarup, M. (1993). *An introductory guide to poststructuralism and postmodernism* (2nd ed.). San Francisco, CA: Pearson Education.

Sharpe, E. K. (2015). Colonialist tendencies in education abroad. *International Journal of Teaching and Learning in Higher Education, 27*(2), 227–234.

Smith, L. T. (2002). *Decolonizing methodologies: Research and indigenous peoples.* New York, NY: Zed Books.

Smitherman, G. (1977). *Talkin and testifyin: The language of Black America.* Detroit, MI: Wayne State University Press.

Strassburg, J. (2000). Shamanic shadows: One hundred generations of undead subversion in southern Scandinavia, 7,000–4,000 BC. *Stockholm Studies in Archaeology, 20.* Stockholm, SE: Stockholms Universitet.

Wood, C. A., & Schroeder, K. (2017, July). Avoiding collateral damage: Education abroad programs and their impacts on host communities. *NAFSA Trends & Insights.* Available from http://www.nafsa.org/Professional_Resources/Research_and_Trends/Trends_and_Insights/Avoiding_Collateral_Damage__Education_Abroad_Programs_and_Their_Impacts_on_Host_Communities/

Zemach-Bersin, T. (2007). Global citizenship & study abroad: It's all about U.S. *Critical Literacies: Theories and Practices, 1*(2), 16–28.

Žižek, S. (1990). Rossellini: Woman as symptom of Man. *October, 54,* 18–44.

Žižek, S. (2000). History against historicism. *European Journal of English Studies, 4*(2), 101–110.

PART TWO

SUPPORTING STUDENT LEARNING ALONG THE EDUCATIONAL CONTINUUM

5

ADULTS STUDYING
ABROAD THROUGH
COMMUNITY COLLEGES

Rosalind Latiner Raby

In the United States, community colleges serve an essential educational function and role as they offer options for university overflow and provide a "second chance" for nontraditional students to achieve a higher education (Cohen, Brawer, & Kisker, 2015). Most community college educational programs are designed to be terminal and as such become the sole venue for higher education as well as the only opportunity to introduce and to build international literacy skills (Raby, 2008). In 2017, there were 1,600 community colleges with 13 million students in the United States, of whom 7.7 million were enrolled in credit programs and 5 million in noncredit programs (American Association of Community Colleges [AACC], 2017).

Community colleges have multiple missions to serve a diverse range of student goals (Cohen, Brawer, & Kisker, 2015). Credit programs culminate in an associate degree, transfer degree/certificate, or certificate for vocational or occupational workforce preparation. Noncredit programs include developmental (remedial) education, English as a second language, community service courses, basic skills development, and lifelong learning services (AACC, 2017). Each community college gives a different weight to each mission and some may be stressed more than others. Not all community colleges have as their primary mission the intent to transfer.

One characteristic of a nontraditional student is being an adult (Cross, 1981; Hagedorn, 2005; Ross-Gordon, 2011). Students younger than 23 years of age are referred to as traditional students (Justice, 2001). The literature is not consistent as to when adult status begins (Allen & Zhang, 2016), with an age range of 23 to 28 (Cross, 1981; National Center for

Education Statistics, 2014). In that the average community college student is 28 years old, most community college students are identified as adults (AACC, 2017). Those surveyed for this chapter concur that the age of "24 is a good indicator of adult or not" (California Colleges for International Education [CCIE], Respondent A, 2017). Literature defines 4 distinct categories for adults including the term *older adult*, for students over the age of 46 (Hagedorn, 2005). Fifteen percent of community college students are defined as older adults and about 88% of older adults are enrolled in noncredit or work-force training programs that are certificate oriented (AACC, 2017). In recent years there has been a decline in adult for-credit enrollment as a result of economic recovery, which has instead attracted adults back into the labor market.

Laanan (2003) showed that adults attend community college for the convenient location, low tuition, comprehensive course offerings, and flexible schedules that allow them to take a minimal number of courses, which can enable them to return quickly to the workforce. This is the opposite of the goals of full-time traditional students. Little is known about community college adult students who study abroad aside from the fact that they do study abroad. To learn more, an informal survey was administered, in November 2017, to members of CCIE, a nonprofit consortia of California community colleges, with responses from 12 directors of education abroad. The following questions were asked: (a) Is the definition of *adult* and *older adult* consistent at your college? (b) What percentage of students studying abroad are "adults"? (c) Are there any notable differences in adult students (their needs, their achievements)? (d) What are best practices in providing optimal learning abroad for adults? A focus on California community colleges is valid because more than half of all U.S. community college education abroad programs are offered by a California community college (Institute of International Education [IIE], 2017). While the responses cannot be generalized, they do provide context to a discussion on adult students who study abroad.

Education Abroad in Community Colleges

In 2017, about 147 community colleges in the United States offered education abroad programs (IIE, 2017). Using the open-access philosophy, community colleges transformed education abroad from a university junior-year abroad with admission constraints (class standing, GPA, prerequisites), to a program that serves all students at all ability levels (Raby, 2008). Access is given to community members not enrolled as students, enrolled students, university students, and concurrently enrolled high school students. Supporting open access are low costs and enrollment with a GPA as low as 1.7 to 2.0. In California, programming includes semester, short-term winter and/or summer programs of 3+ weeks, and 7 to 14-day programs with credit awarded in general education transfer courses as well as in technical, vocational, and occupational courses such as nursing, culinary arts, oenology (wine production), and cosmetology. Although all education abroad is credit bearing, not all adult students want that credit. Most community college education abroad uses the faculty-led model because it is believed that faculty develop special bonds with students who build group affinity (Brenner, 2016; Robertson, 2015; Willis, 2016). Group affinity is important because it provides a safe place to learn and because adults strongly relate to one another due to similar backgrounds and experiences (Zhang, Lui, & Hagedorn, 2013). It is quite common for some faculty who offer education abroad courses to "gain a following and have repeat students annually" (CCIE, Respondent L, 2017).

Community College Education Abroad
Age Ranges in the Literature

Although both adult and older adults study abroad, older adults tend to study more in summer programs. In five published studies, adult students between the ages of 23 and 46 comprised 30% of education abroad students (Raby, Rhodes, & Biscarra, 2014), 76% (Brenner, 2016), 58% (Willis, 2016), 30% (Amani & Kim, 2017), and 14% (Robertson & Blasi, 2017). Within these studies older adults were recognized with 3 students age 50 to 59, 4 students age 62+ (Raby et al., 2014), 1 student age 78 (Brenner, 2016), 4 students age 38 to 49, and 1 student age 62 (Willis, 2016). Survey respondents shared that in the previous year 2 colleges had 25% of summer students age 60 to 84 (CCIE, Respondents D and I, 2017), while a third college had 12 older adults (61–74) in one summer program, and 6 adults and 2 older adults in another summer program (CCIE, Respondent B, 2017). Another college had 20 older adults who studied in the summer and 4 in a semester program (CCIE, Respondent C, 2017). Both community college and community college education abroad literature confirm that adult and older adult learners need to be explored separately from other student populations as age leads to unique educational experiences (Compton, Cox, & Laanan, 2006; Hagedorn, 2005).

Deficit Narratives and Adult Students

Many concur that a primary barrier to participate in community college education abroad is that nontraditional students are less interested and/or unable to study abroad (Commission on the Abraham Lincoln Study Abroad

Fellowship Program, 2005). *Nontraditional* is defined by socioeconomic status levels, race and ethnicity, first-generation, full-time working, or adult (Ross-Gordon, 2011). Any one of these characteristics can mark a student as nontraditional. Unfortunately, there are often low expectations for nontraditional students, resulting in a deficit narrative that limits their chances of success. Community college research acknowledges that a deficit narrative contributes to the "cooling-out" process (Clark, 1960) in which specific programs channel some students into courses with differential outcome expectations. An example is the "sorting" of privileged students to credit programs and students of color, low-income students, and adults to noncredit programs (Brint & Karabel, 1989). Community college administrator expectations about student choices to study abroad are also defined by deficit stereotypes (Raby & Valeau, 2016). Institutional sorting includes education abroad not being included as part of a college pathway, not being a for-credit offering, not being linked to college success programs, and not maintaining the same visibility as other educational programs.

Counterdeficit narratives challenge the deficit narrative as being stereotypical and obsolete since nontraditional students possess multiple forms of capital, some of which are unique to racial, ethnic, and gendered groups, and use these forms of capital to succeed in college (Modood, 2004; Yosso, 2005). Both community college and community college education abroad literature confirm that it is not student personal characteristics but institutional obstacles that hinder student success (McClenney, Marti, & Adkins, 2012; Raby, 2008). The following discussion provides examples of counternarratives relevant to the education abroad context: (a) adults want to learn; (b) adults know how to navigate a balance among work, home, and college; and (c) nontraditional students want to study abroad.

Adults Want to Learn

All community college students choose to attend a community college to better themselves. Counterdeficit research shows that community college adult students have positive self-identity and that this identity leads to college success (Gonzalez, Stein, & Huq, 2013). Adult students, no matter their race, ethnicity, or economic status, have social and cultural capital based on life experiences that contribute to building a strong sense of self-determination (Gipson, Mitchell, & McLean, 2017; Modood, 2004). When past experiences are combined with newly gained knowledge from college experiences, adults routinely achieve success along academic pathways (Dumais & Ward, 2010; Morest, 2013; Moschetti & Hudley, 2015).

Although adults want to learn, it is important to note that each student comes with varying degrees of expertise and will have a differential learning experience. Some of these experiences are negatively defined by existing institutional stratification that varies across racial, class, gender, and age distinctions. Stratification, in turn, contributes to underrepresentation in some college programs (Hodara & Jaggars, 2014; McClenney et al., 2012). Even well-intended institutional policies can discriminate through exclusion of nontraditional students who are already marginalized by inequalities in curriculum and through hostile campus environments (Harper & Quaye, 2009). At the same time, when institutional programs are designed for success, nontraditional students will succeed (Hodara & Jaggars, 2014; Moschetti & Hudley, 2015).

Adult students know how to make sound decisions and choose to study because they want to improve themselves (Bailey, Jaggars, & Jenkins, 2015). Similarly, adult students know that studying abroad is an educational experience they need to become part of (Oberstein-Delvalle, 1999; Zamani-Gallaher, Leon, & Lang, 2016). Adults also are mature, and they realize the importance of taking advantage of college activities (Moschetti & Hudley, 2015; Soria & Stebleton, 2012) and demonstrate this with a "sense of understanding what they want out of the study abroad program" (CCIE, Respondent E, 2017). Willis (2016) found that older students who study abroad were "fairly secure in their racial and ethnic identities prior to departure, which might be a characteristic of the community college population, particularly due to their older average age" (p. 178).

The implication for adult students in education abroad is twofold. First, institutional practices in community college are based on the deficit belief that barriers to studying abroad are mostly student centric and that, as a result, the college will have difficulty attracting students to study abroad. Subsequent adoption of institutional policies that are designed to support the nontraditional student often ends up discriminating against them. For example, to support working students, the length of many programs is shortened. This ends up providing a differential experience for those identified as nontraditional. Second, "sorting" continues directly or indirectly as a result of deficit-based institutional practices. In application to education abroad, the poorly supported or nonexistent programs, in turn, negatively affect student interest (Raby & Valeau, 2016).

Adults Know How to Navigate a Balance
Among Work, Home, and College

A stereotype about adult students is that they have competing needs due to work and/or home and cannot give due attention to school. Although conflicting attention is part of an adult world, research suggests that university students who work are still fully devoted to their studies (Richardson, Kemp, Malinen, & Haultain, 2013). Community college research shows that adults are acutely aware of the need to balance competing forces in their lives (Próspero & Vohra-Gupta, 2007; Silverman, Sarvenaz, & Stiles, 2009) and that they achieve this balance through family support (Strayhorn & Johnson, 2014) and support from friends (Dennis, Phinney, & Chuateco, 2005). Adult students are also often motivated to succeed out of a desire to serve as role models to younger siblings, to their own children, and to grandchildren (Gipson et al., 2017). Finally, student success is increased by engagement with faculty (Wood & Harris, 2015).

Community college education abroad research has similar findings. Most community college students work and are able to navigate both educational and working worlds. They can thus find a way to study abroad. In fact, in the Raby and colleagues (2014) qualitative study, all students were able to "negotiate the tensions between their concerns and the desire for a global experience and sought solutions that allowed them to study abroad" (p. 9). The ability to balance includes the choice to leave children, spouses, and even jobs to take advantage of studying abroad (Amani & Kim, 2017). The support and encouragement they receive from their parents, friends, spouses or significant others, and children for their educations extends to study abroad (Amani & Kim, 2017; Drexler & Campbell, 2011; Raby, 2008; Robertson & Blasi, 2017).

Nontraditional Students Want to Study Abroad

It is often suggested that nontraditional students need to be taught to appreciate the idea of studying abroad. However, research does not support this. Instead, research shows that students know about studying abroad, even prior to enrollment in the community college. Nontraditional community college students know about the benefits gained from studying abroad in terms of career readiness (Zamani-Gallaher et al., 2016). Many students consistently describe studying abroad as an opportunity of their lifetime (Amani & Kim, 2017; Oberstein-Delvalle, 1999). As seen previously, adult students already know how to navigate work and family obligations. It is not surprising then that they are encouraged by faculty to study abroad (Brenner, 2016), by senior administrators who themselves studied abroad (Raby & Valeau, 2016), and by family members and/or close friends who studied abroad (Amani & Kim, 2017; Raby & Rhodes, 2018).

An accepted belief is that community college students have no interest in traveling abroad and in fact rarely travel beyond their own neighborhoods. While limited travel may be true for some students, most know of the world via media, social media, and military service. Student surveys also show that many first-generation students travel back home and travel often (Raby & Rhodes, 2018; Robertson & Blasi, 2017). Especially for older adults, travel is not novel. In one college, "older adults had traveled together before on noncollege-sponsored trips with one of our professors, and on credit classes with another" (CCIE, Respondent F, 2017). In another college, "adults enroll to revisit countries where they were born and/or previously worked" (CCIE, Respondent H, 2017).

Discussion

The deficit narrative is at the foundation of many policy choices at community colleges to offer (or not offer) education abroad. This is dangerous. A deficit narrative can result in institutional practices reminiscent of the "cooling-out" process. Thus, the decision to not offer education abroad disadvantages students by placing them into differential pathways, especially when compared to colleges that define education abroad as a necessity. Four examples of dangers that result from using a deficit narrative follow.

Institutional Choice to Offer Differential Pathways That Exclude Education Abroad

Community college education abroad is often interpreted as an unnecessary luxury for adult students who are perceived to have social, financial, and cultural capital deficiencies (Raby, 2008). Some community college stakeholders oppose education abroad because they see it as superfluous to the career pathway of adults. In colleges whose missions emphasize a short school–to–work career education pipeline to get adults back into work, time spent doing anything else is seen to be inessential. This thinking does not take into account the strong link between studying abroad and career advancement as study abroad participation can enhance career pathway preparation (Raby & Valeau, 2016). Further, many adults "sign up for community college as a one-time thing to take the study abroad course. These adults are not looking for a change in career pathways" (CCIE, Respondent A, 2017). For these adults, the opportunity to study abroad is life enhancing. Another assumption is that education abroad's high cost puts it out of reach for community college students, including adult students. While cost may be a concern, a college that does not offer the same educational opportunities to low-income students as to richer ones is discriminatory on many different levels. Further, not all adult learners are low income, and research suggests that cost is less a deciding factor when students are given an opportunity to understand the cost/benefit of the programs (Amani & Kim, 2017).

Institutional Choice to Use Community College Student Stereotypes to Influence Education Abroad Design Choice

Stereotypes of student characteristics directly influence institutional decisions about the design of education abroad programs. These characteristics include low academic preparation, financial limitations, insular attitudes to leaving home, competing time with work and/or family, and a lack of cultural capital to see education abroad as a link to future careers. There is an unchallenged belief that the only option for working adults is programming of under two weeks. As a result, some community college education abroad programs are noticeably shorter than in the past. This deficit narrative is problematic; students claim that when given the opportunity, they will go on longer programs. In fact, in California, programs longer than two weeks dominate in community colleges (CCIE, 2017). In a 2015 survey, community college students indicated that they were highly likely to participate in short-term (27%), summer (23%), semester (23%), or internship (20%) programs (Robertson & Blasi, 2017). Research suggests timing is more important than length (Amani & Kim, 2017). Further, the optimal time for adult students varies because for some it is time off from work, time in between jobs, when kids are grown, or when a parent can leave the kids (Amani & Kim, 2017).

Institutional Choice to Believe That Adult Students Can Succeed

Research consistently shows that institutional obstacles negatively impact completion more than personal characteristics. However, adults have an interest in education and use social and cultural capital to help them along their academic and career pathways. Literature shows that characteristics that adults bring with them into the community college, while negatively stereotyped by some, in fact contribute to eventual college success. All CCIE survey respondents were unanimous in the opinion that adults bring strengths to study abroad programs. As one respondent said, "Age impacts the student's maturity to deal with the unknown" (CCIE, Respondent D, 2017). The deficit model in which nontraditional students at community colleges will not study abroad needs to be challenged with new institutional policies that support equity.

Differential Experiences of Adult Students While Studying Abroad

Adult students share similarities with younger students in terms of their needs abroad or performance in the classroom. However, programs for students of multiple ages also need to take differences into consideration in their design. This becomes possible when the assets adult and older adult students bring to education abroad are foregrounded, rather than being any assumed deficits. First, adult students have a maturity that allows for a more immersive experience (Willis, 2016). One survey respondent said that because "older students have prior experiences, they see things and act differently in new situations" (CCIE, Respondent J, 2017). Second, adult students influence group dynamics. Positively, maturity allows bonding with peers. In Brenner's (2016) study, the older adult commented that "I was just astounded at how generous and close and open the students were. . . . I could ask any of them, 'Could I hang out with you tonight?' and I would enjoy it" (p. 378). One respondent said that "older students raise the bar for all the younger folks" and at the same time, the younger students seek out friendships with the older students (CCIE, Respondent I, 2017). Adult students "often have a social gift of bridging generational differences easily" (CCIE, Respondent K, 2017) and "if adult students are properly informed and prepared, they integrate well with the group and add a positive dimension to the make-up of our groups" (CCIE, Respondent N, 2017). In the negative, "age can become a dividing line" (Willis, 2016, p. 141). An adult student reported, "There was an age divide with older and younger students studying for a semester in Korea, particularly in connection with drinking under age and lack of responsibility in drinking" (author interview with a student studying in Korea, 2012). Finally, a few respondents noted a problem in which maturity can lead an adult student to becoming a counselor and the "de facto assistant leader or house mom/dad for younger colleagues [which refers to younger students]" (CCIE, Respondents C, F, and N, 2017). "Faculty should not rely on the adult student maturity because they too are students" (CCIE, Respondent L, 2017).

There are also best practices that work well with adult students. First, all survey respondents said that adults, and particularly older adults, want their own housing and prefer to stay in homestays/apartments rather than hotels/dorms. One respondent said that adults should be placed in the nicest housing (CCIE, Respondent L, 2017). Second, some adults have difficulty with technology during the application process. "Extra assistance and flexibility in applying help set the tone for a successful learning experience" (CCIE, Respondent B, 2017). Third, age may impact the ability to "keep up with a packed itinerary" and alternate activities may need to be planned. Yet the same respondent noted that in a Cuba program "there was an 86-year-old who danced rings around people half her age, but her 'boyfriend,' who was 84, went at a much slower pace" (CCIE, Respondent E, 2017). Finally, adults are often resistant to course requirements of writing papers, taking exams, and doing lengthy projects. One respondent noted, "Most of our older adults are studying abroad for personal development, already have their degrees, and either are not interested in earning credits, or are using them for continuing education credits to move up the salary scale (usually college instructors)" (CCIE, Respondent D, 2017). There was general agreement that "counsel on all program features will result in adults that [*sic*] are fully engaged and have a better impact on all participants" (CCIE, Respondent G, 2017). Another respondent suggested giving different assignments for those seeking Pass/No Pass (Respondent K, 2017). Yet another respondent suggested to specifically "counsel to explain that this is not a Road Scholar trip in which one is lectured to in an entertaining and informative manner, but never, ever required to do evaluated written work or extensive graded projects" (CCIE, Respondent A, 2017).

Conclusion

There is a need to learn more about adult and older adult students who study abroad at community colleges because open access demands availability to all students. Community college research shows that stereotypes about adult students are not always correct. In fact, adults are interested in education, they can balance work and school, they participate in a variety of college programs, and they are capable of success. There is no indication that adult students cannot study abroad. Moreover, research shows that many adults have had previous international experiences including travel, work, living abroad, and military deployment. Many also have close family and friends who previously studied abroad and serve as models. It is time to acknowledge deficit narratives that have guided policies and to eliminate them.

There is an urgent need to change community college education abroad policies that have largely been built around a deficit narrative. This is even more important because there are known benefits to education abroad outcomes that enhance effective citizenship, no matter one's age. New program options need to be based on impact surveys of the current generation of students rather than on archaic stereotypes. In addition, specific training for faculty and staff will help them overcome existing preconceptions of students' limitations (Willis, 2016). There also needs to be a reexamination of any policy or program design that negatively impacts enrollment options. Alternative practices can be learned from comparative research of students who attend community colleges and global counterparts. These students are mostly nontraditional in that they are older, have nontraditional entry qualifications, work full-time, have family commitments, come from low-income and minority populations, are immigrants, and are often first-generation students (Raby & Valeau,

2018). It is also important to note that the United States is not the only country in which education abroad is offered within the community college or global counterpart sector. Student mobility programs occur in institutions in this sector in Germany, Portugal, Brazil, and China. All around the world, participation in education abroad is important for all students, including nontraditional students. These mobility programs are done with success and provide options for learning.

In conclusion, it is central to a discussion on adult students that, as one survey respondent said, "Adults are very different, in terms of what they want to get out of the program" (CCIE, Respondent B, 2017). At the same time, it is critical to understand that adult students are "serious students who study abroad for personal enrichment purposes" (CCIE, Respondent G, 2017). The more that the field learns about adult students who study abroad, the more knowledge will showcase where philosophical and structural changes need to be made to enhance community college education abroad programs. Change begins with policy to eliminate existing obstacles that inhibit expansion of programs and limit opportunities for student participants. Countering myths and stereotypes will support new approaches to maintain open access and inclusivity of all students. Evolving definitions of how to achieve student success should acknowledge the role of adult interests and needs. Finally, new constructs need to be created to include education abroad as part of a combination of strategies that colleges adopt to counter historic achievement gaps in student success. These patterns are a reflection of institutional choice in which community colleges choose to not support education abroad.

References

Allen, T. O., & Zhang, Y. (L.). (2016). Dedicated to their degrees: Adult transfer students in engineering baccalaureate programs. *Community College Review, 44*(1), 72–86.

Amani, M., & Kim, M. M. (2017). Study abroad participation at community colleges: Students' decision and influential factors. *Community College Journal of Research and Practice, 41*(10), 1–15.

American Association of Community Colleges (AACC). (2017). *Fast facts from our fact sheet.* Available from http://www.aacc.nche.edu/AboutCC/Pages/fastfacts factsheet.aspx

Bailey, T. R., Jaggars, S. S., & Jenkins, D. (Eds.). (2015). *Redesigning America's community colleges: A clearer path to student success.* Cambridge, MA: Harvard University Press.

Brenner, A. (2016). Transformative learning through education abroad: A case study of a community college program. In R. L. Raby & E. J. Valeau (Eds.),

International education at community colleges: Themes, practices, research, and case studies (pp. 370–390). New York, NY: Palgrave Macmillan.

Brint, S., & Karabel, J. (1989). *The diverted dream: Community colleges and the promise of educational opportunity in America, 1900–1985.* New York, NY: Oxford University Press.

California Colleges for International Education (CCIE). (2017). *Study abroad.* Available from http://ccieworld.org/saprograms.php

Clark, B. (1960). The cooling-out function in higher education. *The American Journal of Sociology, 65*(6), 569–576.

Cohen, A. M., Brawer, F. B., & Kisker, C. B. (2015). *The American community college* (6th ed.). San Francisco, CA: Jossey-Bass.

Commission on the Abraham Lincoln Study Abroad Fellowship Program. (2005). *Global competence and national needs: One million Americans studying abroad.* Washington, DC: U.S. State Department.

Compton, J., Cox, E., & Laanan, F. (2006). Adult learners in transition. *New Direction for Student Services, 114*, 73–80.

Cross, K. P. (1981). *Adults as learners: Increasing participation and facilitating learning.* San Francisco, CA: Jossey-Bass.

Dennis, J. M., Phinney, J. S., & Chuateco, L. I. (2005). The role of motivation, parental support, and peer support in the academic success of ethnic minority first-generation college students. *Journal of College Student Development, 46*(3), 223–236.

Drexler, D. S., & Campbell, D. F. (2011). Student development among community college participants in study abroad programs. *Community College Journal of Research & Practice, 35*(8), 608–619.

Dumais, S. A., & Ward, A. (2010). Cultural capital and first-generation college success. *Poetics, 38*(3), 245–265.

Gipson, J., Mitchell, D. Jr., & McLean, C. (2017). An investigation of high-achieving African-American students attending community colleges: A mixed methods research study. *Community College Journal of Research and Practice, 41*(3), 1–13.

Gonzalez, L. M., Stein, G. L., & Huq, N. (2013). The influence of cultural identity and perceived barriers on college-going beliefs and aspirations of Latino youth in emerging immigrant communities. *Hispanic Journal of Behavioral Sciences, 35*(1), 103–120.

Hagedorn, L. S. (2005). Square pegs: Adult students and their "fit" in postsecondary institutions. *Change, 37*(1), 22–29.

Harper, S. R., & Quaye, S. J. (2009). Beyond sameness, with engagement and outcomes for all: An introduction. In S. R. Harper & S. J. Quaye (Eds.), *Student engagement in higher education: Theoretical perspectives and practical approaches for diverse populations* (pp. 1–15). New York, NY: Routledge.

Hodara, M., & Jaggars, S. S. (2014). An examination of the impact of accelerating community college students' progression through developmental education. *The Journal of Higher Education, 85*(2), 246–276.

Institute of International Education (IIE). (2017). *Community college education abroad data tables.* Available from https://www.iie.org/en/Research-and-Insights/ Open-Doors/Data/Community-College-Data-Resource/Community-College ---Study-Abroad/Leading-Institutions/2006-07

Justice, E. M. (2001, May). Metacognitive differences between traditional-age and nontraditional-age college students. *Adult Education Quarterly, 51*(3), 236–249.

Laanan, F. S. (2003). Older adults in community colleges: Choices, attitudes, and goals. *Journal of Educational Gerontology, 29*(9), 757–776.

McClenney, K., Marti, C. N., & Adkins, C. (2012). *Student engagement and student outcomes: Key findings from CCSSE validation research.* Available from http://www .ccsse.org/aboutsurvey/docs/CCSSE%20Validation%20Summary.pdf

Modood, T. (2004). Capitals, ethnic identity and educational qualifications. *Cultural Trends, 13*(50), 87–105.

Morest, V. S. (2013). *Community college student success: From boardrooms to classrooms.* Lanham, MD: Rowman & Littlefield.

Moschetti, R. V., & Hudley, C. (2015). Social capital and academic motivation among first-generation community college students. *Community College Journal of Research and Practice, 38*(2), 235–251.

National Center for Education Statistics. (2009). *Digest of Educational Statistics 2009. Table 192. Total fall enrollment in degree-granting institutions by control and type of institution, age, and attendance status of student: 2007.* Available from http://nces.ed.gov/programs/digest/d09/tables/dt09_192.asp ?referrer=list

Oberstein-Delvalle, E. (1999). *Study abroad programs in three California community colleges* (Unpublished doctoral dissertation). Pepperdine University, California.

Próspero, M., & Vohra-Gupta, S. (2007). First generation college students: Motivation, integration, and academic achievement. *Community College Journal of Research and Practice, 31*(12), 963–975.

Raby, R. L. (2008, September). *Meeting America's global education challenge: Expanding education abroad at U.S. community colleges.* Institute of International Education Study Abroad White Paper Series 3. New York, NY: Institute of International Education.

Raby, R. L., & Rhodes, G. M. (2018). Promoting education abroad among community college students: Overcoming obstacles and developing inclusive practices. In H. B. Hamir & N. Gozik (Eds.), *Promoting inclusion in education abroad* (pp. 114–132). Sterling, VA: Stylus.

Raby, R. L., Rhodes, G. M., & Biscarra, A. (2014). Community college study abroad: Implications for student success. *Community College Journal of Research and Practice, 38*(2–3), 174–183.

Raby, R. L., & Valeau, E. J. (Eds.). (2016). *International education at community colleges: Themes, practices, research, and case studies.* New York, NY: Palgrave Macmillan.

Raby, R. L., & Valeau, E. J. (Eds.). (2018). *International handbook on comparative studies on community colleges and global counterparts.* Dordrecht, The Netherlands: Springer.

Richardson, J. J., Kemp, S.; Malinen, S., & Haultain, S. A. (2013). The academic achievement of students in a New Zealand university: Does it pay to work? *Journal of Further and Higher Education, 37*(6), 864–886.

Robertson, J. J. (2015). Student interest in international education at the community college. *Community College Journal of Research and Practice, 39*(5), 473–484.

Robertson, J. J., & Blasi, L. (2017). Community college student perceptions of their experiences related to global learning: Understanding the impact of family, faculty, and the curriculum. *Community College Journal of Research and Practice, 41*, 697–718.

Ross-Gordon, J. M. M. (2011). *Research on adult learners: Supporting the needs of a student population that is no longer nontraditional (returning adult students).* Available from https://www.aacu.org/publications-research/periodicals/research-adult-learners-supporting-needs-student-population-no

Silverman, S. C., Sarvenaz, A., & Stiles M. R. (2009). Meeting the needs of commuter, part-time, transfer, and returning students. In S. R. Harper & S. J. Quaye (Eds.), *Student engagement in higher education: Theoretical perspectives and practical approaches for diverse populations* (pp. 223–242). New York, NY: Routledge.

Soria, K. M., & Stebleton, M. J. (2012). First-generation students' academic engagement and retention. *Teaching in Higher Education, 17*(6), 673–685.

Strayhorn, T. L., & Johnson, R. M. (2014). Black female community college students' satisfaction: A national regression analysis. *Community College Journal of Research and Practice, 38*(6), 534–550.

Willis, T. Y. (2016). Microaggressions and intersectionality in the experiences of Black women studying abroad through community colleges: Implications for practice. In R. L. Raby & E. J. Valeau (Eds.), *International education at community colleges: Themes, practices, research, and case studies* (pp. 167–186). New York: NY: Palgrave Macmillan.

Wood, J. L., & Harris, F. III. (2015). The effect of academic engagement on sense of belonging: A hierarchical, multilevel analysis of Black men in the community colleges. *Spectrum: A Journal on Black Men, 4*(1), 21–47.

Yosso, T. J. (2005). Whose culture has capital? A critical race theory discussion of community cultural wealth. *Race Ethnicity and Education, 8*(1), 69–91.

Zamani-Gallaher, E. M., Leon, R. A., & Lang, J. (2016). Self-authorship beyond borders: Reconceptualizing college and career readiness. In R. L. Raby & E. J. Valeau (Eds.), *International education at community colleges: Themes, practices, research, and case studies* (pp. 146–166). New York, NY: Palgrave Macmillan.

Zhang, Y. L., Lui, J., & Hagedorn, L. S. (2013). Post transfer experiences: Adult undergraduate students at a research university. *Journal of Applied Research in the Community College, 21*, 31–40.

6

ENGAGING WITH SELF, OTHERS, SPACE, AND PLACE

Leveraging the Geographic Imagination in Education Abroad

Anthony Gristwood and Darren Kelly

It is good to have an end to journey towards; but it is the journey that matters, in the end.
—Ursula K. Le Guin, *The Left Hand of Darkness* (1969, p. 150)

Education Abroad, Ambilocation, and Geography's Promise

One might be forgiven for thinking that the value of education abroad in a globalizing world is self-evident. Interconnectivity, notions of the shrinking globe, and the acceleration of all kinds of exchanges across geographical borders—of people, goods, and information—saturate everyday experience and are transforming politics, economics, and cultural identities in complex and often contradictory ways. New transport and communications technologies have created new forms of mobility and unprecedented opportunities for students to encounter and engage with difference.

Contemporary American education abroad operates as a globalist project (Tsing, 2000), taking this interconnected world as a given and as a signifier of progress. Intercultural experience is valorized, and students are expected to develop qualities of global competence, global consciousness, and ultimately to achieve global citizenship (Lewin, 2009; Schattle, 2008). This paradigm has not been without critique from both within and beyond the field (Doerr, 2012, 2013; Woolf, 2010) but has become predominant, irreducibly bound up with the neoliberal logic of higher education as a commodified form of cultural capital offering personalized self-actualization.

Yet, as interconnectivity and transnational mobility have expanded, opportunities for authentic encounters appear, simultaneously, to have shrunk. As Engle and Engle (2002) have memorably argued, the commodification of higher education and the hegemony of consumer-driven models of education abroad have facilitated experiences that, despite the proliferation of potential destinations and foci of study, are "neither significantly international nor truly educative" (p. 25). As a result, students risk both physical and social isolation from their host locations, because they lack the self-understanding and geographic imagination—and perhaps also the will—required to engage successfully with others and navigate the spaces and places that they encounter when studying abroad. In essence, geographic relocation paralyzes and isolates them, rather than inviting them to learn.

This chapter's contributors are cultural geographers, one British, one Irish, located in their respective home countries and working closely with American colleagues, students, and partner institutions. As such, we are positioned ambivalently both professionally and disciplinarily. Located at disciplinary and professional intersections, we are abroad, yet, simultaneously, at home. Such *ambilocation*—a term coined to describe the displaced subjectivity and sensibility of in-between-ness in the work of Northern Irish writer Ciaran Carson (S. Smith, 2005)—while sometimes problematic, is potentially of great value for personal and professional development (if framed productively). Specifically, in this chapter we propose that concepts, ideas, and perspectives from the discipline of geography provide a framework for navigating the ambilocation of education abroad, in which students (and education abroad scholar-practitioners) experience a complex and ambiguous borderland between two or more simultaneous and overlapping states of being. Geography can move education abroad above and beyond traditional concerns with intercultural understanding and community engagement. Indeed, it can be a powerful mechanism to help students advance along the educational continuum toward lifelong learning.

The Challenge of Globalism: Geographic Illiteracy and Positionality

> *I think you recognise cities better on the atlas than when you visit them in person.*
>
> —Italo Calvino, *Invisible Cities* (1974, p. 137)

The relative geographic illiteracy of the American population has been widely observed and criticized (Alsop, 2014; Stephens, 2017). For example, a 2016 survey found that while 72% of U.S. college-aged respondents believed it was important to be knowledgeable about geography, world events, and other cultures, the average score when asked about these was only 55%. Nearly a third (29%) earned only a "minimal pass" score of 66% (Council on Foreign Relations, 2016). Yet, as the British geographers Dorling and Lee (2016) argue, "the great challenges of the twenty-first century are geographical in their formulation, analysis and consequence," and the wide range of methodologies and subject matter covered by the discipline makes it uniquely suited to tackling them (p. 33).

As such, we would argue that few disciplines have a stronger case to be placed at the heart of an educational continuum intended to foster active citizenship, personal responsibility, and public contribution to a diverse society. The obvious challenge is that few U.S. undergraduates have been exposed to geographic concepts and ideas, much less majored in geography. Linked closely with the rise of globalization and American global hegemony, growth in U.S. education abroad has inversely mirrored the decline of geography in the country's high school and university curricula. When represented in recent years in the U.S. academy, geography is typically rebranded as global studies (Gaile & Willmott, 2003), or subsumed into technocratic disciplines such as geographic information systems (GISs), urban studies, cartography, or environmental planning (A.B. Murphy, 2007).

This decline is closely connected with the country's path to global hegemony in the twentieth century (N. Smith, 2003). While the acquisition and management of geographical knowledge was central to the development of U.S. hegemony, the relationship between the discipline of geography and the global vision it produced is equivocal. For N. Smith, American Empire (globalism) sees itself as beyond geography; geography is eclipsed as a meaningful discourse of global power. "Old constraints" of geography, such as locational difference or national boundaries, are apparently transcended. Geography survives as mere nostalgia (N. Smith, 2003). Paradoxically, the antigeographical nature of this worldview implies an assumed geographical privilege and exceptionalism for the United States, which as the prime motor and beneficiary of American-dominated globalization, is imagined to be the "natural" pivot for global history (Baudrillard, 1988; Fukuyama, 1992; Hardt & Negri, 2000; R. Smith, 1997).

This globalism has had important implications for the development of education abroad, reconfiguring abroad and home as the rest of the world becomes a foil. "Possessing this new global power . . . meant not having to care about the world's geography. . . . Precisely as geography was everything . . . it was simultaneously nothing" (N. Smith, 2003, p. 18). This imperial worldview is ironic; American globalism established itself as an explicitly anticolonial ideology, yet it constructs cultural and societal difference through an

Orientalist lens similar to that of European colonialism. Indeed, U.S. education abroad, particularly in the context of nontraditional destinations in the Global South, may be marketed as "adventure," portraying students "in the position of explorer . . . bravely penetrating the depths of other lands to discover new knowledge" (Zemach-Bersin, 2009, p. 307). As Neriko Musha Doerr (2012) also notes, the consumerist and highly gendered discourses offered by such marketing strongly influence students' "expectations and views of their experience" (p. 260).

The term *colonial student* encapsulates some of these expectations and unexamined assumptions about students' own subjectivity in relation to the people and places they encounter: "a sense of entitlement, as if the world is theirs for discovery, if not for the taking" (Ogden, 2007, p. 38). As Other, the host location is rendered an "anachronistic space" to be compared and contrasted with the modernity of home (McClintock, 1995, p. 40). Heritage students are not immune; Irish Americans returning to their imagined ancestral home in Dublin are dismayed to discover its contemporary transformation by globalized modernity (Kelly, 2013). To counteract these tendencies, we contend that programmatic and curricular design needs explicitly to focus students' attention on the ways in which their perspectives are influenced by their own subjectivity as Americans abroad (Glass, 2015), as well as the complex impacts of globalization reshaping host locations.

If home constitutes the vanguard of history, contemporary globalization transforms home into a mobile category, as new communication technologies facilitate the transmission of the familiar into abroad. In this context, education abroad's traditional emphasis on culture and cultural difference as ontologically fixed categories and foci of investigation becomes problematic; instead, students find themselves inhabiting complex milieux constructed through a series of competing flows of experiential and mediated information symptomatic of the "complex, overlapping, distinctive order" of the global economy (Appadurai, 1996, p. 32). The local they encounter is always already constructed relationally with the global, a process termed *glocalization* (Soja, 2000, p. 199; Swyngedouw, 1997).

The intersection of the globalist worldview and the collapse of the ontological separation between home and abroad triggers a crisis of subjectivity in students studying abroad today. Dominant intercultural paradigms of education abroad are unable to address productively the cognitive dissonance, disaffection, and disengagement that result from students' ambilocation. Without suitable pedagogical or programmatic structures, students tend to remain closeted in their comfort zones, both physical and virtual, isolated from their environment. The most effective education abroad programs take a holistic approach to both the student as subject and the locations they encounter, and intentionally facilitate opportunities to investigate the ways in which those locations are glocally constructed. As will be argued, geography can provide an effective framework for program design and student engagement.

Defining *Geography*: An (In)Discipline

Geography is the study of space, place, and the environment (American Association of Geographers, 2018). It encompasses the socially constructed and natural worlds (human and their various subdisciplines, including the authors' specialism, cultural geography) and the complex interface and interplay between them. Thus, geography can be difficult to define and locate precisely, transcending as it does traditional disciplinary boundaries. This can be to its detriment: We have already noted how it has often been rebranded or subsumed in the United States, challenging geographers to find departmental homes. However, geography's multi/transdisciplinarity confers an important strategic advantage in the context of education abroad.

Gilbert (2005) celebrates human geography as an "indiscipline" (p. 104), a subversive transgression of traditional disciplinary silos. Perhaps better defined as a broad field of inquiry, geography covers a huge range of topics and offers a distinctive, multifaceted lens through which to analyze the world and everything in it. Moreover, geography has always been a colonizing discipline. Historically, its roots lie in late-nineteenth-century knowledge-gathering imperatives of imperial expansionism. More recently, it has expanded its boundaries explicitly into the territory of the humanities, addressing questions of cultural identity, representation, and power by using concepts and ideas from postcolonial theory (Bhabha, 1994; Soja, 1989). Conversely, in recent years the arts and humanities have colonized geography to address questions of space and identity central to their agenda. This heritage makes geography a field highly sensitive to, and reflexive about, the complex implications of representing difference, whether of place or people. As ideas and concepts from the field have been adapted and developed under different disciplinary labels, such as literature and cultural studies, a potentially rich and fluid terrain for inter- and transdisciplinary dialogue has emerged across the continuum of social and political sciences and humanities.

Applying Geography in Education Abroad

The inherent inter- and transdisciplinarity of geography, as well as its focus on space and place, confers an obvious advantage as an organizing framework in education abroad. Moreover, the subject's openness to reflexivity and self-reflection, praxis of experiential fieldwork, as well as focus on the spatial and cartographic make it uniquely suited to enhance student engagement. Geography can also use students' home campus learning to augment and challenge their existing disciplinary perspectives and experiences, although the shifting composition of students studying abroad presents a challenge to this agenda, and necessitates a very careful and intentional integration of geographic elements into program and course design.

Situated Knowledge and Place: Geography and Experiential Fieldwork

Experiential fieldwork is central to geography, generating situational knowledge and understanding embedded in place. Thematic foci of globalization, urban change, and cultural identities enable students to understand the sociopolitical and economic contexts of their host locations, and to appreciate both their dynamic nature and the sociopolitical conflicts defining their histories and emergent futures. Geography's conceptualization of place is rich and multilayered, indicating many fruitful directions for experiential research. Tuan's (1974) conceptions of *topophilia*, "the affective bond between people and place or setting" (p. 4), focus on the roles of perception, imagination and memory in creating a distinctive sense of place, while Cresswell's (2004) work on social transgression explores how the notion of place has been used to construct ideas of belonging and exclusion. "Moral geographies . . . map particular kinds of people and practice" (p. 13) to particular places. For Massey (1994, 2007), places are best understood in terms of mobility rather than fixity, conceptualized as open and hybrid products of interconnecting flows of people, information, and capital. This mobility forms complex power geometries, whose uneven social relations create a distinctive politics of place.

There has been growing interest in education abroad in drawing on theory and practice from geography to engage with these complex dynamics in urban environments (see, e.g., the various papers in Brewer & Monahan, 2011, or Gristwood & Woolf, 2012). The contributors have written elsewhere about ways to teach students to read the multilayered text of the city, and to contribute to its writing by drawing on their own varied experiences and interactions. This optimizes their experiential learning (Gristwood & Woolf, 2011; Kelly, 2009b). As Whelan (2003), analyzing Dublin's streetscape and iconography, attests:

> The cultural landscape can be read interpretively as a text which expresses a distinctive culture of ideas and practices, of often oppositional social groups and political relationships, in order to reveal the ideas, contexts of the society that produced it. (p. 13)

The Geographic Self: Managing Affect

Human geography stresses the imperative to acknowledge and reflect on the self as a geographic subject, thereby deconstructing taken-for-granted worldviews and considering the self's roles in relation to Others and engagement with them. Reflexivity—reflecting on the self in relation to space and society—has become central to geographic praxis and pedagogy and is especially significant in an international context (Sultana, 2012). To Cloke (2005), three strategies are central to successful self-reflexive practice. First, *positionality* identifies where the individual is coming from, contextualizing the individual's interpretations of experience. Second, *autoethnography* facilitates the interpretation of people, places, and events through the perspective of personal involvement. Third, *intertextuality* pays attention to voices and perspectives beyond the self, thereby decentering it. In this way, Joyce (1922) uses a Jewish outsider's view (Bloom's) to offer a critique of Dublin's streetscape and sociopolitical dynamics, while, as Bhabha (1994) notes, for Rushdie, it is the migrants' hybrid "double vision" that is the truest eye (p. 5).

For Doerr and Taïeb (2018), understanding in practical terms how student subjectivities are shaped before, during, and after education abroad is a question of affect (and its management). They highlight the importance of feelings and emotions in creating the intense affective load of studying abroad, which influences students' attitudes and motivations predeparture, the nature of their experiences in-country, and their postdeparture evaluation of the experience. Designing effective education abroad thus becomes a question of how best to "generate, shape, or transform" affect so that students fully "understand their sociocultural surroundings and participate in wider social activities . . . [rather than] . . . withdraw into transient observer or consumer positions" (Doerr & Taïeb, 2018, p. 3) that dehumanize their encounters with people and place. The geographic approaches outlined previously greatly enhance the management of student affect.

Challenges to Geographic Practice in Education Abroad

Geographic practice in education abroad faces several challenges. In the context of fieldwork, flexible and appropriate assignment briefs are required to develop the capacity of students to reflect on their observations, and to overcome discomfort or skepticism with self-critique (Glass, 2015). This takes time, always at a premium, especially for short-term programs. Here, the educational continuum becomes a crucial support: Exploration and experimentation abroad can be scaffolded by preparatory courses and activities predeparture that develop reflexive praxis and minimize the number of required contact hours abroad (Brewer & Solberg, 2009; Glass, 2015). Likewise, island or direct-enrollment education abroad experiences characterized by segregated ex-pat dorms and recreational spaces, and/or curriculum focused closely on particular languages or disciplinary courses, lack the facilitated reflection and conceptual mortar (geographic imagination) needed to cement together the contextual bricks of learning.

It is difficult to establish with any certainty what motivates U.S. students to study abroad, and therefore to track changes in motivation over time or to assess their effects on learning and development outcomes. P.H. Anderson, Hubbard, and Lawton (2015) suggest that there are four key dimensions to student motivation: learning about the world (world enlightenment), personal growth, career development, and entertainment.

Education abroad's roots in the European Grand Tour have been thoroughly documented (Doerr & Taïeb, 2018). Europe has long constituted an imaginative space for the cultivation of knowledge of high culture and intellectual life of the mind—highly partial and selective forms of engagement (Gristwood & Woolf, 2013). This process of accruing cultural and social capital (Bourdieu, 1986), according to Freire's (1970) banking model of education, would then be transformed through the world of work into enhanced income (financial capital), an interchange of forms of capital even more apposite in the globalizing world of turbo capitalism. Yet today, cultural capital and social capital have been superseded by a neoliberal discourse of utilitarianism. Its dominant imperative has become students' acquisition of specific hard skills for particular jobs, as well as the cultivation of forms of emotional intelligence or soft skills deemed necessary for effective job performance in global, diverse workplaces (see, e.g., Loveland & Morris, 2018).

Unsurprisingly, then, there has been a significant increase in the number of students interning abroad in recent years (Rubin, 2009; Taft, 2015). Internships mediated through rigorous academic courses have the potential to enhance students' personal and professional development and enable them to synthesize and articulate their experiences. However, as student numbers grow and providers proliferate, it is timely to question the effectiveness of internships that comprise too much busywork, lack adequate supervision and mentorship, and are unsupported by coursework that encourages and assesses student engagement and reflection. Internships abroad have to go beyond parents' and advisers' advice to students that the experience will be good for them or look good on their résumés (Toral, 2009).

Thus, students engaged in internships abroad need to be intentional in their aims to be successful in globalized workplaces. To help students navigate (neoliberal) demands of self-management and personal branding, predeparture preparation should focus closely on related aspects of professional performance and display, such as résumé development and appropriate use of social media such as LinkedIn profiles. Moreover, support needs to be attentive to—and manage—student affect, for example, by addressing explicitly the ways in which business practices and work cultures abroad differ from those at home. Student disengagement is exacerbated when working with local colleagues at a placement. It is an error to assume that even well-meaning and motivated students will naturally have the nuanced soft skills to be successful, particularly in high-context cultural workplace environments. The cultivation of emotional intelligence and cultural intelligence is essential here. In the United States, "46% of new employees will fail within 18 months of hire. Eighty-nine percent of the time it is for attitude, and low emotional intelligence ranks second in why they fail" (M. Murphy, 2016). Emotional literacy and mindfulness are crucial for navigating the magnified challenges of internships abroad. Overcoming these challenges is a way for students to maximize the value of education abroad experience for their personal and professional development, and to cultivate competencies highly sought after by employers, such as independence and the ability to think critically and creatively.

The implications of this paradigm shift for today's education abroad students and their motivations are clearly reflected in the 2017 *Open Doors* report, which lists the relative percentages of U.S. education abroad students' fields of study (Institute of International Education, 2017). Accordingly, in 2015–2016, 25.2% of U.S. students who studied abroad majored in science, technology, engineering, and mathematics (STEM) fields, 20.9% in business and management, and 17.1% in social sciences. A mere 3.7% studied the humanities. Moreover, since 2005–2006, STEM has represented the only significant area of growth (8.8%), whereas the social sciences (–5.8%) and humanities (–7.6%) have declined significantly. (*Open Doors* reclassified fields of study beginning in 2013–2014; thus, prior figures are not entirely comparable.)

Counts of geography majors studying abroad are not readily available, nor is straightforward data about students' exposure to geographic content prior to studying abroad. However, existing data strongly suggest that geography students compose a small minority of students studying abroad. According to the Association of American Geographers, degrees conferred in geography in the United States peaked in 2012 at 4,807, reflecting an annual increase of 3.75% since records began in 1948. The number in 2015 was just 4,203. The growing popularity of GIS and cartography notwithstanding, the numbers compare negatively to overall trends in social sciences (Revell, 2017). Given geography's low status as an academic discipline in the United

States, the majority of U.S. students lack knowledge or exposure to basic geographic concepts and ideas available for translation abroad. This significant gap in the U.S. undergraduate curriculum correlates with the challenges of disengagement discussed here.

Shrinking Time? The Challenge of Short-Term Programs

Due in part to rising costs, programs are increasingly structured as short term and intensive. Differentiating programs are aspects such as program length, the style of intervention, and facilitation of program leaders (P. H. Anderson et al., 2015). Student experiences can also be constrained by imperatives such as health and safety; normative disciplinary frameworks (silo-based preparation); or an exclusive focus on specific goals, such as professional development.

Short-term programs can be valuable for students, particularly those restricted by finances and family, sport, work, or other commitments. They can also serve as stepping-stones to longer term experiences. Nevertheless, their time-limited nature constrains in-depth sociocultural investigation, giving rise to concerns about their effectiveness. Indeed, they epitomize education abroad's tendency to construct an essentialized and tightly demarcated abroad space that is consumed within a compartmentalized time period (Doerr, 2016). Short-term programs offer fewer opportunities for students to move proactively beyond comfort zones or to observe and critically reflect on their experiences, particularly when tightly packed with class work and field trips that do not move far beyond the tourist trail. Students cannot address the complex glocal interplay they encounter in the field, nor easily take into account the impact of their presence on the surroundings they are observing.

Questions of money and time also have an impact. Every spare minute must be filled with excursions and learning activities to maximize return on investment and ensure no moment is wasted. Arguably, dominant American sensibilities of time also come into play; a hurried pace is valorized over the kind of unstructured time that facilitates effective exploration of the self and the textures and sensuous geographies of the environment. Yet, "a critical openness lies at the heart of a reflexive approach" and syllabi should be "intentional about creating spaces between structured activities" (Glass, 2014, p. 84).

Here it is helpful to consider the practice of *flânerie,* famously described by Benjamin (1993) as "botanising the asphalt" (p. 36), that is, reflexively investigating the minutiae of the life of the street. The term *flâneur* itself comes from the French verb *flâner,* "to wander aimlessly." In her book

Flâneuse, Elkin (2017) recounts her own experience as an American abroad, drawing attention to the gendered specificity of *flâneur* and to its geographic emergence in nineteenth-century Paris. For her, "coming from suburban America, where people drive from one place to another, walking for no particular reason was a bit of an eccentric thing to do" (p. 4). Similarly, discussing the importance of tourists taking time to explore their new surroundings in the mode of the *flâneur,* White (2001) notes that "Americans are ill-suited to be *flâneurs*. They're good at following books outlining architectural tours . . . or visiting scenic spots . . . but they are always driven by the urge of self-improvement" (p. 40).

Neuroscientist Peter Whybrow's (2006) trenchant critique of contemporary American society applies well in this context: "The 'free moments' that once glued together a busy life have disappeared" (p. 156). Thus, education abroad program design needs to afford students and faculty time to engage with the complex sociocultural contexts they encounter. Additionally, particularly in challenging contexts, space and time must be incorporated into short-term program design to permit the "strong, active, . . . frequent and spontaneous" (C. L. Anderson, Lorenz, & White, 2016, pp. 12–13) facilitation by faculty that will enable positive outcomes in student learning and intercultural development.

Integrative Learning and Interdisciplinarity

Faculty-led home campus courses, which precede or follow study abroad experiences, arguably forge a more lasting connection between academic and experiential learning, enabling critical engagement to take place and leveraging the educational continuum to maximize the potential impacts of education abroad. For Newell (2010), this is a question of "integrative learning," which provides "outside-the-classroom activity" on and off campus to give students experiences "through which they are confronted with new perspectives and are challenged to integrate insights from divergent perspectives." Further, interdisciplinary study, by exposing students to multiple, diverse viewpoints on a complex situation, is central and necessary for integrative learning, encouraging them to synthesize their insights.

Such a holistic approach to shaping pre– and post–study abroad teaching and learning cuts across the grain of discipline-specific preparation that focuses on specific majors, or utilitarian emphasis on core skills or competencies for professional development. Yet, this approach is also complementary to disciplinarity, as each individual discipline provides a partial, if valuable, insight into the situation being studied. It is the function of inter- or trans-disciplinarity to provide the framework within which these conflicting and complementary insights can be molded into a holistic picture. For education abroad providers, there is an inherent tension in creating inter- or transdisciplinary courses for students when they may be curtailed in their course choices by disciplinary constraints. The task for providers, then, is to take what has at times been the *invisible* curriculum within certain courses—such as positive outcomes and skill development gained from assignments related to experiential fieldwork—and translate this into learning outcomes recognizable to disciplines granting credit.

It is illuminating to consider the disciplinary backgrounds of students who study abroad in relation to the soft skill sets (e.g., intercultural and emotional intelligence) required to maximize the education abroad experience. Curriculum integration efforts have led to a focus on the value education abroad can add to students' majors. Yet, in practice, when abroad most students become generic, rather than students of a specific discipline. This tendency is exacerbated when home campus faculty are not actively involved in their students' education abroad and unhelpfully suggest that students park their major, and in some cases their whole university education, in favor of travel (Brewer & Cunningham, 2009).

Shrinking Space? Challenging Geographies of Comfort and Fear

Students' affective disengagement with the people and places they encounter is also the result of the proliferation of comprehensive support services provided on home campuses and by international education organizations abroad. As a recent Association of Study Abroad Providers in Ireland (ASAPI, 2017) workshop noted, education abroad has "followed the trend of U.S. higher education by providing a more structured and supportive experience" for students. The focus of the workshop was to develop strategies to counteract such structure to encourage students' independence, resilience, and engagement in host locations. For ASAPI (2017), a key question was how to leverage "the opportunities presented by discomfort, ambiguity, and struggle in developing intercultural skills . . . [to help] today's young adults develop the resilience and independence that past generations were given the opportunity to learn at a much younger age."

An increasingly competitive education abroad industry, driven by student and parent consumer demand as well as comprehensive legal frameworks focused on compliance and accountability, has escalated an already risk-averse culture. Students are continuously monitored and spatially funneled throughout their time abroad. This monitoring and the highly-structured programming previously discussed discourage students from wandering freely through their host locales. Particularly for students who have grown up in environments of acute sociospatial segregation, staying safe is synonymous with staying put; to move off the beaten path or to become lost is equated, understandably, with threats to personal safety. As the focus of the ASAPI workshop attests, there are also significant pressures on the U.S. education abroad community in Ireland to replicate the housing bubbles of many American campuses, even as studying abroad may be perceived as providing a break from these. For city-based programs, some suburban and rural Americans' negative views of cities and urban living are a further complication. U.S. antiurban sentiment has long been fueled by negative representations of cityscapes and diverse neighborhoods in the media and popular culture, portrayed overwhelmingly as the home for threatening "Others" in TV shows such as *Cops* (N. Smith, 1996). Such threats are potentially exacerbated abroad when students may be challenged to take public transport or live in multiethnic areas in new and unfamiliar locations.

The emphasis on stranger danger drastically shrinks students' available experiential learning space both temporally and spatially (Kolb & Kolb, 2005). This reflects broader societal trends: Heightened concerns over crime and international terrorism have contributed to a kind of moral panic (Cohen, 2002) that actively excludes difference and dangerous Others (Sibley, 1995). Virilio (2005) has noted the ways in which this "campaign of panic" acts to restructure both the experience of urban spaces (such as proliferating surveillance and gated communities) and, critically, individual subjectivities. The result is emotionally and physically stymied "city-dwelling internauts" who are "completely cut off from reality . . . cosmonauts insulated weightlessly in their capsules in a real or simulated void" (p. ix).

The critical deconstruction of such trends and stereotypes is an urgent imperative, providing an opportunity for education abroad to take a holistic approach to shaping student perception and experience. For example, "studentification" of inner-city spaces is proliferating in university towns and cities across Ireland and the United Kingdom (D. Smith, 2002, 2008), a trend to which education abroad contributes. Dublin is experiencing high demand for purpose-built education abroad housing. Thus, several fully serviced, fortified, luxurious (en-suite private rooms, study facilities, gyms, cinema, and Wi-Fi) housing complexes have sprung up, primarily in historically working-class tight-knit neighborhoods that have been in physical decline and are characterized by high unemployment and related social disadvantage. While the nature of these newly built student housing complexes is highly attractive for U.S. education abroad providers, colleges, and universities, they contribute to student disengagement and social segregation.

The Challenge and Promise of Technology

The intersection of geographical isolation with digital technologies is particularly challenging for education abroad practitioners. Growing use of smartphone technologies and apps to pinpoint students' locations within seconds cuts both ways: It's not only an enhanced safety net but also an unbroken umbilicus. It is now the (enforced) responsibility of students while abroad to be contactable at all times, by providers (and helicopter parents) and, therefore, in some sense, never alone. Spatial sequestration and ambilocation are further exacerbated when students studying abroad use social media, Skype, or FaceTime to communicate with friends and parents back home; watch Netflix; play online games; and/or take home institution courses online. Thus, they physically reside in the host city (albeit potentially in segregated accommodation) but are mentally engaged with home (Kelly, 2009b). Widespread use of smartphones and apps impedes the development of skills of self-navigation through urban space, becoming another conduit of spatial funneling; students fail to see what lies between points A and B as they follow their phones to their destinations. The comforting safety net afforded by ubiquitous Internet access can help students become more adventurous while abroad but can also prevent them from becoming more independent.

Nevertheless, technology offers significant opportunities to mediate students' ambilocation and enhance, rather than dilute, their engagement with people and place while abroad—if appropriately scaffolded. For example, in the context of professional development, there is real potential to demonstrate to prospective employers sharpened time management skills, ability to work remotely across different time zones, and enhanced online communication skills and etiquette.

Indeed, the experiential and the virtual are not necessarily in conflict if harnessed imaginatively to foreground the complex interconnections that global and local students encounter, address questions of individual perception and subjectivity, and deepen self-reflection and intercultural sensitivity. Collaborative mapmaking offers one way to bridge the experiential and the virtual, and can be employed both in a single education abroad location and across locations (as well as with cohorts at home institutions engaged in similar inquiry) for comparative analysis.

Using Google Maps

For several years now, the chapter contributors have used Google Maps to provide a specific focus for this learning. Google Maps is a simple, freely available form of GIS technology. The basic platform it provides enables students to capture, manipulate, analyze, and present different types of geographical data; map the spatial location of real-world features; and by overlaying multiple data sets simultaneously visualize the spatial relationships among them. Collaborative mapmaking encourages student ownership of knowledge creation and enhances their ability to integrate the complex mix of experiential and mediated information they need to synthesize while abroad. Embedded photographs, text, and video clips focus attention on the interplay of global and local in shaping dynamic environments, and track students' growing self-awareness as they interrogate their initial perceptions and reflect on their own cognitive and imaginative responses to the experience. The resulting multimedia-rich maps become a tool for visualizing and sharing students' developing geographic imaginations, and for showcasing their field-based research.

Crucially, students thereby combine qualitative and quantitative research methods to interrogate critically what Urry and Larsen (2011) call the tourist gaze that so powerfully frames their initial perceptions. They also examine closely the soft city of memory and imagination that they subsequently construct through their own embodied experiences (Raban, 2008), deepening their understanding of the objective and subjective dimensions of place, and contextualizing their wider ethnographic field research. By drafting their own mental maps or spatial narratives of personal engagement in the city, students can analyze the spatial patterns of collective familiarity and anxiety the maps reveal, as well as the everyday routes by which they navigate urban space, thereby revealing the roads less traveled.

Students can also use Google Maps to create a visual palimpsest of urban change by overlaying historic maps onto templates of contemporary cities (Kelly, 2009a). This requires students to undertake primary field research collaboratively and to utilize a range of secondary sources to explore the dynamic and contested nature of the cityscape, patterns of growth and decline, as well as the social geographies associated with them (Figure 6.1). Supported by required academic reading, students gain more nuanced understandings of the various processes that have transformed the city's sociocultural morphologies, such as the social displacements of gentrification and studentification, as well as *ethnification*—the processes of social displacement and segregation driven by the influx of migrant populations into specific neighborhoods (Kuran & Sandholm, 2008). They can also trace the role of global commerce and politics in reshaping the city's character and skyline.

Feedback from students illustrates the positive and self-reflexive effects of learning to read and write the host city in this way. To quote one student: "I had a chance to step out of my bubble I call America, and see myself, my society for what it truly is." Another writes:

Figure 6.1. Example of students' map of Dublin portraying urban change through space and time.

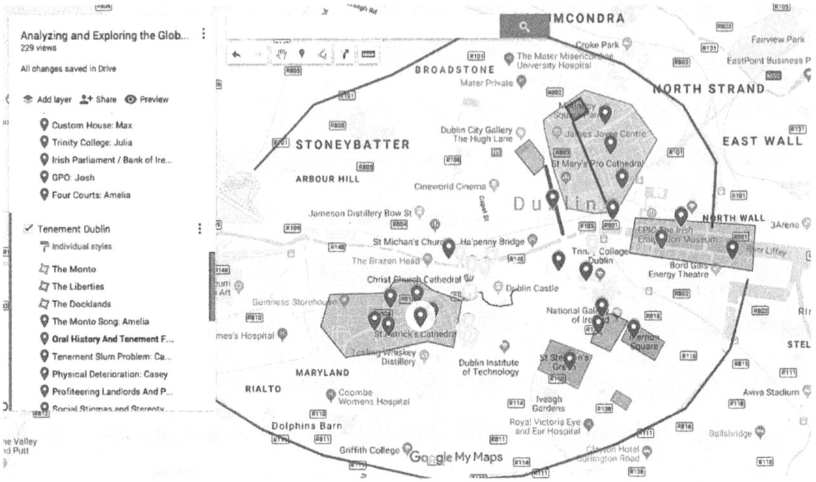

> This course taught me to be uncomfortable with what I didn't know, and to face curiosity with excitement rather than fear. This . . . helped me orient myself within Irish culture and history, . . . critically engage with the city, and . . . better understand the context in which I was living.

More recently, with colleagues Julia Miller in Sydney, Australia, and Adriano Boncompagni in Florence, Italy, we have begun to explore the added value of cross-locational comparative collaboration. There is significant potential here to articulate the educational continuum by virtually connecting cohorts abroad and on the home campus to facilitate synchronous or asynchronous collaboration. For example, as part of institutional initiatives in globally networked learning, the CAPA course *Analyzing and Exploring the Global City*, which runs concurrently at centers in Dublin, Florence, London, and Sydney, requires students to work collaboratively across sites to produce a shared multilayered Google Map. The map analyzes the global and transterritorial character of their respective host cities, and compares and contrasts their initial perceptions of place with later observations as the semester progresses.

Individual students in each city analyze each other's perceptions and the spatial narratives they produce to chart initial observations and evolving relationships with their host cities (see Figure 6.2). They trace a shifting focus from the tourist gaze to the everyday experiences of commuting, streetscape, and daily rhythms (Figure 6.3).

Figure 6.2. Map showing selected students' initial perceptions of London.

Figure 6.3. Later impressions of Sydney: Using public transport.

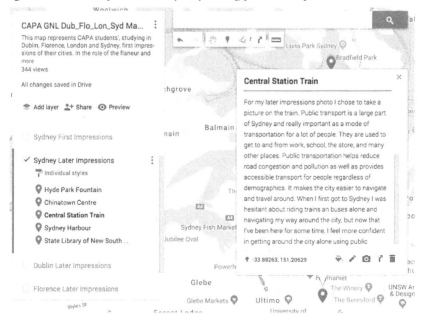

In groups, students then use the maps to explore the interplay of local and global forces. This requires integrating their local fieldwork into a comparative, thematic global analysis of topics such as diversity, public art, nature, and heritage, considering both the specific context of locality and global political, economic, and cultural variables. The triangulation with other host cities allows students to begin to finely tune their critical lens onto their host (and home) locations, and consider reflexively their own performances and encounters in the city (Figure 6.4), then share their findings cartographically as well as in presentations and written work.

Techniques from geography (experiential fieldwork, autoethnography, basic cartographic methods) enable students to engage more deeply with the places and communities they encounter within and across geographic spaces and scales. The digital maps help the students to take ownership and responsibility for their knowledge, demonstrate their developing understanding and engagement with host cities, and facilitate comparative analysis.

Figure 6.4. Examples of thematic map content from Sydney: ethnicity (a) and art (b).

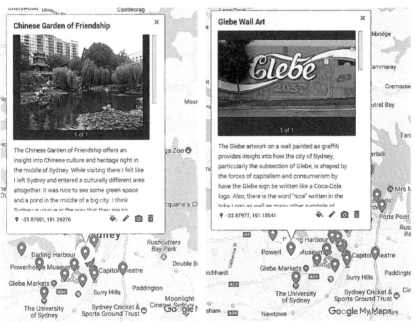

Conclusion

As cultural geographers working in international education, we have noted declining student engagement with the spaces, places, and communities encountered while studying abroad. The roots of this disengagement are to be found in the contradictions inherent in the history of education abroad and dominant ideologies of American globalism. Globalization, technological change, and the twin imperatives of neoliberal consumerism and skills-based utilitarianism have exacerbated these tendencies, with a concomitant shift in the backgrounds and objectives of students studying abroad, and the packaging, time budgeting, and daily management of education abroad experiences.

We suggest that concepts, methods, and pedagogies from geography and its cognate disciplines have the potential to greatly enhance students' engagement with their host locations, and to encourage more self-reflexive and ethnorelative perceptions of the Other in the complex milieux they encounter abroad, particularly in urban environments. Together, experiential fieldwork, globally networked collaboration, and digital mapmaking can enhance students' geographical literacy, reflexive self-awareness, and affective management. The resulting skills students gain will reap significant benefits for their future academic and professional endeavors across the educational continuum. To quote again the late, great writer and feminist Ursula Le Guin (1969), "It is the journey that matters" (p. 150).

References

Alsop, H. (2014). *Americans surveyed: Misunderstood, misrepresented or ignorant?* Telegraph.co.uk. Available from http://www.telegraph.co.uk/news/worldnews/northamerica/usa/10640690/Americans-surveyed-misunderstood-misrepresented-or-ignorant.html

American Association of Geographers (AAG). (2018). *Overview, AAG.* Available from http://www.aag.org/cs/jobs_and_careers/what_geographers_do/overview

Anderson, C. L., Lorenz, K., & White, M. (2016, Fall). Instructor influence on student intercultural gains and learning during instructor-led, short-term study abroad. *Frontiers: The Interdisciplinary Journal of Study Abroad, 28,* 1–23.

Anderson, P. H., Hubbard, A., & Lawton, L. (2015, Fall). Student motivation to study abroad and their intercultural development. *Frontiers: The Interdisciplinary Journal of Study Abroad, 26,* 39–52.

Appadurai, A. (1996). *Modernity at large: Cultural dimensions of globalization.* Minneapolis: University of Minnesota Press.

Association of Study Abroad Providers in Ireland (ASAPI). (2017). *Autumn workshop: Encouraging resilience and independence in study abroad.* Available from https://asapireland.org/2017/11/10/autumn-workshop-encouraging-resilience-and-independence-in-study-abroad/

Baudrillard, J. (1988). *America*. London, UK: Verso.

Benjamin, W. (1973). *Charles Baudelaire: A lyric poet in the era of high capitalism*. London, UK: Verso.

Bhabha, H. (1994). *The location of culture*. London, UK: Routledge.

Bourdieu, P. (1986). The forms of capital. In J. G. Richardson (Ed.), *Handbook of theory and research for the sociology of education* (pp. 241–258). New York, NY: Greenwood Press.

Brewer, E., & Cunningham, K. (Eds.). (2009). Introduction. In *Integrating study abroad into the curriculum: Theory and practice across the disciplines* (pp. xi–xxvi). Sterling, VA: Stylus.

Brewer, E., & Monahan, M. (Eds.). (2011, Spring). Study abroad and the city [Special issue]. *Frontiers: The Interdisciplinary Journal of Study Abroad, 20*. Available from https://frontiersjournal.org/past-volumes/vol-xx/

Brewer, E., & Solberg, J. (2009). Preparatory courses for students going to divergent sites: Two examples. In E. Brewer & K. Cunningham (Eds.), *Integrating study abroad into the curriculum: Theory and practice across the disciplines* (pp. 41–62). Sterling, VA: Stylus.

Calvino, I. (1974). *Invisible cities* ([1st edition] ed., Harvest books) (W. Weaver, Trans.). New York: Harcourt Brace Jovanovich.

Cloke, P. (2005). Self-other. In P. Cloke, P. Crang, & M. Goodwin (Eds.), *Introducing human geographies* (2nd ed., pp. 61–77). Oxford, UK: Hodder Arnold.

Cohen, S. (2002). *Folk devils and moral panics: The creation of mods and rockers* (3rd ed.). London, UK: Routledge.

Council on Foreign Relations. (2016, September). *What college-aged students know about the world: A survey on global literacy*. Available from https://www.cfr.org/global-literacy-survey

Cresswell, T. (2004). *Place: A short introduction*. Oxford, UK: Blackwell.

Doerr, N. M. (2012). Study abroad as "adventure": Globalist construction of host–home hierarchy and governed adventurer subjects. *Critical Discourse Studies, 9*(3), 257–268.

Doerr, N. M. (2013). Damp rooms and saying "please": Mimesis and alterity in the host family space in study-abroad experiences. *Anthropological Forum, 23*(1), 58–78.

Doerr, N. M. (2016). Chronotopes of study abroad: The cultural Other, immersion, and compartmentalized space-time. *Journal of Cultural Geography, 33*(1), 80–99.

Doerr, N. M., & Taïeb, H. D. (2018). Affect and romance in study and volunteer abroad: Introducing our project. In N. M. Doerr & H. D. Taïeb (Eds.), *The romance of crossing borders: Studying and volunteering abroad* (pp. 3–34). New York, NY: Berghahn Books.

Dorling, D., & Lee, C. (2016, March 24). Geography's place in the world. *Times Higher Education*. Available from https://www.timeshighereducation.com/features/geographys-place-in-the-world

Elkin, L. (2017). *Flâneuse: Women walk the city in Paris, New York, Tokyo, Venice and London*. London, UK: Vintage.

Engle, J., & Engle, L. (2002). Neither international nor educative: Study abroad in the time of globalization. In W. Grünzweig & N. Rinehart (Eds.), *Rockin' in Red Square: Critical approaches to international education in the age of cyberculture* (pp. 25–39). Münster, Germany: LIT.

Freire, P. (1970). *Pedagogy of the oppressed.* New York, NY: Herder and Herder.

Fukuyama, F. (1992). *The end of history and the last man.* New York, NY: Free Press.

Gaile, G. L., & Willmott, C. J. (2003). *Geography in America at the dawn of the twenty-first century.* Oxford, UK: Oxford University Press.

Gilbert, D. (2005). Science–art. In P. Cloke, P. Crang, & M. Goodwin (Eds.), *Introducing human geographies* (2nd ed., pp. 104–122). London, UK: Hodder Arnold.

Glass, M. R. (2014). Encouraging reflexivity in urban geography fieldwork: Study abroad experiences in Singapore and Malaysia. *Journal of Geography in Higher Education, 38*(1), 69–85.

Glass, M. R. (2015). Teaching critical reflexivity in short-term international field courses: Practices and problems. *Journal of Geography in Higher Education, 39*(4), 554–567.

Gristwood, A., & Woolf, M. (2011). Experiential approaches to the global city: London as social laboratory. In E. Brewer & M. Monahan (Eds.), *Study Abroad and the City [Special Issue], Frontiers: The Interdisciplinary Journal of Study Abroad, 20,* 17–36.

Gristwood, A., & Woolf, M. (Eds.). (2012). *The city as text: Urban environments as the classroom in education abroad.* Boston, MA: CAPA International Education.

Gristwood, A., & Woolf, M. (2013). Introduction: Interrogating the cosmopolitan, engaging diversity. In A. Gristwood & M. Woolf (Eds.), *Cosmopolitanism and diversity: Concepts, practices and policies in education abroad* (pp. 12–19). Boston, MA: CAPA International Education.

Hardt, J., & Negri, A. (2000). *Empire.* Cambridge, MA: Harvard University Press.

Institute of International Education (ITE). (2017). Fields of U.S. study abroad students, 2005/6–2015/16. *Open Doors report on international educational exchange.* Available from https://www.iie.org/Research-and-Insights/Publications/Open-Doors-2017

Joyce, J. (1922). *Ulysses.* Paris, France: Shakespeare & Company.

Kelly, D. (2009a). Lessons from geography: Mental maps and spatial narratives. In E. Brewer & K. Cunningham (Eds.), *Integrating study abroad into the curriculum: Theory and practice across the disciplines* (pp. 21–40). Sterling, VA: Stylus.

Kelly, D. (2009b). Semiotics and the city: Putting theories of everyday life, literature, and culture into practice. In E. Brewer & K. Cunningham (Eds.), *Integrating study abroad into the curriculum: Theory and practice across the disciplines* (pp. 103–120). Sterling, VA: Stylus.

Kelly, D. (2013). Still haven't found what you're looking for? American students' search for authenticity in contemporary Ireland. In A. Gristwood & M. Woolf (Eds.), *Cosmopolitanism and diversity: Concepts, practices and policies in education abroad* (pp. 68–78). Boston, MA: CAPA International Education.

Kolb, A. Y., & Kolb, D. A. (2005). Learning styles and learning spaces: Enhancing experiential learning in higher education. *Academy of Management Learning and Education, 4*(2), 193–212.

Kuran, T., & Sandholm, W. H. (2008). Cultural integration and its discontents. *The Review of Economic Studies, 75*(1), 201–228.

Le Guin, U. K. (1969). *The left hand of darkness.* St. Albans, UK: Panther.

Lewin, R. (Ed.). (2009). *The handbook of practice and research in study abroad: Higher education and the quest for global citizenship.* New York, NY: Routledge.

Loveland, E., & Morris, C. (2018). *Study abroad matters: Linking higher education to the contemporary workplace through international experience.* Institute of International Education. Available from https://www.iie.org/en/Research-and-Insights/Publications/Study-Abroad-Matters

Massey, D. (1994). A global sense of place. In *Space, place, and gender* (pp. 146–156). Cambridge, UK: Polity.

Massey, D. (2007). *World city.* Cambridge, UK: Polity.

McClintock, A. (1995). *Imperial leather: Race, gender and sexuality in the colonial contest.* London, UK: Routledge.

Murphy, A. B. (2007). Geography's place in higher education in the United States. *Journal of Geography in Higher Education, 31*(1), 121–141.

Murphy, M. (2016, July 15). *Two interview questions to test if job candidates have emotional intelligence.* Forbes.com. Available from https://www.forbes.com/sites/markmurphy/2016/07/15/2-interview-questions-to-test-if-job-candidates-have-emotional-intelligence/#46fdee376346

Newell, W. H. (2010). Educating for a complex world: Integrative learning and interdisciplinary studies. *Liberal Education, 96*(4), 6–11. Available from https://www.aacu.org/publications-research/periodicals/educating-complex-world-integrative-learning-and-interdisciplinary

Ogden, A. (2007). The view from the veranda: Understanding today's colonial student. *Frontiers: The Interdisciplinary Journal of Study Abroad, 15*, 35–56.

Raban, J. (2008). *Soft city.* London, UK: Picador.

Revell, M. (2017). *Long-term trends in degrees conferred in geography.* Disciplinary Data Dashboard. Available from http://www.aag.org/galleries/disciplinary-data/Longterm_trends_in_degrees_conferred_in_geography.pdf

Rubin, K. (2009, May–June). Overseas internships jumpstart. *International Educator*, 58–70. Available from https://global.lehigh.edu/sites/global.lehigh.edu/files/ai_ie_overseas_internships_jumpstart.pdf

Schattle, H. (2008). *The practices of global citizenship.* Lanham, MD: Rowman & Littlefield.

Sibley, D. (1995). *Geographies of exclusion.* London, UK: Routledge.

Smith, D. (2002). Patterns and processes of studentification in Leeds. *Regional Review, 12*(1), 14–16.

Smith, D. (2008). The politics of studentification and "(un)balanced" urban populations: Lessons for gentrification and sustainable communities? *Urban Studies, 45*(12), 2541–2564.

Smith, N. (1996). *The new urban frontier: Gentrification and the revanchist city.* New York, NY: Routledge.

Smith, N. (2003). *American empire: Roosevelt's geographer and the prelude to globalization.* Berkeley: University of California Press.

Smith, R. (1997). The end of geography and radical politics in Baudrillard's philosophy. *Environment and Planning D: Society and Space, 15*(3), 305–320.

Smith, S. (2005). *Irish poetry and the construction of modern identity: Ireland between fantasy and history.* Dublin, Ireland: Irish Academic Press.

Soja, E. W. (1989). *Postmodern geographies: The reassertion of space in critical social theory.* London, UK: Verso.

Soja, E. W. (2000). *Postmetropolis: Critical studies of cities and regions.* Oxford, UK: Blackwell.

Stephens, J. (2017, January 23). Geographical literacy and the rise of Trump. *Huffington Post.* Available from https://www.huffingtonpost.com/entry/geographic-illiteracy-and-the-rise-of-trump_us_587fef14e4b0aa1c47ac280c

Sultana, F. (2012). Reflexivity, positionality and participatory ethics: Negotiating fieldwork dilemmas in international fieldwork. *ACME: An International E-Journal for Critical Geographies, 6,* 374–385.

Swyngedouw, E. (1997). Neither global nor local: "Glocalization" and the politics of scale. In K. R. Cox (Ed.), *Spaces of globalization: Reasserting the power of the local* (pp. 137–166). New York, NY: Guilford/Longman.

Taft, R. (2015, May 8). *Are international internships on the rise?* GoOverseas.com. Available from https://www.gooverseas.com/blog/are-international-internships-on-the-rise

Toral, P. (2009). Synthesis and career preparation: The international relations senior thesis. In E. Brewer & K. Cunningham (Eds.), *Integrating study abroad into the undergraduate curriculum: Theory and practice across the disciplines* (pp. 191–208). Sterling, VA: Stylus.

Tsing, A. (2000). The global situation. *Cultural Anthropology, 15*(3), 327–360.

Tuan, Y.-F. (1974). *Topophilia: A study of environmental perception, attitudes, and values.* Englewood Cliffs, NJ: Prentice-Hall.

Tuan, Y.-F. (1979). Space and place: Humanistic perspective. In S. Gale & G. Olsson (Eds.), *Philosophy in geography* (pp. 387–427). Dordrecht, The Netherlands: Reidel.

Urry, J., & Larsen, J. (2011). *The tourist gaze 3.0.* London, UK: SAGE.

Virilio, P. (2005). *City of panic.* Oxford, UK: Berg.

Whelan, Y. (2003). *Reinventing modern Dublin: Streetscape, iconography and the politics of identity.* Dublin, Ireland: Dublin University College Press.

White, E. (2001). *The flâneur.* London, UK: Bloomsbury.

Whybrow, P. C. (2006). *American mania: When more is not enough.* New York, NY: W.W. Norton.

Woolf, M. (2010). Another *Mishegas*: Global citizenship. *Frontiers: The Interdisciplinary Journal of Study Abroad, 19,* 47–60.

Zemach-Bersin, T. (2009). Selling the world: Study abroad marketing and the privatization of global citizenship. In R. Lewin (Ed.), *The handbook of practice and research in study abroad: Higher education and the quest for global citizenship* (pp. 303–320). New York, NY: Routledge.

7

LEARNING TO NAVIGATE

Lessons From Student Development

Paige E. Butler

S tudents today change and evolve at a rapid pace requiring educators to reflect continually on the programs, services, guidance, and support provided across higher and international education. Today's undergraduates are increasingly diverse and face complex obstacles as they navigate into adulthood and the global economy following graduation. To develop intentional programs and support students in ways that foster growth and development, education abroad practitioners and stakeholders must understand who students are today, what their needs are, and how to best support those needs as students advance through their education. Student development theory provides a framework to address student needs at different points of their cognitive, psychological, and social identity development. Education abroad practitioners who understand and can apply student development theory to practice will help emerging adults who study abroad to take advantage of powerful learning and development opportunities.

This chapter highlights selected theories relevant and applicable to the education abroad context. First, foundational, psychosocial, and cognitive development theories are presented as key references that can benefit education abroad practitioners in their work with program development, assessment, student advising, and support services. Second, social theories and newer research showcase more integrative and holistic methods of understanding students, particularly related to students' social and emotional development. Third, emerging adulthood theory is presented to educate readers about clear generational shifts and expectations that can impact students during their time abroad. Examples of application of theory to practice are provided to help practitioners enhance practice through theoretical grounding.

Student Development Theory

Student development theory offers valuable insight and guidance into understanding today's college students. Student development refers to "the ways that a student grows, progresses, or increases his or her developmental capabilities as a result of enrollment in an institution of higher education" (Rodgers, 1990, p. 27). Student development research is interdisciplinary in nature. Closely connected with current and foundational research from psychology, sociology, intercultural studies, business, and higher education, it examines students' growth and shifting needs as they progress through their education. Better understanding of the needs and culture of students today can help lead to strategies to both support their learning and assuage their and their families' fears and demands related to participation in on- and off-campus learning experiences.

Student development theory has evolved and become increasingly sophisticated over the last 30+ years. While foundational student development theories are typically cognitive, structural, psychosocial, or vocational in nature, later theories take a more integrative approach to examine the holistic nature of how students learn and change during their college years. They explore common traits and characteristics of students and identify specific aspects of the educational environment that can foster change. Further, by identifying specific learning-oriented outcomes and milestones for students to achieve throughout their education, student development theories provide a road map for students, families, and educators. The theories continue to grow in nuanced ways, helping educators better understand the complex identities of undergraduates. For a more detailed overview of a full range of student development theories, the author suggests the textbook *Student Development in College: Theory, Research, and Practice* by Patton, Renn, Guido, and Quaye (2016).

Foundational Theories in the Education Abroad Context

The early student development scholar Nevitt Sanford's (1962, 1966) theory of challenge and support posits that students must be ready for growth, the environment must create the appropriate amount of challenge for students to learn, and the amount of challenge a student can accept is based on the corresponding amount of support offered. Challenge and support is a critical theory for education abroad professionals to understand and apply in practice; students' needs vary according to their developmental stage and individual characteristics. Coupling challenge and support with other developmental theories helps elucidate ways in which educators can encourage learning and growth. The most appropriate candidates for education abroad are students prepared for its challenges. Understanding the inputs students bring (prior knowledge, experiences, attitudes, etc.) and their location in their development journey helps educators prepare students for the challenges they will encounter before, during, and after studying abroad. Educators must create learning environments that challenge students at appropriate levels, recognizing that individual students have different thresholds for challenge. First-time traveler students may find getting on an airplane and flying to another country solo a major challenge, while for others, challenges may involve language barriers, academic differences in the classroom, signing a contract for housing, or making friends in a new cultural environment. When students are underchallenged or undersupported, they may disengage, retreat or regress, or stagnate in their current development stage. Figure 7.1 highlights four quadrants that represent results of challenge and support. Maximum growth occurs when the appropriate amount of challenge and support exists.

To meet students where they are developmentally, education abroad professionals must provide advisement and learning environments that offer varying degrees of challenge and support. Further, scaffolded support, up front and early on in the experience, can help students transition to unfamiliar cultural environments and work through early challenges. Support can be scaled back over time as students build their own support systems and seek out support tools independently to maximize growth. Students must and can invest in their own learning and development when appropriately challenged and supported.

Figure 7.1. Support and challenge grid.

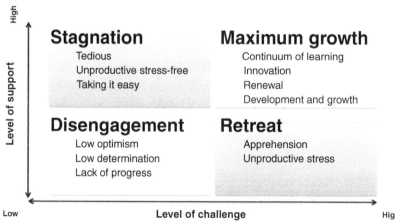

Note. Image from "Why Great Leaders Must Support and Challenge People and Teams" by E. Rubio (2016). Reprinted with permission.

Alexander Astin's (1984) theory of student involvement expands on the importance of students investing energy into the educational experience: "The amount of student learning and personal development associated with any educational program is directly proportional to the quality and quantity of student involvement in that program" (p. 298). While students' degrees of interest and willingness to invest energy will vary, Astin's work teaches that education abroad is enhanced through engaging students in their own preparation and learning directly, in terms of both *quantity* and *quality*. For example, students ready for higher levels of challenge can create or cocreate predeparture or on-site orientation sessions alongside peers or professionals, peer leaders can provide student-to-student assistance during education abroad, and students can become involved abroad in clubs or other opportunities. All of these align with good practices in enhancing student engagement and involvement in the learning and development process. Moving beyond transactional information sharing from authority to student is critical. This requires that educators move into stronger developmental roles that offer space to coach and mentor students; provide guidance and feedback; and, at times, allow students to struggle with the learning challenges and experiences they encounter.

Some dissonance and disorientation is normal and necessary to learning, but the threshold varies by student, environment, and available support. Astin (1984) suggests that students build connections and engage in the learning process in and outside of the classroom (1984). Person-environment interaction theory suggests the importance of education practitioners in helping students embrace being safely uncomfortable, or *comfortably uncomfortable,* while abroad in order to maximize learning and development.

Applying Foundational Theory to Practice: Two Case Studies

The student profiles in Figure 7.2 can help education abroad professionals learn to apply Sanford's and Astin's foundational theories to assess student readiness, develop individualized advising strategies, and tailor support. For example, Alejandra is likely "connecting" her academic work from her major and minor and has strong social capital with her professor and peers in the program. Alex is likely "experimenting" to test his academic interests and explore a new challenge academically and personally by traveling abroad for the first time.

As Alejandra and Alex demonstrate, students bring different needs based on prior international experiences, language abilities, social capital, and their identity development. Basic information about students, their backgrounds, and their study abroad plans can help educators anticipate the level of challenge

Figure 7.2. Theory to practice: Student profiles.

Alejandra, 21, female	Alex, 19, male
Student Information: Undergraduate Level: Rising Senior Major: Latin American Studies Minor: International Relations Language(s) Spoken: Bilingual Spanish/ English (speaks Spanish at home) Cumulative GPA: 3.6; Major GPA: 3.75	*Student Information:* Undergraduate Level: Rising Sophomore Major: Business Minor: N/A Language(s) Spoken: English +2 Semesters of College-Level Japanese Language Classes Cumulative GPA: 3.75; Major GPA: 3.8
Study Abroad Program Plans: Study Abroad Program: Faculty-Led Program Location: Argentina and Chile Term: Summer; Length: 5 weeks Housing: Host Family (1 per location) Credit(s): 3 cr; 1 course Direct Credit–Home University Other Program Notes: 8 Students Enrolled, Led by Latin American Studies Professor	*Study Abroad Program Plans:* Study Abroad Program: University Exchange Location: Japan Term: Fall; Length: Semester (16 weeks) Housing: Residential Hall With Japanese Roommate; Local Students Credits: 12–16 cr; 4–5 courses Transfer Credit–Host University Other Program Notes: Direct Enrollment, Courses in Japanese History, Language and Culture in Japanese; Business and Psychology Courses in English
Student Background Information: Prior International Experience: Yes (personal travel) Prior Experience in Host Country: No Other Notes: Co-President of the Coalition of Latinx Students Winner of Latino Student Achievement Scholarship for Leadership and Advocacy	*Student Background Information:* Prior International Experience: No Prior Experience in Host Country: No Other Notes: Considering Adding a Japanese Minor Member of the Undergraduate Business Student Association

students may encounter abroad and the supports they might require before, during, and after studying abroad. Next explored are theories related to psychosocial and cognitive dimensions of student development that can help frame strategies to promote growth and learning throughout the educational experience.

Psychosocial Development: Theories and Implications for Education Abroad

Psychosocial student development theories examine inter- and intrapersonal aspects of development: the relationships people develop, how they define themselves, and what they choose to do with their lives (Evans, Forney, Guido, Patton, & Renn, 2010). Stemming from Erik Erikson's work in the 1950s, the theories posit a series of development stages across the human life span (Erikson, 1950). Common markers of adulthood include progress toward intimacy and commitments. Students thus place importance on building relationships during their college years. Marcia (1966, 1980) expanded on Erikson's work (1966, 1980) to explore how individuals formulate their own identities, separating from parental/family values to choose their own pathways and establish clear commitments. Observing elements unique to women's identity formation in adulthood, Josselson (1978/1989) concluded that women's identity development differs from men's, with relationship development more important. Astin's theory of involvement and Josselson's women's identity theories can be paired to create strong educational environments that foster development. Research has found that women's identity achievement is linked closely to involvement in organizations, activities, and leadership roles (Weston & Stein, as cited in Marcia, 1980, p. 173). Similarly, in the education abroad context, the Georgetown Consortium Project (Vande Berg, Connor-Linton, & Paige, 2009) found that while females made significant gains in intercultural development abroad, males did not. Together, student development theory and education abroad research offer a strong argument for considering gender differences in advising, training, and programming, although uncertainty exists as to which resources should be offered. Further, nascent research on nonbinary gender identities must be considered if gender is to be utilized in a developmental context.

The works of Erikson, Marcia, and Josselson serve as foundational theories of college-student identity formation, reminding educators that in addition to classroom knowledge acquisition, students are negotiating and exploring their identities, ideologies, occupational interests, sexuality, behaviors, and relationships as they emerge into adulthood. In fact, Chickering "saw the establishment of identity as the core developmental issue with which students grapple during their college years" (Evans et al., 2010, p. 65). Chickering's (1969; Chickering & Reisser, 1993) identity theory research identifies seven vectors of psychosocial development during college years: developing competence, managing emotions, moving through autonomy toward interdependence, developing mature interpersonal relationships, establishing identity, developing purpose, and developing integrity. Similar to Sanford (1962, 1966) and Astin (1984), Chickering (1969) believes student development is influenced significantly by learning environment. Influences include institutional objectives, institutional size, student-faculty relationships, curriculum, teaching, friendships, and student communities (Chickering & Reisser, 1993).

Like Sanford, Chickering and Reisser (1993) highlight the need for disequilibrium for growth to occur: Encounters with disorientation and discomfort are important stimuli for learning. Subsequent research on disequilibrium and student development stresses the need to individualize interactions and interventions to reflect the diversity of students' needs and stages of development.

Navigating discomfort can be challenging for students and educators alike. Space for reflection can help, as can clearly stated missions and goals that help students understand expectations for learning and align opportunities with their goals. Differences in the learning environment between the home and host settings must be considered: As indicated, faculty and curriculum greatly impact undergraduate learning and development, along with social aspects related to housing, roommates, or relationships at home and abroad.

Cognitive Development: Theories and Implications for Education Abroad

Knowledge acquisition is a major component of student identity development. Undergraduates gain new disciplinary content knowledge and build metacognitive skills around how to learn, think critically, and reflect on learning as part of the knowledge acquisition process. Cognitive structural theorists examine this intellectual development beginning with Inhelder and Piaget (1960) and including Perry (1970, 1981), Kohlberg (1976), Gilligan (1993), Baxter Magolda (2001, 2002, 2007), and King and Baxter Magolda (2005). In education abroad, cognitive structural theories are useful for program and course development and assessing student learning.

Common themes distilled from each theory's insight into student learning and intellectual, moral, and ethical development can help orient practitioners around general stages of cognitive development and their implications for education abroad. Cognitive development stages highlighted by Perry (1970) include dualism, multiplicity, relativism, and commitment. However, caution must be exercised: Much student development research focused on a more homogeneous population than today's wide range of learners from diverse backgrounds.

Considering the implications for education abroad, first- or second-year students in stages of exploration and experimentation may likely present more *dualistic* or dichotomous thinking tendencies, although it is important to not stereotype learners, who in fact may differ. Nonetheless, in early development, learners may see two concrete possibilities in which the world operates and classify information and exchanges as right or wrong, good or bad, or factual or fiction. Learning may be experienced as transactional, with authorities, usually professors, providing correct information and right answers. Multiple answers or the absence of a clear answer can easily frustrate dualistic students and lead them to question the credibility of the authority figure. Cognitive dissonance (uncertainty) helps dualistic students advance their intellectual development by questioning their default mode of thinking. Students will need help navigating dissonance abroad, such as when comparing home and host countries.

At the cognitive development stage of *multiplicity,* students recognize that they do not know the answer and acknowledge that different, equally valid answers may exist. In this stage, different sources of information, including peers and self, become more important and valid in the learning process. Education abroad is ideal in allowing students to question dualistic thinking and wrestle with multiple perspectives, as specific examples between the home and host culture quickly emerge for comparison. This may begin with thinking, "Everyone in the world should eat lunch at noon," progress to "People in some places eat lunch at different times in the day," and move to confronting more challenging concepts, such as the role of gender in a culture or views on LGBT+ rights. Multiplistic students may struggle to evaluate differing perspectives, defer contentious issues, and conclude everyone is entitled to unopposed opinion. Assistance in questioning opinions, discerning information sources, and formulating arguments to challenge viewpoints can help students advance beyond multiplistic thinking. Assignments that push students to establish, support, and/or defend a position and argue points and counterpoints, whether in oral and/or written contexts, can meet education abroad outcomes and goals from advancing linguistic proficiency to deepening critical thinking.

Advanced students recognize that not all opinions are fully equal, thus demonstrating a more *relativistic* perspective. Relativism recognizes diverse opinions and requires critical information in their support, whereas opinions unsupported by sufficient evidence become invalid. It is okay to disagree, particularly when considering complex issues. Indeed, complex problems do not have right or wrong answers. Thus, relativistic thinkers make meaning by critically examining ideas, questioning information—even when coming from an authority figure—and starting to adopt and reject information based on their own understanding and synthesis. *Commitment* is demonstrated when relativistic students integrate knowledge from various sources with their own personal experience and reflection, and commit to certain beliefs and values.

Perry (1970) also suggests that rest periods advance learning when development stagnates or slows. Students may retreat or temporarily return to previous stages to manage feelings when overwhelmed by challenge. A successful balance of information processing, questioning, and acceptance can be difficult to achieve when students transition to more relativistic cognitive thinking. Supportive assignments and ongoing reflection about concepts and metacognitive processes can alleviate frustration, help students understand their growth, and encourage ongoing examination of information and beliefs.

Applying Psychosocial and Cognitive Theory to Practice

Figures 7.3 and 7.4 present two scenarios. These, along with the student profile information in Figure 7.2, can help education abroad professionals apply psychosocial and cognitive theories to practice.

In the scenarios, Alejandra and Alex demonstrate different levels of cognitive development and responses to encountering challenges abroad. They remind education abroad professionals to meet students where they are developmentally, and elucidate differences witnessed as students encounter cognitive dissonance or critical incidents that confront their current stage of thinking. Advisers must consider these developmental stages to adequately challenge and support students to advance their learning.

Education abroad professionals can challenge dualistic students to practice critical thinking by avoiding oversimplification or overgeneralization and considering the validity of other perspectives. Examples and opportunities to practice complex thinking can support students in earlier stages of thinking.

Figure 7.3. Alejandra at dinner: A cognitive development perspective.

Alejandra is enjoying dinner with her host family when her younger host brother makes a comment about *gypsies* bothering him and his friend in the park after school. Alejandra's host mother tells her that gypsies are illegal immigrants and tells her to stay away from them "because most of them are criminals." Alejandra knows that the term is used derogatively to refer to people from neighboring countries without legal status, as well as people of indigenous descent. Feeling uncomfortable with the conversation, Alejandra excuses herself from the table and goes to her room. She jumps online to chat with two of her friends who are also program participants and relays the conversation. One friend tells her she needs to report the conversation and request to move immediately. Another friend tells her to ignore it and suggests they didn't mean it to come off insensitively—after all, the host family has welcomed Alejandra into their home like a family member, so obviously they aren't racist or xenophobic. Alejandra goes to sleep feeling uneasy; at home she proudly advocates for Latinx students and strives to raise awareness around issues of discrimination and equity. After another day or two, she decides to speak to her professor for advice about how to address this with her host family.

Figure 7.4. Alex and authorities: A cognitive development perspective.

Alex debates leaving his Japanese history class early for the second time in a week. An international student from South Korea asked his professor a question about a reading that discussed the history of war and some contentious topics between South Korea and Japan. Alex thought the question was really important as the reading seemed inconsistent with the history he had learned. The professor simply responded with a vague response and didn't answer the question at all. Alex thought it was really disrespectful to the student and his culture for the professor to ignore the question. After class, he made it a point to speak to the other international student and said, "What a joke, I can't believe the professor didn't know how to answer your question—he's not qualified to teach a history class like this—you know way more than he does!" The international student shrugged and said he didn't really expect a direct answer, but he was happy the professor acknowledged his question at least. Alex was baffled—he knew before coming to Japan that indirect communication styles were common, but he assumed that in class professors would have clear answers. Alex sends an angry e-mail to his study abroad adviser at home, stating that the program professors aren't credible or knowledgeable, and he doesn't think this is a good study abroad program so he's thinking about returning home early instead of continuing to waste his time and money "not learning anything."

Faculty can help multiplistic students distinguish between strong and weak arguments, explore and construct knowledge together with peers, and seek alternative interpretations and question assumptions to deepen perspectives and demonstrate higher order thinking skills. In general, practitioners can strengthen students' experience and practice with higher order thinking by promoting interaction among students, sharing real-life examples and case studies, asking probing questions, encouraging reflection, and sharing feedback. As students develop, they often experience disequilibrium and discomfort. This stimulates learning and development for longer term growth when matched with the right level of support. Intentional design and articulation of desired learning outcomes help students navigate key developmental stages during study abroad.

Integrative Student Development Theories: Social and Emotional Development for Emerging Adults

Changes in technology, access to education, student diversity, and more have led to a deeper understanding of students' social identities and engagement with the world. Thus, this section considers a burgeoning area within student development theory related to students' myriad social identities. Social identity theory provides valuable information and guidance about working with students, but practitioners must avoid overgeneralization and stereotyping, emphasize individuation, and honor the multiple identities of learners.

Social Identity Development

Over the last few decades, student development researchers have questioned the applicability of foundational human and student development theory for increasingly diverse college student populations, as much of the early research focused on primarily White, male, U.S. student populations, often studying at more elite institutions. Newer research seeks to account intentionally for the varied institutional environments and experiences students encounter as undergraduates. More work remains, but researchers have made significant strides in better understanding students' multiple social identities including race/ethnicity, gender, and sexual orientation and expression, among other social and cultural identities (ability, religion, nationality, legal status, socioeconomic status, etc.). Social identity is a rich area of study highlighting important differences among learners. Social identities impact psychosocial and cognitive development, and diverse student identities require differentiated support to fully consider intersectional identities in a holistic and integrative manner. Integrative and social identity development theory, along with foundational theories, helps educators improve advising, student services, and programming across institutions to better support diverse learners and create inclusive and welcoming educational environments for them.

Social identity theory sheds light on how individuals both make sense of and express their unique social identities. Social identities and their expression impact students' abilities to navigate other areas of their development. Social identities are challenging and evolving, as they reflect judgments—internal and external—based upon cultural norms relevant to the time and place under which the identities are observed or expressed. As such, social identities are continuously shifting and evolving. Social identity formation requires examining issues of power, privilege, and oppression, and recognizing that both visible and invisible identities factor into student identity formation. As such, social identities are complex to understand and practice, yet social identities play a significant role in how students see themselves, make decisions, and interact with others (Evans et al., 2010).

In the education abroad context, social identity presents a layer of complexity as the element of time and place change during the abroad experience, as do cultural and community expectations of social identity. It is particularly important to prepare students for transitions before, during, and after studying abroad as the social constructs of identity can vary significantly between cultures. As an example, consider Eric, a rising junior planning to study abroad. Eric identifies as an American, White, male, gay, Christian student and plans to study abroad in Tanzania. His identities related to his gender, religion, sexual orientation and expression, nationality, race, and socioeconomic status may all be interpreted differently in a country where he would potentially experience intersectional minoritization based on his various social identities.

No matter students' development in relation to their social identities, traveling abroad and encountering new social constructs and norms can raise new or different issues impacting student development. Perhaps Eric has progressed through his sexual and gender identities to openly identify as a member of a lesbian, gay, bisexual, or transgender community in the United States. While abroad, however, he may struggle with how his defined social identity is perceived in a more conservative community that does not accept homosexuality and enforces laws reflecting this ideology. Eric may also experience being a racial minority for the first time, and consider race differently as its social construct shifts between home and host country. Eric's intersecting social identities may negatively impact his education abroad if he is underprepared or undersupported to navigate challenges.

As another example, Kimmi identifies as a female, third-generation Korean American, native-English speaker. She attends a small, private, predominantly White liberal arts college in the Midwest near her small, rural hometown. Kimmi is excited to study abroad in South Korea and to visit for the first time the country and region from which her family emigrated decades prior. While comfortable with her Korean American and other social identities at home, Kimmi may experience new perspectives about these while abroad, depending on interactions with locals and the perception of her national, racial, and ethnic identities. If her American identity is more prominent in interactions with locals and causes her to feel like an outsider, Kimmi may question her sense of belonging to the Korean culture that has been part of her family heritage. She may in turn question her American identity and sense of belonging. Kimmi's example signals that when students of color, particularly those who attend predominantly White institutions or live in predominantly White communities, study abroad in locations where their own racial or ethnic identities are the dominant population, they may experience and evaluate their identities in new ways. Some may lean toward their American or their ethnic identity more strongly, while others may look toward a third culture to reflect their identity (Hisano, 2015; Meier, 2015). In the United States, students may be accustomed to having a specific social identity that creates a certain in-group or out-group status or affiliation, often based on more visible identities such as race, gender, or physical ability. Abroad, direct and indirect shifts among in-group or out-group status can significantly influence student development and learning. Predeparture conversations about identity and transitioning between home and host cultures; cultural mentoring pre–, during, and post–study abroad; and opportunities for reflection upon return are critical aids to social identity development.

Emerging Adulthood

Emerging adulthood theory (Arnett, 2014; Bluth, Roberson, & Gaylord, 2015) helps inform educators about today's college entrants. *Emerging adulthood* is defined as "a new life stage between that of adolescence and of young adulthood—lasting from age 18 years to about age 29 years" (Arnett, Žukauskienė, & Sugimura, 2014, p. 569), and the theory focuses on developmental tasks that occur as emerging adults explore their identities and relationships. Arnett suggests that traditional markers of adulthood such as marriage, job security, and buying a home are no longer the key priorities they once were for individuals in their early 20s. Instead, emerging adulthood frames students' interdependence upon parents or families until later in their 20s; the segue into adulthood becomes more self-focused. It is a time of exploration and risk taking, prolonged well beyond college. Identity exploration features prominently in this "in-between" age, with emerging adults optimistically pursuing dreams and goals before they feel constrained by relationships, careers, families, or other responsibility. Emerging adulthood serves as a valuable framework to understand student experiences and relationships and provides a helpful lens to blend student development and the international education context. Emerging adulthood is "a period of heightened instability" (Arnett et al., 2014, p. 569). Such instability is normal and healthy, but educators must be prepared to support emerging adults as they transition through new experiences, explore their identities, and take risks. Education abroad can provide students an opportunity to practice increasing autonomy and responsibility and learn new skills with long-term benefits.

Emotional Development

While the transition into adulthood can signify a time of uncertainty, education abroad also represents a time of exploration: new sights, sounds, smells, tastes, experiences, and more. These changes can also lead to disorientation by creating a heightened sense of mental and emotional arousal, leading to the influx of emotional highs and lows common in transitioning among cultures. This level of change and stimulation can become overwhelming; navigating the nuanced stressors associated with cultural transitions requires skills. Preparation and training can help emerging adults be in a mind-set that is prepared for growth and development.

If unprepared or undersupported, students may experience emotions abroad that negatively impact their success and development. Sixty-two percent of undergraduate students already report "overwhelming anxiety," while one-third of adolescents and adults report ongoing anxiety (Tate, 2017). Education abroad professionals must use a variety of tools and strategies to foster student growth, and support students as they navigate through stressors and learning challenges abroad.

The clinical psychologist Abarbanel (2009) suggests the importance of facilitating disengagement from high-arousal situations abroad. When overly stressed or anxious, the brain struggles with language, scheduling, planning, and reasoning—all critical functions of successful navigation abroad. Abarbanel suggests limiting phones and electronics, practicing healthy eating, exercising, and engaging in arts (music, dancing, painting, etc.) as respites from high emotional states of being. Students must learn to self-regulate and to calm down when uncomfortable situations arise. Having an "emotional passport" while abroad enables students to gain better perspective, embrace multiple viewpoints, and reframe interpretations. An emotional passport refers to students' ability to develop "skills to regulate intense emotional challenges experienced in cultural transitions" (2009, p. 133).

To foster positive development abroad, educators can help students develop the emotional resilience critical for learning and growth. Abarbanel (2015) shares 12 prompts to engage students in conversations about emotional health, such as: "Reflect on an experience where everything was new, and you figured out/had help with ways to get comfortable. . . . What was the challenge? How did you approach the situation? What worked? Who helped you? What was especially hard? Something learned?" Another valuable prompt helps orient students around curricular and cocurricular experiences: "Describe what in your daily routine helps you get things done and stay focused. What would help you maintain your best self abroad—what do you need in your routine?"

Cues can signal when students are struggling abroad. Typical behaviors that intervene with learning and wellness abroad include boredom, withdrawal, excessive sleeping, compulsive eating or drinking, being homesick, overgeneralizations or stereotyping, inability to work effectively (Abarbanel, 2015). Interventions can help students navigate through the experience. Abarbanel's research converges with that of Arnett and other student development theorists to emphasize that undergraduates' experiences are impacted by the surrounding environment and encounters. While a heavy focus on exploring and experimenting with identities, building social networks, skill development, and finding belonging in new communities, transitional stages and feelings of disconnection can elicit depression and anxiety for emerging adults (Arnett et al., 2014).

Conclusion

Educators today serve diverse student needs; student learning and development theory can help them develop programs and advise and support students. This chapter presents an overview of past and present relevant theories, and applies these to practice in the education abroad context. To maximize learning before, during, and after education abroad, students must be appropriately challenged and supported in their cognitive, psychosocial, and emotional development. Practitioners must engage students to take agency in their own learning experiences and embed support structures throughout the international experience. Support expands beyond academic content, culture, and logistics to information and tools that benefit knowledge and identity development. Individuation of advising, mentoring, reflection, and programming encourages students to develop the broader skills of critical thinking and emotional resiliency that will sustain them through the periods of discomfort that are essential to learning.

Education abroad provides the ideal environment to engage with diverse others and explore the new and different—important concepts for today's emerging adults studying abroad. Educators must help prepare students for the disequilibrium normal in studying abroad, recognizing that disequilibrium is often exactly what leads to new insight and growth. However, students often are insufficiently prepared to navigate through intense new experiences abroad and may regress or stagnate if discomfort, uncertainty, and ambiguity overpower their abilities to think critically, reflect, withhold judgment, and process information and emotions. This can lead students to engage in self-destructive behaviors and derail positive growth. Individuation is essential to supporting students and ensuring learning can occur.

Deeper understanding of students and student development theory serves to improve education abroad programming and maximize student experiences and learning abroad. It gives educators key insight to provide high-quality advising and support student needs. Theory and experience aid educators in predicting and responding to challenges students encounter before, during, and after studying abroad. Education abroad practitioners' ability to apply theory to practice is critical to maximizing student learning and development abroad.

References

Abarbanel, J. (2009). Moving with emotional resilience between and within cultures. *Intercultural Education, 20*, 133–141. Available from http://www.tandf online.com/doi/abs/10.1080/14675980903371035

Abarbanel, J. (2015). *For study abroad professionals, supporting resilience in transition: A guide for conversations with students about emotional health.* Available from http://www.slideshare.net/cieeorg/reinventing-wellness-a-guide-for-conversations -with-students-about-emotional-health

Arnett, J. (2014). *Emerging adulthood: The winding road from the late teens through the twenties* (2nd ed.). New York, NY: Oxford.

Arnett, J., Žukauskienė, R., & Sugimura, K. (2014). The new life stage of emerging adulthood: An international perspective. *Lancet Psychiatry, 1*, 569–576. Available from http://www.jeffreyarnett.com/azk.lancet.2014.pdf

Astin, A. W. (1984). Student involvement: A developmental theory for higher education. *Journal of College Student Personnel, 25*(4), 297–308.

Baxter Magolda, M. B. (2001). *Making their own way: Narratives for transforming higher education to promote self-development.* Sterling, VA: Stylus.

Baxter Magolda, M. B. (2002). Helping students make their way to adulthood: Good company for the journey. *About Campus, 6*(6), 2–9.

Baxter Magolda, M. B. (2007). Self-authorship: The foundation for twenty-first-century education. *New Directions for Teaching and Learning, 109*, 69–83.

Bluth, K., Roberson, P., & Gaylord, S. (2015). A pilot study of a mindfulness intervention for adolescents and the potential role of self-compassion in reducing stress. *The Journal of Science and Healing, 11*(4), 186–198.

Chickering, A. W. (1969). *Education and identity.* San Francisco, CA: Jossey-Bass.

Chickering, A. W., & Reisser, L. (1993). *Education and identity* (2nd ed.). San Francisco, CA: Jossey-Bass.

Erikson, E. H. (1950). *Childhood and society.* New York, NY: Norton.

Evans, N. J., Forney, D. S., Guido, F., Patton, L., & Renn, K. (2010). *Student development in college: Theory, research and practice.* San Francisco, CA: Jossey-Bass.

Gilligan, C. (1993). *In a different voice: Psychological theory and women's development.* Cambridge, MA: Harvard University Press.

Hisano, Y. (2015). The narratives of adult third culture kids: Cultural identity development and psychological support upon reentry to one's home country. *Theses, Dissertations, and Projects.* Northampton, MA: Smith Scholar Works. Available from https://scholarworks.smith.edu/cgi/viewcontent.cgi?article=1764&context =theses

Inhelder, B., & Piaget, J. (1960). *The growth of logical thinking from childhood to adolescence.* Available from https://doi.org/10.1111/j.2044-8295.1960.tb00727.x

Josselson, R. (1989). *Finding herself: Pathways to identity development in women.* San Francisco, Jossey-Bass CA. (Original work published 1978)

King, P. M., & Baxter Magolda, M. B. (2005). A development model of intercultural maturity. *Journal of College Student Development, 46,* 571–592.

Kolhberg, L. (1976). Moral stages and moralization: The cognitive-developmental approach. In T. Lickona (Ed.), *Moral development and behavior: Theory, research, and social issues* (pp. 31–53). New York, NY: Holt.

Marcia, J. E. (1966). Development and validation of ego-identity status. *Journal of Personality and Social Psychology, 3*(5), 551–558.

Marcia, J. E. (1980). Identity in adolescence. *Handbook of Adolescent Psychology, 9*(11), 159–187.

Meier, C. R. (2015). *Third culture kids and social media: Identity development and transition in the 21st century.* ProQuest Dissertations and Theses Global. Available from https://search.proquest.com/docview/1687190092?accountid=26417

Patton, L., Renn, K. A., Guido, F., & Quaye, S. J. (2016). *Student development in college: Theory, research, and practice* (3rd ed.). San Francisco, CA: Jossey-Bass.

Perry, W. G. Jr. (1970). *Forms of intellectual and ethical development in the college years: A scheme.* New York, NY: Holt, Rinehart and Winston.

Perry, W. G. Jr. (1981). Cognitive and ethical growth: The making of meaning. In A. Chickering (Ed.), *The modern American college* (pp. 76–116). San Francisco, CA: Jossey-Bass.

Rodgers, R. F. (1990). Recent theories and research underlying student development. In D. G. Creamer & Associates (Eds.), *College student development: Theory and practice for the 1990s* (pp. 27–79). Alexandria, VA: American College Personnel Association.

Rubio, E. (2016) *Why great leaders must support and challenge people and teams.* Available from: https://www.linkedin.com/pulse/why-great-leaders-must-support-challenge-people-teams-enrique-rubio/

Sanford, N. (1962). *The American college.* New York, NY: Wiley.

Sanford, N. (1966). *Self and society: Social change and individual development.* New York, NY: Atherton.

Tate, E. (2017, March 29). Anxiety on the rise. *Inside Higher Ed.* Available from https://www.insidehighered.com/news/2017/03/29/anxiety-and-depression-are-primary-concerns-students-seeking-counseling-services

Vande Berg, M., Connor-Linton, J., & Paige, R. M. (2009). The Georgetown Consortium project: Interventions for student learning abroad. *Frontiers: The Interdisciplinary Journal of Study Abroad, 18,* 1–75.

8

USING ASSESSMENT TO ALIGN AND INTERWEAVE CORE CURRICULUM OBJECTIVES AND EDUCATION ABROAD LEARNING OUTCOMES

Katherine N. Yngve

This critical perspective chapter is dedicated to expanding the dialogue on education abroad assessment beyond its recent laser-like focus on better research design and its partisan and sometimes polarizing discussions about differing survey instruments. Therefore, it dose not, as prior studies have accomplished, attempt to define the competencies that may be correlated to education abroad and the myriad options for measuring them (namely Fantini, 2009; Sinicrope, Norris, & Watanabe, 2007), nor does it review research relating to said outcomes (cf. Salisbury, 2015; Vande Berg, Paige, & Lou, 2012). Attempting in these ways to pin down what the purpose and outcomes of education abroad *ought to be* is arguably not the best way to address the concerns raised throughout this book. Prematurely focusing on how to document an outcome restricts one's ability to think clearly and creatively about educational questions that are often overlooked and far more important, such as: *Which* of the desired outcomes of an undergraduate curriculum might best be taught through structured encounters with persons from another culture? How? When? For which kind(s) of learner? In short, colleges and universities would do better to "first expand the range of available and 'acceptable' learning outcomes [of education abroad] and then find ways to measure their achievement" (Salisbury, 2015, p. 25).

For at least 60 years, outcomes research has periodically suggested that education abroad is not, in fact, a reliable conveyor belt to linguistic proficiency, mutual understanding across cultures, or reduced ethnocentrism (Churchill, 1958; Freed, 1995; Robinson, 1978; Vande Berg et al., 2012). For roughly the last 20 years, educators' reaction to such troublesome findings has been to design more rigorous studies and complex survey instruments or to develop better explanatory models (Fantini, 2009; Salisbury, 2015). From these efforts, much useful information has been generated. In the end, however, even the most rigorously designed and analyzed survey of education abroad outcome "merely explains the *relative proportion of the experience's impact on the outcomes*. The findings do not tell us anything about how complex learning might emerge over the course of a series of singular experiences" (Salisbury, 2015, p. 19; emphasis added). Most outcomes studies tell the reader only the degree to which a group has changed (or hasn't) as a result of a particular program. Even the best education abroad outcomes studies, as published, do not adequately differentiate between the learning needs and processes of students at different developmental stages or of different ethnicities, genders, or majors. Yet, perspective transformation, a key element of mutual understanding and/or reduced ethnocentrism, is a deeply personal, contextual process (Mezirow, 1991). Accordingly, education abroad and the institutions that seek to harness its pedagogical benefits to enrich their curricular offerings would be well advised to become better acquainted with formative assessment and the key assessment principles outlined in the next section.

Four Key Assessment Principles

In seeking to better integrate education abroad into the educational continuum, it is useful to bear firmly in mind the following four key principles of good assessment:

1. Alignment of the assessment instrument with instructional objectives, curriculum design, and delivery of the curriculum is absolutely fundamental. If they are misaligned, education is compromised (Fantini, 2009); that is, students do not reliably learn what the instructor intended.
2. "Assessment works best when the programs it seeks to improve have clear, explicitly stated purposes" (Hutchings, Ewell, & Banta, 2012, para. 8). To be more direct, unless one is measuring across a multiyear period (or

perhaps measuring free-throw percentage), competence is not a realistic learning objective. Students and instructor-mentors benefit from being able to focus on learning objectives that are more SMART: specific, measurable, attainable, realistic, and time-bound (Deardorff & Deardorff, 2016).

3. In order to be useful, assessment must be connected to issues, problems, or concerns that people care deeply about (Suskie, 2009). For example, education abroad assessment might seek to determine the degree to which prehealth students develop the empathy and communication skills to connect to patients from a variety of ethnic or national backgrounds.

4. "Student learning is a campus-wide responsibility, and assessment is a way of enacting that responsibility" (Hutchings et al., 2012, para. 11). Quite simply, assessment can create better learning (Rust, 2002). Therefore, it should similarly be a campus-wide responsibility to be able to enact formative assessment, for example, to appraise students' efforts and provide supportive feedback for being effective across cultures (assuming for the moment that cross-cultural effectiveness is your curricular and/or education abroad goal).

Education Abroad and Formative Assessment

There are over 150 instruments, by this contributor's count, that can be used to measure some component or type of culture-crossing competence; these include predictive, normative, summative, and formative options (Fantini, 2009; Paige, 2004). This chapter focuses primarily on rubric-based assessment and on formative assessment, in addition to mentioning roughly eight specific instruments that the contributor's faculty colleagues have found to support student-centered, process-based learning (and research). This is by no means intended to cast aspersions on instruments not mentioned or on predictive, normative, and summative assessment techniques; it is meant instead to address perceived weaknesses in both the outcomes literature and standard education abroad professional practice.

Why rubrics? A *rubric* has been defined as "a coherent set of criteria for students' work that includes descriptions of levels of performance quality" (Brookhart, 2013, p. 4). Students learn better when they have assistance in setting specific and concrete goals that build gradually toward a larger goal, such as developing the building block skill of correctly formulating a topic sentence (and similar elements of writing a good research paper), rather than setting broad goals, such as contracting to earn an A in the same course (Clark, Gill, Prowse, & Rush, 2017). In an education abroad context this might mean pledging to use the conditional tense of a new verb in conversation at least once a week, rather than vowing to become fluent in Spanish during one's semester abroad. Good rubrics give educators a way to turn complex competencies into SMART learning goals, an approach that helps students build a sense of self-efficacy and increases internalized motivation toward ever-increasing levels of mastery.

Why formative assessment? Formative assessment, as a pedagogical practice, aligns well with the findings of recent education abroad research, which suggest that students, in order to develop, need frequent feedback, guided reflection, and mentor-supplied strategies for improvement (Paige & Goode, 2009; Vande Berg et al., 2012). Formative assessment involves using a range of formal and informal appraisal, review, or diagnostic procedures to improve students' uptake and eventual mastery of skills or behaviors. It is a change-oriented teaching method that has been found to accommodate individual learner differences and foster a disposition toward lifelong learning (Rust, 2002). Formative assessment may use observation and drills, qualitative methods (reflection exercises, instructor debriefs, formal or informal focus groups, etc.), and/or quantitative instruments (quizzes, inventories, predictive assessments, etc.), in order to assist the learner and the instructor in measuring either proficiency gaps or gains in competency. The feature that most clearly distinguishes formative from other kinds of assessment is prompt feedback: For example, a free-throw drill is a formative assessment when the player's coach uses it as an opportunity to suggest techniques for improvement; when used to determine the composition of the team's starting five, however, it's a summative assessment. A few well-known survey instruments that are designed to easily be used for formative assessment of competencies related to education abroad are the Intercultural Conflict Style Inventory (ICS Inventory, 2018), the Intercultural Effectiveness Scale (Kozai Group, n.d.), and the Beliefs, Events, and Values Inventory (Bevi, 2018).

Case Study: Embedding "Intercultural Competence" at a Land-Grant University

In 2011, the Indiana state legislature mandated that all public institutions of learning, K–16, adopt a standards-based core curriculum. At Purdue University, this resulted in the faculty senate approving a university-wide core curriculum that required several higher order competencies, including intercultural competence, be embedded in all undergraduate degree programs. The method of assessment that the senate suggested for documenting students' mastery of these embedded higher order outcomes was a set of rubrics devised by the Association of American Colleges & Universities (AAC&U; Rhodes, 2009); collectively these rubrics are known as the AAC&U VALUE (Valid Assessment of Learning in Undergraduate Education) Rubrics. In other words, the faculty senate suggested that departments use the rubrics to evaluate direct evidence of student learning (essays, presentations, projects, etc.) from existing courses, rather than adding content to courses, using surveys, or restructuring degree programs.

The AAC&U Intercultural Knowledge and Competence VALUE Rubric is composed of a set of six easy-to-understand interpersonal dexterities: cultural self-awareness, knowledge of cultural worldview frameworks (sometimes called "other awareness"), empathy, communication (both verbal and nonverbal), curiosity, and openness. An example is given in Table 8.1.

For Purdue, these dexterities comprise "the ability to work effectively with persons who define problems differently" (Downey et al., 2006, p. 1). Purdue's efforts to implement the four assessment best practices referenced previously, beginning from the mandate of this shared and rubric-based definition of *intercultural competence*, have taken place in multiple contexts, of which three are elucidated in the following sections.

Short-Term Study Abroad: Connecting Faculty and Student Interests

For many years, study abroad participation at Purdue has trended strongly toward short-term departmental programs led by faculty (or qualified student-support administrators). Current short-term participation rates come to about 80% of Purdue's study abroad totals, and roughly two-thirds of short-term participants select departmental programs. These range in length

TABLE 8.1
Intercultural Knowledge and Competence VALUE Rubric Example Item

Item	Level One	Level Two	Level Three	Level Four
Attitude: Curiosity	States minimal interest in learning about other cultures.	Asks simple or surface questions about other cultures.	Asks deeper questions and seeks out answers.	Asks complex questions; seeks out and articulates answers that reflect multiple cultural perspectives.

Note. Example adapted from AAC&U Intercultural Knowledge and Competence VALUE Rubric (Rhodes, 2009). Complete rubric available from www.aacu.org/value/rubrics/intercultural-knowledge

of time spent abroad from 1 to 6 weeks; roughly 75% of the program leaders come from science, technology, engineering, and mathematics (STEM) disciplines. Short-term study abroad programs are often seen as semirecreational endeavors, inherently less impactful than semesters abroad (Donnelly-Smith, 2009). For STEM students, however, short-term faculty-led programs have some distinct advantages. When developed "in house," they automatically count for home-university credit in a STEM discipline, reducing anxieties about timely graduation. Also, they often take advantage of a faculty member's overseas scholarly networks, actively demonstrating that the ability to find common ground has yielded benefits to the careers of at least two STEM professionals (the program leader and the host-country collaborator). In other words, short-term programs can be "hard-wired" into STEM students' educational continua, illuminating the career-enhancing value of international experiences in ways that the traditional semester abroad program often does not (being more focused on language-and-culture studies). Introducing rubric-based formative assessment into such STEM faculty-led programs means Purdue is measuring what all participants really care about: the interpersonal skills of collaborative STEM excellence.

However, even very cosmopolitan professors seldom have training in teaching or measuring intercultural or interpersonal skills, and rarely does the tenure process support them in developing these skills. This is ironic, given that a number of professional standards societies strongly encourage degree programs to build students' intercultural competence including ABET (the Engineering and Technology accreditation body), the American Academy of Nursing, the American Association of Medical Colleges, and the American Veterinary Medical Association. Clearly, then, it would behoove a college or university to provide support to faculty for better nurturing of said competencies in their students. How might this be done without "stepping on" faculty sensibilities?

Since 2010, Purdue has addressed quality concerns by requiring both new and recurring departmental programs receive formal approval by the faculty leader's departmental business officer, chair, and dean. Additionally, the university's associate dean of study abroad and the dean of international programs must approve each program proposal. Purdue had not, however, gathered data as to which nondisciplinary skills these key stakeholders intended to teach by venturing abroad with students, nor had it actively supported leaders in embedding intercultural competence into their program's curriculum or cocurriculum. Accordingly, in late summer 2014, the departmental program proposal process was altered to require each aspiring leader to select one or more of the six components of the AAC&U Intercultural Knowledge and Competence VALUE Rubric as a learning objective, and to commit to incorporating a suitable formative or summative assessment method into the program. To help scaffold the teaching and assessment decisions of the program leaders, an intercultural learning objectives planning worksheet was created. The worksheet supported the faculty program leader in matching any element of the intercultural learning rubric (e.g., curiosity or empathy) with a reliable related assessment tool. Leaders could choose from a list of 20 research-derived quantitative instruments (most of them cost free) and 4 research-derived rubrics. Many of these instruments were selected with an eye toward their possible use as predeparture discussion starters between the leader and participating students about potential behavioral or affective competency gaps. Other, more widely known, intercultural assessment instruments were included to encourage faculty to connect their education abroad leadership to a large body of scholarly research, and potentially publish in this area. Finally, a behavioral inventory (Ruben, 1976) was added in response to comments by experienced leaders that they often observed, but could not quantify, changes in students' culture-crossing behavior as the program unfolded. In short, although it also facilitates institutional data collection, the emphasis of this worksheet has been to (a) be attentive to faculty motivations such as procuring tenure and teaching effectively, (b) encourage them to operationalize the Intercultural Knowledge and Competence VALUE Rubric as an addition to their pedagogy tool kit, and (c) lead to productive conversations across institutional siloes about improving students' disciplinary and intercultural learning.

Faculty and Staff Development: Creating a Shared Culture of Evidence-Based Learning

Regardless of whether they are cocurricular staff, academic staff, or faculty, those who serve as instructors, coaches, and mentors need practice in order to give effective feedback to students, thus enabling students to operationalize feedback toward higher skill levels (Driscoll & Wood, 2007; Suskie, 2009). In the education abroad literature, it has been found that even individuals who are very experienced culture-crossers (and recognized for disciplinary teaching excellence) may need assistance to reliably facilitate students' intercultural development (Anderson, 2016). Therefore, it was not unexpected when the first year of assessment results indicated that, while they were indeed learning on Purdue's short-term programs, students were in general not making noteworthy gains in intercultural competence. To be specific, students were often becoming more confident about travel, were sometimes forming mentoring bonds with a professor or friendship bonds with a student from a disparate background, and were occasionally even articulating globalized perspectives on future careers. Each of these personal gains can contribute to the eventual development of intercultural competence. By and large, however, they were not learning to, for example, "ask deeper questions and articulate complex answers" (level three curiosity on the rubric) or to "recognize the intellectual and emotional aspects of more than one worldview" (level three empathy). This disappointing finding had two useful consequences. First, it opened up a collaboration window for identifying ways to better teach reflection and reflective writing to all students. (This problem had also long frustrated faculty and staff who support service-learning.) And second, it persuaded upper administration to allocate funding to incentivize faculty development in formative assessment of intercultural competence (which was framed as "focusing on undergraduate mentoring" in order to better align with evolving promotion and tenure standards). A rubric-based intercultural pedagogy workshop series, totaling 10 hours of interactive instruction, has been provided every fall since 2016 to at least 50 Purdue program leaders and has proven popular enough that members of the initial cohort requested creation of an advanced pedagogy series in 2017. Also in 2017, rubric-based meta-analysis of students' education abroad essays or journals indicated that faculty development of this sort can improve student learning outcomes: The reflection products of 2017 students whose short-term program leaders were workshop-series "graduates" exhibited twice the number of component qualities of intercultural competence, and exhibited them to a higher average level of proficiency than the reflection products of students whose leaders had not participated in a workshop series.

Staff Development for On-Campus Learning: In Support of "Teaching to the Test"

To further support incorporation of intercultural learning into the curriculum and cocurriculum, Purdue University's Center for Instructional Excellence (2017a) has operationalized the six individual constructs of the intercultural rubric into a certificate program of six minilessons. Each minilesson can be assigned as homework, employed as an icebreaker activity, or used to "liven up" a class lecture. Disseminating the rubric in this way has helped advisers and cocurricular staff understand intercultural competence as a set of easily explained interpersonal skills relevant to students' career advancement. For example, creativity, a skill that research shows to be correlated to experience outside one's home country (Maddux, Adam, & Galinsky, 2010), has been recognized by Purdue's College of Science as a key component of being able to think and function as a scientist. Scientific creativity requires a willingness to suspend judgment about new ideas, unusual perspectives, or conflicting data (openness); the ability to recognize when one's habitual ways of thinking may be leading one to confirmatory bias (self-awareness); and the gift of being able to persuade a lab director, dean, or funding agency to commit resources in support of further research or product development (communication). In short, it requires high levels of proficiency in at least three aspects of intercultural competence. Linking the component constructs of the rubric to the college's definition of *scientific excellence* and offering professional development to its academic advisers has greatly augmented the advisers' enthusiasm for connecting education abroad to a budding scientist's career preparation tool kit. Some of these advisers are also adding intercultural activities and assessments to the large-enrollment first-year courses they teach, which means that a greater percentage of College of Science students are being exposed to self-awareness, communication, and openness as core disciplinary skills. In other words, even science students who choose not to study abroad are being mentored in acquiring the skills to interact more effectively across cultural difference.

These staff development experiments strongly suggest that a rubric-based definition of *intercultural competence* can be more motivational to students and staff than more complex concepts such as ethnorelativism or global citizenship (both of which are sometimes mistakenly framed as "political correctness"—and consequently disparaged). However, some staff have voiced concern that operationalizing the rubric in this way is "teaching to the test." In fact, teaching to the test is not necessarily a bad thing (Suskie, 2009). Assessment (testing) is part of a time-honored pedagogical process by which instructors identify the specific things they want students to learn, create engaging opportunities for students to learn those things, and then measure the extent to which students have improved. To put it more bluntly, if a test does not connect directly to what has been taught (and vice versa), there is no value in either endeavor.

Implications for Better Practice

Institutional contexts differ. Can generalizable lessons be drawn from the preceding best-practice maxims and the case study? We argue yes, and provide the following suggestions for building a culture of assessment that supports embedding an identified learning outcome into both the at-home curriculum and its related education abroad programs.

1. *"Have clearly stated learning outcomes and share them with your students" (Suskie, 2000, p. 1).* An embedded purpose of the learning opportunities

provided by Purdue, whether in Indiana or abroad, is to improve all students' cultural self-awareness, understanding of alternate worldview frameworks, communication skills (verbal and nonverbal), curiosity, openness, and intercultural empathy. Other institutions may frame their purposes differently, but in all cases the outcome objectives should be transparent and allow for the setting of SMART goals.

2. *Measure what people care about.* Bearing in mind that the purpose of assessment is to create change (better learning), what does your program leader, institution, or department care enough about to want to continuously improve? Beloit, a liberal arts college, cared deeply about student agency, so faculty and staff codeveloped a rubric that scaffolds reflection, ownership, and curiosity. (The rubric and a description of the creative process are available from https://serc.carleton.edu/acm_face/student_agency/beloitoverview). Purdue, a land-grant research university, has adopted a primary assessment tool, the AAC&U Intercultural Knowledge and Competence VALUE Rubric, which helps faculty and staff explain how intercultural competence aligns with its valued outcomes of scientific inquiry and excellence (curiosity and openness), leadership (self-awareness and empathy), and teamwork (communication and other-awareness). Yet, when faculty members prefer to deepen the teaching of sustainability, social justice, or comfort with difference by doing so in an education abroad context, Purdue offers alternative instruments (among them other AAC&U rubrics) that allow them to focus on what they care about and want their students to care about. Ultimately, it is more important that faculty members engage thoughtfully with the learning process of their students, and align education abroad with disciplinary goals, than that all faculty conform to an institutional decree about particular desired outcomes of education abroad. Yes, this can make institutional meta-analysis a little tricky—but accreditation agencies principally care that institutions focus on improvement of learning. Whether this improvement is easy to measure is not of importance to them; nor should it be to you!

3. *Incorporate backward design principles for better curriculum-to-outcome alignment.* Frequently when designing curriculum, instructors focus on content matter that "needs" to be conveyed rather than on skills that ought to be learned. Yet research indicates learning is "stickier" when content is not king, goals are transparent and concrete, and the focus is on gradually increasing competency (Clark et al., 2017; Rust, 2002). Backward design is a simple three-step curriculum design process that

improves alignment by asking the instructor to, first, identify desired results (e.g., what the student(s) will do better after the learning intervention); second, determine acceptable evidence of mastery; and, third, design a curricular or cocurricular lesson that builds toward the goal (Wiggins & McTighe, 2005).

4. *Use multiple instruments.* Why suggest a variety of assessment instruments rather than standardize upon a single widely used measure? First, faculty can easily become alienated by top-down institutional assessment demands (Weimer, 2013). Second, mixed-methods research yields more reliable understanding of the learning process (Salisbury, 2015). More importantly, however, one-on-one consultations with experienced Purdue program leaders in 2014 revealed that numerous faculty members felt their disciplinary training had not adequately equipped them for teaching and measuring intercultural skills. Accordingly, to support leaders' existing interest in student learning, it was important to indicate that many reliable assessment options were available. Not incidentally, classroom-based research indicates that motivation and the degree to which complex skills are mastered can be increased by allowing learners (in this case the faculty study abroad leaders) to select from multiple ways of completing an assignment (Suskie, 2009).

5. *Harness "locally owned" learning goals.* When one needs a great expanse of fence painted, it can be useful to seek volunteers from a group searching for new ways to develop members' upper body musculature. Put differently, if you can uncover a learning goal that a great many individuals on campus want students to develop (leadership, critical thinking, comfort with difference), you are in a position to help that person or group find ways to measure whether said learning is occurring across the educational continuum of your institution—and to jointly envisage ways that education abroad might lead toward their desired outcome goals. This creates shared ownership of improving learning and interconnects the outcomes of education abroad to the students' educational trajectory.

6. *Whenever possible, begin with a free (but validated!) assessment tool.* Individuals skeptical about measuring complex skills, or about assessment's value for their programs, are unlikely to want to invest time and money into an instrument that they perceive to be both inscrutable and costly. Furthermore, creating an in-house instrument from whole cloth makes no sense; doing so may appear to be cost free but will instead consume your scarcest resource—time. Purdue's experience suggests that almost any learning outcome that can reasonably be hypothesized

as resulting from intercultural encounters can be found, using Google Scholar or Science Direct, to have an associated research-derived survey instrument. Such instruments often have high face and/or construct validity; in other words, they will help skeptics and students begin to deconstruct "intercultural competence" (or "global citizenship") and visualize gradual mastery of the competencies you are attempting to foster. Purdue leaders are particularly fond of the following free instruments for such purposes: the Miville-Guzman Universality-Diversity Scale, or M-GUDS (Fuertes, Miville, Mohr, Sedlacek, & Gretchen, 2000); the Tolerance for Ambiguity Scale (Herman, Stevens, Bird, Mendenhall, & Oddou, 2010); the Attitudinal and Behavioral Openness Scale (Caligiuri, Jacobs, & Farr, 2000); and the Purdue-created Intercultural Attitudes, Skills, and Knowledge Short Scale (the A.S.K.S[2]) and Global Learning Short Scale (the G.L.S[2]), two formative surveys that were each created from an AAC&U rubric to foster competency-oriented self-reflection and support group discussion (Purdue University Center for Instructional Excellence, 2017b). These last two survey instruments (or their associated rubrics) are particularly useful for helping faculty understand the differing constellation of attitudes, skills, and behaviors that contribute to the disparate proficiency profiles of "intercultural competence" and "global citizenship." Finally, when an instructor begins to worry about social desirability bias, it may be time to consider a more complex instrument (and to either make the case for a regular assessment budget or consider charging learners an intercultural assessment "lab fee"). Note, however, that when it comes to crossing cultures, teaching students to recognize what is socially desirable is arguably an extremely fitting learning outcome.

Conclusion

The focus of this chapter has been on rubric-based assessment because it provides transparency of intended learning outcomes and can therefore increase student and faculty buy-in, even in the hard sciences, to pursuing intercultural competency or other education abroad outcomes. Rubric-based assessment has also been cited as fairer to a diverse range of learners (Suskie, 2000) because it evaluates an authentic product of an individual's learning and allows for multiple ways of demonstrating mastery (written work, oral reflection, creative performance, behavioral observation, etc.). Unlike predictive or summative instruments, which seek to reduce face validity in order to avoid biasing the results, rubric-based assessment allows the student and the instructor to easily conceptualize, focus on, and measure the acquisition of transparent, easily understood *building blocks* to competency, which neurocognitive research has shown to be a more reliable way to produce deep learning (Lang, 2016). Finally, as this chapter has demonstrated, rubric-based assessment can help educators more easily interweave core institutional or disciplinary desired outcomes with education abroad (and vice versa).

Readers who leap to the assumption that this chapter (or the institution that employs the contributor) is intending to advocate against the use of complex survey instruments (proprietary or otherwise) and large-scale outcomes studies, however, would be very much mistaken. For example, the use of proprietary survey instruments has helped Purdue leaders demonstrate that faculty, if supported to a higher level of instructional excellence in intercultural mentoring, can change the mean intercultural sensitivity of a group of STEM students *just as significantly* via an on-campus course (Miller & Schellhase, 2017) or a two-week education abroad program (Parker, 2018) as the most cutting-edge, intentional semester-long programs found in the education abroad literature. Subsidizing faculty or staff certification in a widely used instrument has helped staff (from the academic adviser level to the assistant provost level) conceptualize how to more effectively move students away from attitudes of polarization toward the skills of finding common ground across troubling differences. And, as previously mentioned, comparative meta-analysis of qualitative data helped the institution determine that it needed to devote more resources to faculty development and to helping students improve their reflective writing skills. In short, intrainstitutional advocacy is an additional reason to, as recommended before, use multiple instruments and multiple approaches when assessing learning outcomes.

In conclusion, then, this contributor's final piece of advice for international educators or assessment professionals who want to connect education abroad to the educational continuum would be to not horde your expertise, but to instead teach more people on campus "how to fish." Better learning is an outcome that is owed by all members of a college or university to its students and to the communities to which they belong and will come to lead. Assessment, which is critical to better learning, is too important to be cloistered in an education abroad office or an institutional research office. Anyone who mentors, instructs, or otherwise supports students should be able to "do" assessment, at least of the formative kind. Indeed, Purdue's experience suggests that faculty and staff alike will thank you for giving them the assessment tools and training to better understand, mentor, and assist their students.

References

Anderson, C. (2016). *Instructor influence on student intercultural learning during instructor-led short-term study abroad* (Unpublished doctoral dissertation). University of Minnesota, Minneapolis.

Astin, A. W. (1984). Student involvement: A developmental theory for higher education. *Journal of College Student Personnel, 25*(4), 297–308.

Bevi. (2018). *Home page.* Available from http://www.thebevi.com/

Brookhart, S. M. (2013). *How to create and use rubrics for formative assessment and grading.* Alexandria, VA: ASCD.

Caligiuri, P. M., Jacobs, R. R., & Farr, J. L. (2000). The Attitudinal and Behavioral Openness Scale: Scale development and construct validation. *International Journal of Intercultural Relations, 24*(1), 27–46.

Churchill, R. (1958). The student abroad. *The Antioch Review, 18*(4), 447–454.

Clark, D., Gill, D., Prowse, V., & Rush, M. (2017). *Using goals to motivate college students: Theory and evidence from field experiments.* Working Paper 23638. Cambridge, MA: National Bureau of Economic Research. Available from http://www.nber.org/papers/w23638.pdf

Deardorff, D. K., & Deardorff, D. L. (2016). Assessing intercultural outcomes in engineering programs. In K. St. Amant & M. Flammia (Eds.), *Teaching and training for global engineering* (pp. 239–261). New York, NY: Wiley-IEEE Press.

Donnelly-Smith, L. (2009). Global learning through short-term study abroad. *Peer Review, 11*(4). Available from https://www.aacu.org/peerreview/2009/fall/donnelly-smith

Downey, G. L., Lucena, J. C., Moskal, B. M., Parkhurst, R., Bigley, T., Hays, C., . . . & Belo-Nichols, A. (2006). The globally competent engineer: Working effectively with people who define problems differently. *JEE: The Research Journal for Engineering Education, 95*(2), 107–122.

Driscoll, A., & Wood, S. (2007). *Outcomes-based assessment for learner-centered education: A faculty introduction.* Sterling, VA: Stylus.

Fantini, A. (2009). Assessing intercultural competence: Issues and tools. In D. K. Deardorff (Ed.), *The SAGE handbook of intercultural competence* (pp. 456–477). Thousand Oaks, CA: SAGE.

Freed, B. (Ed.). (1995). *Second language acquisition in study abroad contexts.* Philadelphia, PA: John Benjamins.

Fuertes, J. N., Miville, M. L., Mohr, J. J., Sedlacek, W. E., & Gretchen, D. (2000). Factor structure and short form of the Miville-Guzman Universality-Diversity Scale. *Measurement and Evaluation in Counseling and Development, 33*, 157–169.

Herman, J. L., Stevens, M. J., Bird, A., Mendenhall, M., & Oddou, G. (2010). The Tolerance for Ambiguity Scale: Towards a more refined measure for international management research. *International Journal of Intercultural Relations, 34*(1), 58–65.

Hutchings, P., Ewell, P., & Banta, T. (2012). *AAHE principles of good practice: Aging nicely.* Available from http://www.learningoutcomesassessment.org/PrinciplesofAssessment.html#AAHE

ICS Inventory. (2018). *Resolving conflict across cultural boundaries: Using the Intercultural Conflict Style Inventory (ICS)*. Available from https://icsinventory.com/

Kohlberg, L. (1976). Moral stages and moralization: The cognitive-developmental. In T. Lickona (Ed.), *Moral development and behavior: Theory, research, and social issues* (pp. 31–53). New York, NY: Holt, Rinehart and Winston.

Kozai Group. (n.d.). *Intercultural Effectiveness Scale*. Available from https://www.kozaigroup.com/intercultural-effectiveness-scale-ies/

Lang, J. M. (2016). *Small teaching*. San Francisco, CA: Jossey-Bass.

Maddux, W. W., Adam, H., & Galinsky, A. D. (2010). When in Rome . . . Learn why the Romans do what they do: How multicultural experiences facilitate creativity. *Personality and Social Psychology Bulletin, 36*(6), 731–741.

Mezirow, J. (1991). *Transformative dimensions of adult learning*. San Francisco, CA: Jossey-Bass.

Miller, M. L., & Schellhase, E. M. (2017). *Results of a semester-long on-campus intercultural empathy course for health-professions-oriented undergraduates*. Panel presentation at the annual conference of SIETAR-USA, the Society for Intercultural Education, Training and Research in the USA, San Diego, CA.

Paige, R. M. (2004). Instrumentation in intercultural training. In D. Landis, J. M. Bennett, & M. L. Bennett (Eds.), *Handbook of intercultural training* (pp. 85–128). Thousand Oaks, CA: SAGE.

Paige, R. M., & Goode, M. L. (2009). Cultural mentoring: International education professionals and the development of intercultural competence. In D. K. Deardorff (Ed.), *The SAGE handbook of intercultural competence* (pp. 333–349). Thousand Oaks, CA: SAGE.

Parker, H. (2018). *Outcomes of a two-week study abroad program for engineering majors using intercultural mentoring techniques and guided reflection*. Panel presentation at the Purdue Institute on Scaling Up: Intercultural Learning and Mentoring, West Lafayette, IN.

Purdue University Center for Instructional Excellence. (2017a). *Activities and assignments*. Available from https://www.purdue.edu/cie/globallearning/activities.html

Purdue University Center for Instructional Excellence. (2017b). *Assessment—short scales*. Available from https://www.purdue.edu/cie/globallearning/assessments.html

Rhodes, T. (2009). *Assessing outcomes and improving achievement: Tips and tools for using the rubrics*. Washington, DC: Association of American Colleges & Universities. Available from https://www.aacu.org/value

Robinson, G. L. (1978). The magic-carpet-ride-to-another-culture syndrome: An international perspective. *Foreign Language Annals, 11*(2), 135–146.

Ruben, B. D. (1976). Assessing communication competency for intercultural adaptation. *Group and Organization Studies, 1*(3), 334–354.

Rust, C. (2002). The impact of assessment on student learning. *Active Learning in Higher Education, 3*(2), 145–158.

Salisbury, M. (2015). How we got to where we are (and aren't) in assessing study abroad learning. In V. Savicki & E. Brewer (Eds.), *Assessing study abroad: Theories, tools, and practice* (pp. 15–32). Sterling, VA: Stylus.

Sinicrope, C., Norris, J., & Watanabe, Y. (2007). Understanding and assessing intercultural competence: A summary of theory, research and practice. *Second Language Studies, 26*(1), 1–58.

Suskie, L. (2000, May). Fair assessment practices: Giving students equitable opportunities to demonstrate learning. *AAHE Bulletin.* Available from http://citeseerx.ist.psu.edu/viewdoc/download?doi=10.1.1.540.9919&rep=rep1&type=pdf

Suskie, L. (2009). *Assessing student learning: A common sense guide.* San Francisco, CA: Jossey-Bass.

Vande Berg, M., Paige, R. M., & Lou, K. H. (Eds.). (2012). *Student learning abroad: What our students are learning, what they're not, and what we can do about it.* Sterling, VA: Stylus.

Weimer, M. (2013, January 15). The assessment movement: Revisiting faculty resistance. *Faculty Focus.* Available from https://www.facultyfocus.com/articles/educational-assessment/the-assessment-movement-revisiting-faculty-resistance/

Wiggins, G., & McTighe, J., (2005). *Understanding by design.* Alexandria, VA: ASCD.

9

REFLECTION AS A TOOL IN THE EDUCATIONAL CONTINUUM

Victor Savicki and Michele V. Price

Reflective abstraction is the driving force of learning.

— Fosnot and Perry (2005, p. 34)

Education abroad has unique characteristics, yet uses methods and approaches that generalize to multiple learning environments. This chapter focuses not on content that might transfer from a sojourn abroad to a home university, but rather on an approach to learning that can transfer, and whose key component is reflection. Regardless of the educational setting and intended learning goals, unexamined experience does not rise to the level of learning. *Reflection*, however, provides an opportunity for such crucial examination (Bennett, 2012) and by some scholars is defined as the sine qua non of learning as expressed in the chapter-opening quote by Fosnot and Perry (2005). Further, education abroad provides a particularly rich living learning laboratory for experiential and transformative learning theories, both examples of a broader approach to learning called constructivism. During deep reflection, a critical step in these theories, students purposefully construct meaning based on the principles of constructivism. This chapter, therefore, begins with a brief foray into the theory behind reflection, before homing in on its application in the education abroad setting. We list general principles of reflection, and use specific examples to illustrate their application. We provide guidance at discriminating between deep versus superficial reflection and illustrate concrete options for practice. We then generalize this approach to learning to home campus settings, both because reflection is a skill that requires practice over time, and because reflection is key to integrating learning abroad into undergraduate education. But let's consider what reflection is, and why it is so important.

What Is Reflection?

Reflection is critical to ensuring that experiences abroad result in learning, yet the process of reflection is often barely examined by education abroad professionals. This section therefore considers definitions of *reflection*, discusses what it is not, and offers examples of how it can be facilitated in education abroad.

Homan (2006) offers one definition of the concept: *reflection* "refers to the process by which an individual builds meaning by analyzing an experience, evaluating its worth, and conceptualizing its relevance through the synthesis of additional viewpoints and information" (p. 9). Another path to understanding what reflection is can be marked with instances of what reflection is not, as illustrated in Table 9.1. The following discussion draws from Savicki and Price (2017b), and their work over three years assessing reflections and improving reflection prompts in undergraduate reflection courses offered by the service-learning provider IPSL (formerly known as the International Program for Service Learning) (see Price, Savicki, & Barnhart, 2014; Price, Savicki, & Moran, 2015).

TABLE 9.1
Contrasts Between What Reflection Is and Is Not

Reflection IS NOT	*Reflection IS*
Rumination	Shifted perspective, generation of alternatives
Overgeneralized	Disaggregated, well differentiated
Universal/unchangeable	Contextual
Unidimensional/intellectualized/ disconnected	Integrative (emotion, behavior, cognition)
Purely visceral	Descriptive

Rumination, or rethinking an experience over and over again, is not reflection. Rather, reflection requires a shift of perspective (Mezirow, 1991; Pagano & Roselle, 2009) and a consideration of alternative views (Fosnot & Perry, 2005). Often such a shift comes from being able to step away from the event to look at it retrospectively, or by recording it in a medium (e.g., a journal or a photo) that allows the event to be encapsulated in time.

Overgeneralizations lack the detail necessary for a more nuanced consideration of experiences being reflected on. Rather, reflection involves disaggregating events into thoroughly described, well-differentiated parts. The more detail available, the more possibility to find aspects that pique interest and offer threads of narration leading to alternative interpretations that delve beneath initial, simplistic impressions. Adequate description is the clay from which new constructions are molded.

In a similar fashion, language that presumes that events are universal and unchangeable (that's just the way I am/they are) detaches contextual influences from the events being discussed. It is difficult to reach an alternative explanation of events when one's language presumes that they cannot be different. Environment and interpretive concepts influence each other in a reciprocal fashion. Leaving the context out constrains interpretation (von Glaserfeld, 2005). Rather, a focus on the context of the experience presumes that events may be changeable depending on the situation. Describing the external conditions in an education abroad setting also increases the probability of capturing cultural factors.

Descriptions of experiences devoid of emotional content (feelings, values, attitudes) lead to intellectualized, disconnected, and unidimensional statements that lack the full richness of human response. Following Ward (2001), the acculturation process during education abroad impacts affect, behavior, and cognition. As Zull (2012) suggests, "We gain knowledge through feelings that come with the sensory information" (p. 173). Strong reflections link students' responses to the experiences they are writing or speaking about. Those events do not happen in a vacuum. Integrating one's self into reflections increases the probability of meaning-making, a potentially transformative process (Hunter, 2008). Reflection allows experiences to be evaluated, interpreted, and acted upon.

However, an emotions only report ("It was awesome!") will not result in an integrated, meaning-making process. Rather, the full self, affective, cognitive, behavioral, needs to be engaged to construct the meaning that is a goal of reflection.

Additionally, various brain capacities may be involved in reflection (Zull, 2012). "Reflection does not exclusively engage any brain function or anatomic area of the cortex. However, processing our experiences engages the integrative regions of the cortex" (p. 173). Education abroad experiences not subjected to mental processing can lead to "a shallow experiential base" (p. 183). Cognitive complexity sets the stage for reflection both in terms of describing in detail distinctions observed and in terms of integrating all aspects of the self.

Reflection's Importance in Education Abroad and Beyond

Reflecting on their education abroad allows students to become active construers of their experiences (Bennett, 2012). "Moving from simply recording experiences to actively changing and designing them is a major factor in assessing learning" (Zull, 2012, p. 175). Humans are meaning-making beings; thus, experiences gain significance to the degree that students can ascribe meaning to them. Unexamined experiences do not rise to the level of learning that will result in meaningful outcomes. "Our experience of reality itself is a function of how we organize our perceptions" (Bennett, 2012, p. 103).

"Virtually every program identified in the research literature as being effective in helping students develop their intercultural competence embraces reflection as a key principle of learning" (Paige, 2015, p. 566). Thus, reflection emerges as a central factor in student-centered learning abroad (Vande Berg, Paige, & Lou, 2012) and helps students become active participants in their own learning and development. Some will already have the skills necessary to use reflection effectively; others will need to be guided. In either case, reflection helps unlock the process of transformation. Cultural clashes and points of disequilibrium in dealing with a foreign culture provide fodder for meaning-making; and, at home, disequilibrium, clashes of ideas, and challenging frames of reference can also set the stage for reflection. Reflection helps students transfer insights and understandings garnered in education abroad to the home culture and university by helping them shift perspective to think about how their learning might be extended to a different place and time.

Before discussing principles for reflection and providing examples of reflection in practice, we next take up theories underpinning reflection: constructivism and experiential and transformative learning.

Theoretical Underpinnings

Reflection has a solid, well-established theoretical base, and is further advanced in practice by two well-known, though underused, theories of learning. We pause now to briefly delve into this important background.

Constructivism

As a thought experiment, imagine that a long, slithery, green snake falls through a gap in the ceiling tiles onto a conference room table around which five people are seated. One person jumps up and runs screaming from the room. Consumed by a social media app, another ignores the snake. Another hustles around the table to take a selfie with the snake to post on the Internet. Another strokes the snake to examine its texture; yet another holds forth on the name of the snake, its origins, and habitat. Clearly, it is not the snake alone that is responsible for the diverse reactions, but rather the meaning the observers construct about their experience based on both the snake and their histories; the known and the knower.

In a more theoretical vein, consider the following definition:

> *Constructivism* is a theory about knowledge and learning; it describes both what "knowing" is and how one "comes to know." Based on work in psychology, philosophy, science, and biology, the theory describes knowledge not as truths to be transmitted or discovered but as emergent, developmental, nonobjective, viable constructed explanations by humans engaged in meaning-making in cultural and social communities of discourse. Learning from this perspective is viewed as a self-regulatory process of struggling with the conflict between existing personal models of the world and discrepant new insights, constructing new representations and models of reality as a human meaning-making venture with culturally developed tools and symbols, and further negotiating such meaning through cooperative social activity, discourse, and debate in communities of practice. (Fosnot, 2005, p. ix; emphasis added)

This definition leaves a lot to be unpacked. The idea that knowledge is constructed rather than revealed or discovered places heavy emphasis on the meaning-making process, of which reflection is the chief component. Likewise, the notion that "the knower and the known are inseparable" (Kincheloe, 2005, p. 14) places the learner smack in the middle of the context of experience rather than in an intellectualized, abstract, "objective" realm. Meaning includes both the observer and the data; they are inextricably intertwined. Meaning-making is spurred by contrasts, conflicts, perturbations, and discrepancies. Learners bring mind-sets to the process and are challenged by experiences that do not immediately fit into these. Clearly, culture clashes provide a plethora of discontinuities. Finally, meaning-making is not a solitary activity but is based on preexisting experience and the ability to discuss, debate, and negotiate meanings with a mentor, coach, and/or peers in the education abroad context or upon return to home environments.

As educators, at home or abroad, we need to be sensitive to the characteristics and history that students bring to the learning situation. Classic classroom teaching tends to ignore students' individual differences, whereas a constructivist approach emphasizes such differences and uses them when students reflect.

Learning Theories

Two popular theories of learning place reflection at a key juncture in the learning process: experiential learning theory (Kolb, 1984) and transformative learning theory (Mezirow, 1991). Meaning-making, for which reflection is pivotal, lies at the heart of both theories.

In experiential learning theory, the observation and reflection component bridges the gap between concrete experience that launches the learning cycle and forming new knowledge that supplies meaning (Savicki, 2008). The observations need to be sufficiently detailed and described to generate a relatively complete picture of the concrete experience. At this point learners can experiment with "constructive alternativism" (Maher, 1969) in order to generate an array of possible explanations for why the experience played out the way it did and how the learner's values, beliefs, attitudes, and emotions might have influenced the meaning initially ascribed to the event. In this theory of learning, reflection offers a means to shift perspective and generate alternatives.

In transformative learning theory, a specific disorienting dilemma sparks the need to understand an experience. One choice is to try to cram the disorienting event into the student's existing meaning framework. However, reflection can be employed to think about the event creatively, thus paving the way for the student's meaning frame to expand—the definition of *transformation* (Hunter, 2008). This type of change in meaning perspective requires reflecting on the student's premises, presuppositions, and assumptions regarding the event (and the host culture). The result is a deeper, more engaging level of reflection.

Kolb's and Mezirow's theories provide a framework to consider how reflection might be designed to identify and reflect on experiences that are surprising, disorienting, and puzzling.

How to Facilitate Reflection

Reflective learning is not what happens to a student, it is what the student does with what has happened. When we assess reflection, it is important that we do not assess the content of an experience, but rather that we assess what the student has done with the content. (Bourner, 2003, p. 270)

As we explore various methods to aid our students to reflect deeply, we must keep in mind that however intriguing their stories, it is how students deal with the content of their stories that will demonstrate their skill at reflection. Reflection is a skill that can be learned and polished. It does not appear full blown, but rather increases in increments and through repeated iterations. The dramatic "aha" moments usually occur at the end of a trail of questioning and discovery that may span multiple attempts at understanding.

General Principles for Reflection

Educators can guide and coach students in the reflective process. Following are some general principles for fostering deeper reflection during the student's search for meaning. While most of the principles can apply to reflection in any learning context, the principles concerning ethnorelativism and gradualism are particularly relevant to education abroad and other intercultural learning contexts

Provide Feedback

There is no guarantee that student reflections will result in intercultural competence, global awareness, or any other positive outcomes associated with education abroad. Sometimes reflection can, unfortunately, lead to ethnocentric conclusions. For this reason, and because reflection is not a usual pattern of thought in daily life, students need feedback on their reflections, whether from education abroad practitioners, faculty, fellow students, or others. Feedback may be individual, that is, faculty to student, or may be offered in a group setting where others may benefit by observing feedback and discussion. In any case, feedback should be benign and nonjudgmental, with suggestions for how to think more deeply about the experience being reflected upon. Feedback can often take the form of Socratic questioning rather than instructor pronouncements. For example, "It seems that this experience was confusing to you. Why do you think that was the case or what did you find most confusing?" Also, opportunities should be offered for confidential reflection and feedback should the student request it.

Expect Iteration

Although we, as reflection coaches, may wish students to move quickly to realizations that we see clearly, the pace of students' reflection will be influenced by previous experience, values, beliefs, and attitudes. It may be difficult to be patient, but rushing students to conclusions may backfire. Multiple iterations may be necessary for them to come to, what seems to us, an obvious conclusion. Remember to breathe.

Foster the Development of Metacognition
Reflection is "thinking about thinking," or metacognition. We need to encourage students to consider themselves as part of the reflection process. What values, beliefs, attitudes, presuppositions, assumptions, and expectations do they bring to their observations and their evaluation of the experience they are reflecting upon? None of us can be absolutely neutral observers; our histories shape our perceptions. For students to think deeply about an experience, they need to think about their own contributions to how they construe it. Raising this will help students integrate the experience with their perspective and increase the chance that they will come to alternative ways of thinking about the experience. "The reflective process entails bringing students to a point where acquiring new information and building meaning around it involves examining their perceptions and challenging what they currently understand to be true" (Homan, 2006, p. 13).

Encourage Integration
None of us are sliced into disconnected pieces of thinking, feeling, and behaving. We are integrated, holistic beings. Thus, when students reflect, our task is to help them consider all the parts of themselves that may facilitate deep reflection. Reflection is not a pristine, rational, purely cognitive activity. All of one's self is involved. So, noticing and asking for clarification about aspects of self that might be missing in an initial reflection may help students round out their thinking.

Prioritize the Development of Ethnorelativism
An oft-stated goal of education abroad is to increase students' intercultural sensitivity so that they move from ethnocentrism toward ethnorelativism. The developmental model of intercultural sensitivity (DMIS) provides a theoretical base for this movement (Bennett, 1993). Student reflections are likely to bounce around on the developmental scale offered by this theory. Our task is to help students move in an ethnorelative direction. Ethnocentric rants about students' host culture can be difficult to hear but are to be expected. Our task is to point students toward an alternate, more ethnorelative perspective (cf. Arrúe, 2008, Binder, 2008, and Minucci, 2008, for examples of approaches to intercultural sensitivity training).

Employ Gradualism
Deep reflection that examines one's cultural beliefs, values, attitudes, and assumptions may tread on parts of personal identity. Reflecting on cultural differences may be the first time many students have considered what their

culture is and who they are in relation to it. It pays to approach these issues gradually. Cross-culture interactions can feel threatening and uncomfortable (Frey & Tropp, 2006), and students may be worried about being rejected, embarrassed, ridiculed, or exploited—aspects of intergroup contact anxiety (Stephan & Stephan, 1985; Voci & Hewstone, 2003). When studying abroad, day-to-day "foreign" encounters with the host culture may elevate threats to self-identity via symbolic anxiety (Stephan, Stephan, & Gudykunst, 1999). Lou and Bosley (2008) suggest helping students move one step at a time along the DMIS continuum, rather than jumping immediately to the most ethnorelative stage. This step-by-step movement tends to prevent students from being overwhelmed by challenges to their cultural identity.

Deploy Prompts Intentionally

Guiding students to deeper reflection requires developing prompts that move students beyond simplistic description and "what I did today" narratives toward combining an analysis of the target experience/concept/ disequilibrating event with an inward focus on the student's own feelings, beliefs, values, expectations, premises, and assumptions (Hubbs & Brand, 2010). Ideally, students synthesize insights from both dimensions to make meaning of the situation reflected on. Deep reflection combines the known and the knower.

Unfortunately, the tendency in academe is to approach reflective questions or prompts as if they were questions on a knowledge-based essay exam. Or a prompt may begin with the following: "Reflect on . . . ." This can lead students to offer a response they think will satisfy the professor or adviser or to provide a detached observational, intellectualized, "objective" report about what happened on a particular day. Clear, accessible prompts that prompt both content and self-processing are more effective. For example: "Discuss experiences abroad, small or large that were especially meaningful and memorable. Explain why and how these will have a lasting effect on you" (Brewer & Moore, 2015, p. 152).

Often it is useful to ask about specific information rather than general events (Savicki & Price, 2015). To paraphrase examples of common study abroad reflective prompts:

> Discuss insights you may have gleaned about your host culture from your use of public transportation in your host country. Include both specific examples, and how you made sense of them based on your previous expectations of the host culture (See Stemler, Imada, & Sorkin, 2014, for specific examples of common study abroad situations.

It can also be useful to build perspective shift into prompts by asking about a past or future time, such as in this paraphrase of a prompt: "Give a few examples of what you think your host culture will be like and how you see yourself interacting with your host culture. Are you excited, apprehensive, uncertain? Why?" (Savicki & Price, 2017a).

Feedback in Practice

Feedback and coaching can help students round out and deepen their reflections. The next examples are based on actual student reflections, while the suggested feedback illustrates guidelines for reflection discussed earlier in this chapter.

Lack of Integration

A prompt asking students to describe their arrival at their host airport might yield the following:

> I got sick on the plane and felt awful by the time we landed. Getting through immigration was a hassle. Then once I got through, I found out that the university arrival team was meeting students in a different terminal. It took me forever to get there because I had to keep making stops. On top of that, the airport was so large and there were so many people, I didn't know how I would find the team. When I finally arrived at the correct terminal, I saw someone holding a sign for the university. They were glad to see me and were so nice. The day continued this way when I found out I was living in a residence that wasn't on the main campus. I didn't feel well for the rest of the day, so I just slept.

The student does not discuss her emotions, but her anxiety ("I didn't know how I would find the team") and relief ("They were glad to see me and were so nice") are clear. This is where feedback is important. The student was sick, overwhelmed by the large airport, found out she wasn't living on the main campus, and then just slept for the rest of the day, but much of this is not articulated in the reflection. Instead, it is mostly a record of what happened when she arrived.

The adviser could respond by asking about the student's feelings at each stage in the process, and currently. Friendly and conversational follow-up will likely enable the student to reveal some of what she was experiencing internally, and begin to realize emotional reactions are important in reflections.

Lack of Metacognition

Consider this prompt: "Now that you are midway through your program, write a reflection about a program excursion you have recently taken. Where did you go? What did you see? What was interesting or unusual? What host culture values were evident? How did those values compare to how you thought about your host culture before you arrived there?" A possible response might be:

> This week was really busy. We watched a game in the finals for the World Cup. I wanted Argentina to win, but that didn't happen. The rest of the week was fun because the whole group went to Buenos Aires. I had to get up at five in the morning to leave and the trip was really long. The hotel we stayed in is the worst I've ever seen, and we were all unhappy. But the trip itself was fun. We got to watch a tango show, and then the next day, we took a tango lesson.

This student simply writes a travelogue and does not answer the questions. There is no reflection. He reveals that neither he nor the other students were happy about the hotel. Perhaps the student had preconceived notions about hotels based on hotel experiences in the United States. Feedback can prompt important cultural comparison: "Tell me more about the hotel. It seems that all of you were unhappy. What was different for you from hotels where you have stayed in the United States? Based on your U.S. values, what were you expecting when you checked into the hotel and saw your room, and why do you think you felt that way? How did you come to that conclusion?"

Opportunity for Intercultural Sensitivity Development
Reflection on cultural differences might be prompted by "Describe a situation or two in which you found differences from U.S. culture. What thoughts do you have about the differences and how do you feel about them? How did you come to these thoughts and feelings?"

> I took the U-bahn to my class today, and I was shocked at how people just jammed into the cars and stood so close to me. They jostled and crowded together. I could smell someone's garlic breath on me. I was really uncomfortable and maybe a little scared. I never experienced this disgusting behavior in the United States. I don't know if the Viennese are just rude, or insensitive, or what. I was so relieved to get out of the U-bahn and into the fresh air.

The student talks about her difficulties with crowding and personal space impingement. To draw meaning from her feelings, she will need to think about how she came to them. It may be possible to both address her lack of metacognition and encourage a shift of perspective by helping her become more ethnorelative and less ethnocentric. Can she imagine how much personal space she would need to feel more comfortable? Might she experiment with standing closer or a farther away from her Viennese hosts? How does she think her hosts might feel if she stood at that distance? What might they think about her?

These student reflection examples are simple and brief but illustrate what students often produce. The prompts are not uncommon. Adviser questions provide feedback as well as opportunities for iterative reflection.

Implications for Campus-Based Learning Activities

When abroad, students will almost surely experience events that clash with their expectations and assumptions about how "reality" is supposed to function. Such events provide the fodder for reflection. On campus, students may also experience disequilibrium, but not pause to make sense of it. In teaching, faculty present constructs, ideas, and information that will be new, unexpected, and provocative but neglect opportunities for reflection. Both students and faculty often feel constrained to accept course material without question, not considering how it might fit into or expand student frames of reference. It is at these times that reflection prompts that follow the guidelines presented earlier in this chapter may be useful. Students will make class material their own to the degree that they can examine it using reflection. This is not to say that a whole class needs to be designed using the constructivist model, although many have been. (See Fosnot, 2005, for examples in math, literature, and physics.) Course projects, portfolios, journals, essays, videos, and demonstrations are all opportunities to ask students to reflect on how they are processing the information and concepts encountered in class. Reflection is especially relevant for "high-impact" educational activities such as practica and internships, as well as individual exploration such as advising and career counseling. Reflection can help students "craft" their academic focus and extract the most from their educational opportunities. Reflection can help students not only make sense of their experiences abroad but also make connections with their in- and out-of-class experiences before and after their sojourns abroad. Reflection can help them take greater, better informed ownership of the trajectory they envision their lives taking.

Crucial in such situations is reflection that embraces the emotional as well as the cognitive aspects of experience. Traditional courses often view student emotions as barriers to learning; yet emotions can open students to learning that makes a difference to them, and endures far beyond the immediate experience. Analysis of information and experience must be paired with the processing of relevant internal thoughts and feelings. (See Savicki & Price, 2017b, for methods to encourage deep reflection.) As content experts, faculty will determine which aspects of their disciplines offer opportunities for reflection. With creativity and a shift in perspective, advisers and counselors will be able to help students pause to make time for deeper reflection.

Conclusion

This chapter has argued that learning to reflect can be transformative. Further, only through reflection can experience rise to the level of learning. While we have focused on the education abroad context, the same principles and guidelines can be extended to the home campus. Indeed, we would argue that reflection is critical to translating undergraduate educational experiences into learning. Additionally, reflection is a prerequisite for enabling students to make connections between their learning abroad and their learning at home, both in terms of personal growth and cultural learning and in terms of academic knowledge and skills. The key is to craft assignments and activities that help students think about the way they think about events, concepts, experiences, and themselves. This approach stands in contrast to more traditional educational approaches in which students passively receive information to later regurgitate it on tests and papers. Support and training for faculty and advisers may be necessary, as traditional teaching methods do not prompt reflection.

Reflection requires learners' active participation and can transfer across situations. Reflection bolsters a student's active engagement with the world. Ideally, before studying abroad students already will have had some experience with reflection. Even then, they may struggle with the idea of including themselves in their meaning-making (the known *and* the knower). It is imperative, therefore, that we help them learn and affirm reflection as a powerful approach to participating in constructing meaning.

References

Arrúe, C. (2008). Study abroad in Spain viewed through multi-cultural lenses. In V. Savicki (Ed.), *Developing intercultural competence and transformation: Theory, research, and application in international education* (pp. 236–258). Sterling, VA: Stylus.

Bennett, M. J. (1993). Toward ethnorelativism: A developmental model of intercultural sensitivity. In R. M. Paige (Ed.), *Education for the intercultural experience* (2nd ed., pp. 21–71). Yarmouth, ME: Intercultural Press.

Bennett, M. J. (2012). Paradigmatic assumptions and a developmental approach to intercultural learning. In M. Vande Berg, R. M. Paige, & K. H. Lou (Eds.), *Student learning abroad: What our students are learning, what they're not, and what we can do about it* (pp. 90–114). Sterling, VA: Stylus.

Binder, F. (2008). Action methods for integration of experience and understanding. In V. Savicki (Ed.), *Developing intercultural competence and transformation: Theory, research, and application in international education* (pp. 195–214). Sterling, VA: Stylus.

Bourner, T. (2003). Assessing reflective learning. *Education+Training, 45*(5), 267–272.

Brewer, E., & Moore, J. (2015). Where and how do students learn abroad? In V. Savicki & E. Brewer (Eds.), *Assessing study abroad: Theory, tools, and practice* (pp. 145–161). Sterling, VA: Stylus.

Fosnot, C. T. (2005). Preface. In C. T. Fosnot (Ed.), *Constructivism: Theory, perspectives, and practice* (2nd ed.). New York, NY: Teachers College Press.

Fosnot, C. T., & Perry, R. S. (2005). Constructivism: A psychological theory of learning. In C. T. Fosnot (Ed.), *Constructivism: Theory, perspectives, and practice* (2nd ed., pp. 8–38). New York, NY: Teachers College Press.

Frey, F. E., & Tropp, L. R. (2006). Being seen as individuals versus as group members: Extending research on metaperception to intergroup contexts. *Personality and Social Psychology Review, 10*, 265–280.

Homan, A. (2006). Constructing knowledge through reflection. *The Cross Papers, Number 9*. Phoenix, AZ: League for Innovation in the Community College.

Hubbs, D. L., & Brand, C. F. (2010). Learning from the inside out: A method for analyzing reflective journals in the college classroom. *Journal of Experiential Education, 33*, 56–71.

Hunter, A. (2008). Transformative learning in international education. In V. Savicki (Ed.), *Developing intercultural competence and transformation: Theory, research, and application in international education* (pp. 92–107). Sterling, VA: Stylus.

Kincheloe, J. L. (2005). *Critical constructivism primer*. New York, NY: Peter Lang.

Kolb, D. (1984). *Experiential learning as the science of learning and development*. Englewood Cliffs, NJ: Prentice Hall.

Lou, K. H., & Bosley, G. W. (2008). Dynamics of cultural contexts: Meta-level intervention in the study abroad experience. In V. Savicki (Ed.), *Developing intercultural competence and transformation: Theory, research, and application in international education* (pp. 276–296). Sterling, VA: Stylus.

Maher, B. A. (1969). *Clinical psychology and personality: The selected papers of George Kelly*. Huntington, NY: R. E. Krieger.

Mezirow, J. (1991). *Transformative dimensions of adult learning*. San Francisco, CA: Jossey-Bass.

Minucci, S. (2008). Every day another soulful experience to bring back home. In V. Savicki (Ed.), *Developing intercultural competence and transformation: Theory, research, and application in international education* (pp. 215–235). Sterling, VA: Stylus.

Pagano, M., & Roselle, L. (2009). Beyond reflection through an academic lens: Refraction and international experiential education. *Frontiers: The Interdisciplinary Journal of Study Abroad, 18*, 217–229.

Paige, R. M. (2015). Interventionist models for study abroad. In J. M. Bennett (Ed.), *SAGE encyclopedia of intercultural competence* (pp. 563–568). Thousand Oaks, CA: SAGE.

Price, M. V., Savicki, V., & Barnhart, E. (2014, November). *Assessment of students' reflections across their study abroad.* NAFSA Regions I & XII Biregional Conference, Portland, OR.

Price, M. V., Savicki, V., & Moran, M. (2015, November). *Student reflection: Why it is important and how to assess it.* IPSL Symposium, Universidad San Ignacio de Loyola, Cusco, Peru.

Savicki, V. (2008). Experiential and affective education for international educators. In V. Savicki (Ed.), *Developing intercultural competence and transformation: Theory, research, and application in international education* (pp. 74–91). Sterling, VA: Stylus.

Savicki, V., & Price, M. V. (2015). Student reflective writing: Cognition and affect before, during, and after study abroad. *Journal of College Student Development, 56,* 587–601.

Savicki, V., & Price, M. V. (2017a). Components of reflection: A longitudinal analysis of study abroad student blog posts. *Frontiers: The Interdisciplinary Journal of Study Abroad, 29*(2), 51–62.

Savicki, V., & Price, M. V. (2017b). Guiding reflection on cultural experience: Before, during, and after study abroad. In S. L. Pasquarelli, R. A. Cole, & M. Tyson, (Eds.), *Passport to change: Designing academically sound, culturally relevant, short-term faculty-led study abroad programs.* Sterling, VA: Stylus.

Stemler, S. E., Imada, T., & Sorkin, C. (2014). Development and validation of the Wesleyan Intercultural Competence Scale (WICS). *Frontiers: The Interdisciplinary Journal of Study Abroad, 24,* 25–47. Available from http://www.frontiersjournal.com/documents/StemlerImadaSorkinFrontiersXXIV-Fall2014-withappendix.pdf

Stephan, W. G., & Stephan, C. W. (1985). Intergroup anxiety. *Journal of Social Issues, 41,* 157–176.

Stephan, W. G., Stephan, C. W., & Gudykunst, W. B. (1999). Anxiety in intergroup relations: A comparison of anxiety/uncertainty management theory and integrated threat theory. *International Journal of Intercultural Relations, 23,* 613–628.

Vande Berg, M., Paige, R. M., & Lou, K. H. (2012). Student learning abroad: Paradigms and assumptions. In M. Vande Berg, R. M. Paige, & K. H. Lou (Eds.), *Student learning abroad: What our students are learning, what they're not, and what we can do about it* (pp. 90–114). Sterling, VA: Stylus.

Voci, A., & Hewstone, M. (2003). Intergroup contact and prejudice toward immigrants in Italy: The mediational role of anxiety and the moderational role of group salience. *Group Processes and Intergroup Relations, 6,* 37–54.

von Glaserfeld, E. (2005). Introduction: Aspects of constructivism. In C. T. Fosnot (Ed.), *Constructivism: Theory, perspectives, and practice* (2nd ed., pp. 3–7). New York, NY: Teachers College Press.

Ward, C. (2001). The A, B, Cs of acculturation. In D. Matsumoto (Ed.), *Handbook of culture and psychology* (pp. 411–446). New York, NY: Oxford University Press.

Zull, J. E. (2012). The brain, learning, and study abroad. In M. Vande Berg, R. M. Paige, & K. H. Lou (Eds.), *Student learning abroad: What our students are learning, what they're not, and what we can do about it* (pp. 162–187). Sterling, VA: Stylus.

IO

WHY IS THE MISSING LINK STILL LARGELY MISSING IN EDUCATION ABROAD PREPARATION?

The Case for Ongoing Orientation

Bruce La Brack and Anthony C. Ogden

A quarter of a century ago, an article titled "The Missing Linkage: The Process of Integrating Orientation and Reentry," stressed the importance of looking at education abroad preparation in the broadest terms possible (La Brack, 1993). The seminal article made the case that rather than compartmentalize the typical phases (predeparture, in-country, and reentry) as separate, if related, components, such courses should be linked and integrated conceptually and pedagogically across the entire arc of the education abroad experience to improve gains in student learning. The curriculum that underpinned these education abroad gains was established in 1976 as the University of the Pacific's Cross-Cultural Training Program, as it was referred to at the time. (While the program emphasis has shifted to intercultural, the university has retained the original course designation.) By 1993, it had become recognized as a national best practice in providing an ongoing, explicitly linked set of courses. From the program's inception, the predeparture and reentry cross-cultural training courses were credit bearing. Another feature of the program, novel at the time, was that all students who enrolled in a Pacific education abroad program were required to take (and pass) both courses. The program continues to the present day and celebrated its forty-second year of operation in 2018.

The primary motivation in writing the original "missing linkage" article was derived from La Brack's direct experience developing Pacific's curriculum, in addition to administering and teaching in the program, at that point, for 17 years. He wanted to share with education abroad professionals both his core ideas related to structuring and sequencing such courses and his professional excitement about the realization that the more explicitly, thoughtfully, and developmentally focused such coursework became, the better the results for the students. La Brack believed that this approach would be of interest to others also tasked with preparing students to study abroad. Moreover, he expected that many of the exercises and techniques employed in the courses would encourage students to view their time abroad as an ongoing process of exploration, change, and growth, and could be easily adapted elsewhere. Although designed specifically for U.S. undergraduates, he also hoped that the theoretical underpinnings of the courses, grounded in intercultural learning theory, and their overall structure, which links predeparture orientation and reentry activities, might become more widely adopted by others across a variety of international educational contexts.

For the most part this has not occurred, even though there is hardly a university education abroad program in the United States that does not have some kind of predeparture activity termed *orientation* and, increasingly, many institutions are offering some corollary type of postreturn "reentry activities." However, the amount of time allocated to such programming varies wildly. Predeparture orientations are often only a few hours to a day in duration, are generally heavily weighted toward logistical and administrative issues, and frequently contain little intercultural information. Conversely, reentry activities, where they exist, are generally limited to "welcome back" social events and/or job/employment fairs, with little opportunity for group and individual reflections on the meaning of the students' international experiences.

This situation seems at odds with often-expressed program goals of advancing intercultural communication and competency development, while simultaneously providing students with the conceptual tools to help them figure out what is going on in new and novel social contexts. Recent research, most notably the Georgetown Consortium Project, demonstrated that intercultural competence does not automatically occur as the result of students merely being in the vicinity of events (Vande Berg, Connor-Linton, & Paige, 2009). Without a grounded understanding of how different societies' values and communication patterns compare and contrast with one's own, it is difficult for students to accurately interpret unfamiliar behaviors and attitudes and respond appropriately. While the emphasis on intercultural communication per se seems to have lessened recently, it was a primary rationale for education abroad for several decades (see chapter 1).

The current situation seems depressingly familiar. It indicates that in spite of the robust growth in U.S. education abroad programming over the past couple of decades, predeparture orientation is still offered largely in isolation from any postreturn activities. This is complicated by the fact that such activities are increasingly delivered virtually and, unless required, student participation is often low, because at this point, they may not see the need or value. Despite widespread agreement among education abroad professionals that orientation is an important part of preparing students to study abroad, few institutions require courses like the Pacific model; fewer still give academic credit for participation in them; and almost none theoretically link the curriculum across the distinct phases of education abroad: preprogram, while abroad, and upon return.

The purpose of this chapter is fourfold. The first is to offer a brief overview of and reflection on Pacific's cross-cultural program in sufficient detail to enable readers unfamiliar with its main features to understand how they developed and were integrated into a specific curriculum. The second purpose is to discuss how the larger context of education abroad has changed over the past quarter century. In doing so, we will address concerns related to emerging issues such as ever-shorter program duration, and the rise in importance and prominence of health and safety issues and related risk-management concerns. Additionally, we will discuss complications involved in coordinating orientation programming with partner organizations, and the growing questioning of the value of education abroad in terms of cost and career relevance.

The third purpose is to provide an overview of the current state of orientation programming across a broad spectrum of U.S. academic institutional types, specifically examining the extent to which the kinds of linkages suggested in the original article have been implemented (not a large number) and where they have not (a majority). Representative examples of best practices developed at other institutions are noted. The fourth purpose is to discuss current challenges facing education abroad, specifically introducing the concept of *ongoing orientation* programming, which will likely be required in the future to maximize positive and intentional student success outcomes associated with education abroad participation. Suggestions are offered for developing, facilitating, and auditing ongoing orientation programming.

The Organizing Principle of the Pacific Orientation Curriculum

The program at the University of the Pacific in Stockton, California, arose from modest origins. Initially founded primarily as a direct response to student concerns about difficulties in returning home, it soon expanded to encompass both predeparture and reentry. This approach was one possible way to provide timely and appropriate cultural information at all phases of the education abroad experience, as well as reduce students' dissatisfaction with their international studies and return home (Bathurst & La Brack, 2012).

The basic framework of Pacific's orientation/reentry courses has long been quite simple. Since 1986, all education abroad participants have been required to take and pass 2 credit-bearing cross-cultural training courses. In their third or fourth semester, they enroll in Cross Cultural Training (CCT) I: Predeparture Orientation, which meets 3 hours a week for 8 weeks, totaling 24 instructional contact hours. Pacific students generally study abroad beginning in their fifth semester (or later), with their experience ranging from 10 to 15 weeks to 2 to 3 semesters, with some students studying at two different sites sequentially (e.g., Spain and Ecuador). Upon returning home, generally in the seventh or eighth semester, students take Cross Cultural Training (CCT) II: Re-entry Seminar, which meets 3 hours a week for 7 weeks, totaling 21 instructional contact hours.

While specific content, course readings, and exercises changed over time as different instructors revised and adapted the courses, the organizing principle behind the CCT coursework remained remarkably stable, although experimentation was always encouraged. Thus, as the following timeline illustrates, the program foci shifted at several junctures in response to changing circumstances and to adopt emergent best practices:

- 1986–1996. Gradual shift from the original culture-specific focus to a more culture-general approach.
- 2001–present. Strong emphasis on "interventionist" strategies implemented across the curriculum to take advantage of "teachable moments." This is part of a profession-wide commitment to seek and encourage ways that deliver information and feedback to students at the most appropriate time and in the most effective manner.
- 2006–present. Shift from using postreturn, self-reported student satisfaction surveys to tracking attitude shifts and quantifying intercultural competency gains using the Intercultural Development Inventory (IDI) instrument. The IDI is now administered to education abroad students at three points: initially in the first semester, again before students study abroad, and finally postprogram but prior to graduation. It was hypothesized that the students who went through the CCT coursework would demonstrate more significant change in their level of intercultural sensitivity (Bathurst & La Brack, 2012). Data from 2010 support this hypothesis (Sample, 2010, 2013).

Despite the adjustments, it is important to emphasize that, from its inception, the organizing principle of CCT was to provide linkages to ensure that education abroad coursework be mutually reinforcing across the CCT curriculum. For example, the concept of culture shock is initially raised in orientation and then revisited both in-country (did it occur?) and during re-entry (as re-entry shock). In other words, concepts that are primarily theoretical and abstract in predeparture become personal and experiential once abroad and after coming home.

An example of a linking activity is having outbound students create lists of "five things you are most looking forward to while abroad" and "five things that are worrying you the most." This both gives the instructor some quick insights into students' overall expectations and concerns and, when shared with the class, helps lower students' anxieties when they realize they are not alone in their apprehensions. The instructor files these lists away and upon the students' return distributes them to the students. This often results in a very fruitful discussion about the accuracy of their original hopes and fears. The majority of CCT students spontaneously volunteer that neither their positive expectations nor greatest concerns turned out to be anywhere near accurate. Some note ruefully that their positive anticipations did not always materialize; others were very surprised because the issues that most concerned them proved not to be the ones that most seriously bothered them. The instructor can then point out that the students are now beginning another process (re-entry) that most have not had prior experience dealing with. Basically, the students' own words and experiences are used to suggest that their preconceptions of what it will be like to return home might be no more accurate than those involved in originally imagining what education abroad would be like. This mismatch between student projections and reality can also be used to demonstrate the larger point that unrealistic expectations can frequently lead to premature disappointments.

At Pacific, one major conclusion reached was that these types of linkages would help reduce what we saw then, and continue to observe, as the failure of orientation conducted in isolation. Orientation activities that stand alone do not scaffold student learning across the education abroad experience. Unfortunately, conceptually, linkage is a simple idea, but it can be complex to administer and sustain, particularly for smaller education abroad offices and even more so in mammoth ones.

The Changing Landscape of Education Abroad

As discussed in chapter 2, education abroad programming has continued to mature and evolve, and participation rates have grown dramatically over the last 25 years. Students today can study just about any discipline in practically any part of the world for any duration of time. Programming models have also expanded and now, in addition to traditional study abroad, students are increasingly choosing international internships, global service-learning, undergraduate research, and so on. Although students continue to study abroad for a semester or an academic year, today the majority enroll in short-term programs, some of which last just a few days. Currently, 63% of all U.S. students who earn credit abroad participate in programs of less than 8 weeks, most often during the summer months (Farrugia & Bhandari, 2017). Although philosophically and experientially a longer foreign exposure may be better, at least insofar as intercultural learning is concerned, the current reality is that many adult learners, working students, and caregivers may simply not have the luxury of participating in longer-term programs. Others may not see their academic relevance or have the academic freedom to pursue them. Additionally, the question of how short an education abroad experience can be before it ceases to qualify as such must be considered.

What has not changed, however, is the enduring need to prepare students, irrespective of program duration, to maximize their learning abroad and be able to apply that learning upon return. The length of time spent abroad may impact the content and duration of orientation and re-entry training programs. A complicating factor in this equation, particularly in orientation programming, is the growing importance universities and education abroad providers attach to responsibly covering health and safety issues and institutional risk-management concerns. Too much emphasis on logistics reduces the amount of time available for discussing intercultural communication issues, academic integration, or other issues that are relevant to student learning and development.

Irrespective of program duration, a thoughtfully constructed orientation can help prepare students to maximize whatever time is available to them abroad. Coupling predeparture preparation with re-entry debriefing will increase significantly the potential for additional cultural understanding, personal growth, and integration with ongoing academic courses. As short-term programs become the new normal for many institutions, it is unclear how this might impact the way institutions will adapt their orientation programming to this new reality.

How much or in what format orientation programming short-term programs require remains an open question. An argument can be made that preparation for programs that have limited intercultural exposure might require commensurately shorter training, but a counterargument can also be made: When the cultural engagement aspect of an education abroad program is reduced, both the predeparture and re-entry orientation might need to be *longer* to maximize culture learning while abroad. This may be especially relevant because short-term faculty-directed programming may be primarily structured around disciplinary learning. Further, debriefing opportunities continue to be necessary to solidify learning and discuss how students might seek additional opportunities to extend and apply their new knowledge and skills more broadly.

Other Approaches to Education Abroad Orientation

The most common education abroad types today include reciprocal student exchanges, consortia, provider, and faculty-directed programs. Orientation and re-entry programs across these quite different models vary enormously in terms of content, duration, and the degree of coordination, if any, between orientation/re-entry offerings at a student's home campus and abroad. Program types are too diverse to generalize, but it is possible to highlight a few orientation programming models in which the kinds of linkages suggested by the Pacific approach have been successfully implemented (see Figure 10.1). These include serving single institutions as well as virtual programs designed for use across multiple institutions.

Institutional Programs

Creative orientation programs where linkages are explicit include the Intercultural Distance Learning courses developed jointly by Bellarmine University and Willamette University (1995 to the present), and the University of Minnesota's Maximizing Study Abroad project (1999 to the present) that resulted in a popular undergraduate textbook and related online components discussed in the following paragraphs. Pacific's program was included in a review of programs deploying best practices (Vande Berg & Paige, 2009) and has been the focus of numerous articles and commentary over the years.

The Bellarmine/Willamette courses employ distance learning pedagogy, are linked, include required pre- and postimmersion workshops on campus, and employ frequent virtual interaction with faculty and other students. Taught via e-mail and computer-based software, the courses link education abroad participants enrolled in the same course at different locations in the United States and abroad. The overall intent of these courses is for students to develop intercultural skills while immersed in another culture, using a peer-mentoring approach that is faculty monitored. This process provides the space and time for reflection and guided discussion "with one's home culture peers and/or instructors" (Lou & Bosley, 2008, p. 276). Lou and

Figure 10.1. Sample institutions providing ongoing orientation.

Many education abroad offices across the country are shifting the methods they use to prepare and support education abroad participants. The following is a brief list of institutions that offer orientation courses. Some courses focus on all phases of the education abroad experience—*predeparture, while abroad,* and *re-entry*—while others may focus on only one phase.

- **Bellarmine University**: Perspectives of World Cultures: Predeparture Course (required for academic year and semester program participants). Another course helps foster intercultural development and includes predeparture, while abroad, and re-entry elements.

- **Beloit College**: Action-research re-entry topics courses (optional, 2 credit hours) and reflection/outreach re-entry course for study abroad ambassadors (optional, 1 credit hour).

- **Elon University**: Predeparture course for winter term programs (1 credit hour). Re-entry course option also available.

- **Spelman College**: Predeparture travel seminar (required, 1 credit hour). While abroad and re-entry elements are also required for students.

- **Trinity University** (TX): Preparing for Study Abroad (optional, 1 credit hour). Re-entry (optional, 1 credit hour).

- **University of Kentucky**: Education Abroad at UK: Maximizing Your International Education Experience (required, 1 credit hour). Online orientation course where predeparture, while abroad, and re-entry elements are emphasized.

- **University of Minnesota**: Global Identity: Connecting Your International Experience to Your Future (optional, 1 credit hour). Predeparture, while abroad, and re-entry elements are included in the course.

- **University of the Pacific**: Cross Cultural Training I (predeparture course, required for all students participating in semester or academic year programs, credit bearing). Cross Cultural Training II—Re-entry course that is required for School of International Studies, but optional for all other students.

- **University of Wisconsin, Lacrosse**: Orientation to Study Abroad (required, 1 credit hour). Study Abroad Practicum—Journaling for Credit (1 credit hour). Cross-Cultural Reentry From Study Abroad (1 credit hour).

- **Willamette University**: Maximizing the Study Abroad Experience (required for semester-long participants or longer, 1 credit hour). Predeparture and re-entry elements are emphasized. Intercultural Study Within Cultural Immersion (4 credit hours). For participants in an off-campus, cultural immersion program. Includes predeparture and re-entry elements.

Bosley contend that the importance of the postimmersion workshop cannot be overstated as this is where a great deal of additional intercultural learning can occur.

The Maximizing Study Abroad project takes a somewhat more conventional approach. It evolved through several stages: an original curriculum development phase that resulted in the publication of *Maximizing Study Abroad* (Paige, Cohen, Kappler, Chi, & Lassegard, 2002, 2006); a three-year research phase; and an online, in-country course phase. The entire project was linked and focused on student culture and language learning strategies (Paige, Cohen, & Shively, 2004). Since 2005, the University of Minnesota's Learning Abroad Center, in cooperation with the university's Department of Educational Policy and Administration, has offered an optional one-credit course to students. Its current form, Global Identity: Connecting Your International Experiences to Your Future, is available to all students participating in Learning Abroad Center programs. As far as we know, no other language- and culture-learning materials have been developed that are both as theoretically driven and empirically tested as the Minnesota study abroad projects.

Both of these are examples of theoretically linked training options that view the entire education abroad curriculum as an integrated and cumulative whole. Both use direct training and virtual components to build intercultural skills while abroad, and each provides ways to apply this knowledge postreturn.

Virtual Programs

Offering face-to-face, direct instruction may be preferable to employing a wholly virtual curriculum. However, when numbers of students are so large that direct instruction becomes difficult or impossible, or there are too few staff to deliver the instruction, a thoughtful adaptation of online materials using readily available Internet resources can go a long way toward alleviating such constraints. Students, even on their own, can gain enough culture-general knowledge from online materials to make a difference in the success of their international experience. Ideally, students will be monitored to ensure that the work is actually done, but many institutions have developed ways to facilitate this.

In the past several decades numerous online intercultural training resources have been developed. One early example is the What's Up With Culture? On-line Cultural Training Resource for Study Abroad website (www2.pacific.edu/sis/culture/). Developed by La Brack with support from a three-year grant (2000–2003) from the Department of Education Fund for the Improvement of Postsecondary Education, the website is open access and allows anyone involved in nonprofit, international educational activities to copy, adapt, and distribute the content without permission.

This online training resource drew directly on content from Pacific's 2 cross-cultural training courses and incorporates the theoretical linkages that characterize them. Targeted toward traditional-aged U.S. undergraduates intending to study abroad, the website was designed to be interactive, self-guided, self-paced, self-contained, self-graded, self-assessed, and encyclopedic in scope. It contains 10 modules (6 on predeparture orientation, 1 on in-country adjustment and pre- and re-entry phases, and 3 on the re-entry process), extensive bibliographic resources for both students and faculty, and a glossary of terminology. The focus was on conveying culture-general information, cross-cultural training concepts and instruments, and intercultural communication categories, and providing a resource for students and faculty looking for useful information on ways to increase culture learning. The site was never intended as a stand-alone course, nor as a substitute for culture-specific information. The materials, however, can be supplemented through use of role plays; Describe, Interpret, Evaluate exercises; small-group discussions; reflection papers; video/CD presentations; student exchange of culture-specific information; and a myriad of supporting tools. If direct instruction is not possible, the website can be used by students to gain culture-general information, acquire basic knowledge on the nature and categories of culture, be introduced to intercultural theory, and become sensitized to why cultural differences matter. In addition, there are self-assessment exercises that students can use to reflect upon and increase cultural self-understanding of their values and behavioral preferences.

Another free online resource is the Safety Abroad First–Educational Travel Information (SAFETI) Clearinghouse Project (globaled.us/safeti/index.asp), sponsored by the Center for Global Education, currently hosted by California State University, Dominguez Hills. This is an excellent resource for information to support education abroad program development and implementation. While it emphasizes health and safety issues, it offers a wide range of information including sample orientation/re-entry syllabi. Pacific has had a long association with The Center for Global Education, which has published a number of articles written by La Brack featuring the CCT program (2000a, 2000b, 2000c). For example, one article focused on the "safety incident survey" research project developed and administered by La Brack to a sample of Pacific students who had studied abroad, which showed an average of 2.5 safety incidents per student (2000b). The survey provided clear and detailed information of what is going on around the world in terms of safety, and the kinds of situations and circumstances students faced while abroad. As a result, Pacific instituted a policy that required all students returning from study abroad to complete a Safety Abroad First-Educational Travel Information (SAFETI) survey form as part of their exit interview with Pacific's International Program and Services staff. Furthermore, the survey provided data that could be cited in CCT I (Orientation) to alert students about specific circumstances to be aware of in various locations, as well as to provide suggestions on how to avoid negative consequences and situations. The ability to gather reliable, accurate, and current data during the re-entry process provides educators with practical knowledge about international conditions that can be passed along during the next orientation. This is another example of how linkages can be created and integrated into the entire education abroad process.

What's Next? The Case for Ongoing Orientation

Decades ago, Pacific responded to what was perceived as a pressing need to better support the intercultural learning of students studying abroad by linking predeparture orientation and re-entry training (La Brack, 1993). It has been clear that students needed to continue their learning and development well beyond their time abroad, a goal that remains very relevant today. Preparing students beforehand is only one step in a continuum of learning and reflection that can, and should, continue long after the student's international studies have concluded. Pacific's approach was groundbreaking, especially in offering credit-bearing coursework in tandem with education abroad programming. Although broadly replicating that approach across institutional contexts may not be feasible, the basic purpose and goals of the approach remain absolutely relevant and can be utilized to inform how orientation programming is facilitated today. Looking forward, we propose that orientation programming be linked and continuous as *ongoing orientation*. No matter what form orientation programming takes, however, it is critical that before, during, and after education abroad content be explicitly linked, both theoretically and practically.

As such, the continued use of terminology such as *predeparture orientation* and *re-entry training* might need to be rethought, perhaps being replaced by terminology more reflective of the understanding that studying abroad is less about facilitating international travel, which these terms have been said to connote, and more about structuring learning to achieve intentional educational outcomes, as discussed in chapter 3. In other words, there may be a conflict between terminology that suggests international travel and the current view of education abroad as an educational high-impact practice that is increasingly tied to student success. Ongoing orientation programming that positions education abroad within the broader undergraduate experience and provides iterative, continuous, and intentional support for student learning and development may be better suited and better received by today's undergraduate students. Perhaps predeparture orientation and re-entry training eventually will no longer be seen simply as bookends, but rather as distinct phases in an ongoing orientation process that emphasizes the continuity of learning *preprogram, while abroad,* and *upon return.*

In many ways, the concept of ongoing orientation mirrors that of an academic course. For better or worse, U.S. students understand and are accustomed to receiving course syllabi and recognize that most undergraduate courses are structured around clear objectives and measures of assessment. As with a course syllabus, ongoing orientation can be modeled on a course structure and introduced to students with well-articulated and measurable goals that are supported with explicit pedagogies. In this way, the international study serves as a primary pedagogy framed by the orientation. The ongoing orientation structure outlines the distinct phases of learning, what students will be doing at each phase, and the expectations of them. It should deliver content that deliberately scaffolds learning over time. Ongoing orientation programming must be flexible enough to accommodate the diverse range of education abroad program types, each with a unique purpose and set of learning goals.

Whether credit bearing or not, ongoing orientation aligned with the distinct phases of education abroad allows the content to be tailored more appropriately to each respective phase. Traditional orientation programming seemingly attempts to cover everything preprogram. This can result in long, detailed sessions seemingly more for the benefit and protection of the home institution than of truly supporting student learning and development at a time when students will be most responsive. For example, prior to studying abroad, many students express interest in understanding arrival logistics, making friends, housing, and so on. Once in the destination country, their priorities shift and they become more interested in socializing, making friends, learning the local language, seeking health care, and so on. Upon return, their interests shift again to such matters as academic credit transfer, sharing their experiences, and getting reoriented to campus. The key factor when designing and facilitating ongoing orientation is to understand what content needs to be presented, specifically when, and how to best facilitate student learning and development at each phase. Ongoing orientation can not only help address these valid preoccupations but also help students navigate disorienting challenges while abroad and postprogram, translate these into learning, and help students make curricular connections. The key is tailoring specific content to students when they are most responsive and inquisitive, and recognizing that there may be differences in receptivity among students.

An audit of the orientation curriculum can be helpful here. Implementing effective ongoing orientation requires that the content and pedagogy be determined in advance and in conjunction with well-articulated learning objectives, determined at a time that the content is most relevant to students, and facilitated in a way that motivates participants to engage with the information. A curriculum audit therefore requires breaking down the essential content into the three major phases: preprogram, while abroad, and postprogram. Most orientations cover topics ranging from intercultural learning, health and safety, academic integrations, and so on. Consider, for example, the topic of intercultural learning, which remains an important and common topic for ongoing orientation. While many traditional predeparture programs attempt to generally inform students about intercultural learning and cultural adjustment, a well-structured ongoing orientation may begin by stressing topics such as the cultural iceberg, stereotypes and cultural generalizations, cultural value orientations, and American identity abroad. Once students are abroad, it becomes more appropriate to highlight issues of cultural adjustment, conflict resolution, socialization patterns, intercultural friendships, and so on. Postprogram topics should emphasize reflective exercises, discussions of the styles of re-entry, and identifying sources of support for students to help them articulate what they learned abroad and ways to apply that learning moving forward.

Health, safety, and security are other important topics that must be addressed at all phases of ongoing orientation, and yet specific topics can be highlighted and emphasized at differing phases. For example, during preprogram activities, topics related to health, safety, and security may include discussing the need to determine emergency contact information, reviewing health insurance and evacuation coverage, and immunization needs. While abroad, ongoing orientation may highlight the need to update emergency contact information, what to do in an emergency or a crisis, and how to seek medical treatment. After returning home, students may be more responsive to understanding how to receive follow-up health care, submit health insurance claims, and so on. The question is not parsing out important health and safety information, but rather determining what elements of a particular topic should be presented when students are likely to be most responsive.

Providing ongoing orientation also necessitates the use of approaches that appeal to contemporary student learning styles and preferences. While credit-bearing academic courses may be viable for only smaller institutions, new course management software and advances in distance learning approaches make it more feasible to scale up both credit- and noncredit-bearing ongoing orientation to accommodate larger numbers of students. As mentioned earlier, virtual platforms can be created to allow students to engage with the content and respond to periodic assessments before, during, and post–education abroad.

Although understandably more difficult, it is nonetheless important to develop and facilitate ongoing orientation programming that supports the continuity of learning while students are abroad. It is essential that in-country orientation programming be continuous throughout the time abroad. Additionally, distance-learning platforms can ensure that all students, irrespective of program duration, discipline, and destination, are supported in ways that enable them to maximize their learning abroad. Furthermore, international partners, whether local institutions or affiliated provider organizations, are increasingly active and effective at providing sophisticated orientation that supports student learning and development in context. When selecting international partners, it is important to partner with those who are prepared to provide value-added ongoing orientation that is congruent with student learning and cultural adjustment.

Conclusion

Many education abroad professionals have begun to realize that our singular purpose is not to send students abroad, but rather to partner internally (with faculty, staff colleagues, and institutional leaders) and externally (with higher education organizations, education abroad organizations, and university partners abroad) to educate today's students. Our role is to leverage education abroad programming intentionally to support student learning and development. Education abroad is but one among many high-impact practices that can be used effectively to support the realization of predetermined and well-articulated outcomes that align with the goals and culture of the home institution. In this way, the purpose of education abroad has shifted from an emphasis on trips and travel to one that centers on understanding how education abroad programming might be strategically used, in one or all of its forms, to produce students who understand the international nuances of their disciplines and are prepared for lifelong learning and career success.

Much has changed over the years and challenging circumstances will certainly continue to arise, but what remains is our need to commit to developing well-structured, ongoing orientation programming that supports student learning and development. As is often noted, learning abroad should never be treated in the same way one might store photos on a smartphone to only periodically scroll through them to reminisce about distant memories.

Rather, it should complement and enhance undergraduate education, especially as one leaves the university and moves into the wider, multicultural world. Our role as education abroad professionals has never been to emphasize tourism, but to work as well-intentioned partners to advance the overall education and development of our students. Looking forward another 25 years, the details of these discussions will change, but the need to provide well-structured ongoing orientation, in one form or another, will most certainly persist. Moreover, and most critically, if we can make a deliberate decision to ensure that any such future preparations on our campuses (and off) are appropriately theoretically linked, we may no longer need to ask, "What happened to the missing linkage?" because it will no longer be absent.

References

Bathurst, L., & La Brack, B. (2012). Shifting the locus of intercultural learning: Intervening prior to and after student experiences abroad. In M. Vande Berg, M. H. Paige, & K. M. H. Lou (Eds.), *Student learning abroad: What your students are learning, what they're not, and what we can do about it* (pp. 261–283). Sterling, VA: Stylus.

Farrugia, C. A., & Bhandari, R. (2017). *Open Doors 2017 report on international educational exchange*. New York, NY: Institute of International Education.

La Brack, B. (1993). The missing linkage: The process of integrating orientation and reentry. In R. Michael Paige (Ed.), *Education for the intercultural experience* (pp. 241–279). Yarmouth, ME: Intercultural Press.

La Brack, B. (2000a). The evolution continues: The UOP cross-cultural training courses. *SAFETI Online Newsletter, 1*(1). Available from http://globaled.us/safeti/v1n12000ed_evolution_continues.asp

La Brack, B. (2000b). How do we really know what happens to our students overseas? The University of the Pacific SAFETI survey and its relation to cross-cultural training courses. *SAFETI Online Newsletter, 1*(2). Available from http://globaled.us/safeti/v1n22000ed_how_do_we_really_know_what_happens.asp

La Brack, B. (2000c) The missing linkage: The process of integrating orientation and reentry. *SAFETI Online Newsletter, 1*(1). Available from http://globaled.us/safeti/v1n12000ed_missing_linkage.asp

Lou, K., & Bosley, G. (2008). Dynamics of cultural contexts: Meta-level intervention in the study abroad experience. In V. Savicki (Ed.), *Developing intercultural competence and transformation* (pp. 276–296). Sterling, VA: Stylus.

Paige, R. M., Cohen, D., Kappler, B., Chi, J., & Lassegard, J. (2002, 2006). *Maximizing study abroad: A student's guide to strategies for language and culture learning and use*. Minneapolis: University of Minnesota.

Paige, R. M., Cohen, A. D., & Shively, R. (2004). Assessing the impact of a strategies-based curriculum on language and culture learning abroad. *Frontiers: The Interdisciplinary Journal of Study Abroad, 10*, 253–276.

Sample, S. (2010, October 28–30). *Study abroad and the international curriculum: Assessing changes in intercultural competence.* Paper presented at the Intercultural Development Inventory Conference, Minneapolis, MN.

Sample, S. (2013). Developing intercultural learners through the international curriculum. *Journal of Studies in International Education, 17*(5), 554–572.

Vande Berg, M., Connor-Linton, J., & Paige, R. M. (2009). The Georgetown Consortium Project: Intervening in student learning abroad. *Frontiers: The Interdisciplinary Journal of Study Abroad, 18,* 1–75.

Vande Berg, M., & Paige, R. M. (2009). The evolution of intercultural competence in U.S. study abroad. In D. K. Deardorff (Ed.), *The SAGE handbook of intercultural competence* (pp. 419–437). Newbury Park, CA: SAGE.

PART THREE

PARTNERSHIPS IN EDUCATION
ABROAD INTEGRATION

II

THE INTERSECTION OF EDUCATION ABROAD AND CAREER READINESS, AND THE ROLE OF INTERNATIONAL EDUCATORS

Anne M. D'Angelo and Mary Pang

Education abroad (EA), embracing long- and short-term international study, is potentially such a transformational juncture in life that its significance may be viewed analogously as a motivational vehicle, serving to carry students along an educational continuum. While the EA experience constitutes but one brief segment of a student's higher education journey, the effects of such learning can be long lasting by preparing students for their careers and boosting their employability.

Indeed, EA is an opportunity for student learning to occur on personal and professional levels to enhance their *career readiness*, defined by the National Association of Colleges and Employers (NACE, 2018) as "the attainment and demonstration of requisite competencies that broadly prepare college graduates for a successful transition into the workplace." Facing the challenges of participating in EA and being outside one's comfort zone in an unfamiliar country and culture can stimulate a student's sense of curiosity and exploration, and help the student acquire abilities generally recognized to augment employability. The twenty-first-century job skills identified by the Institute of International Education's (IIE) Center for Academic Mobility Research and Impact report include "intercultural skills, curiosity, flexibility & adaptability, confidence, self-awareness, interpersonal skills, communication, problem-solving, language, tolerance for ambiguity" (Farrugia & Sanger, 2017, p. 5). Adaptability has been labeled a "metacompetency" (Morrison & Hall, 2002), while adaptability and flexibility have been posited as the foundations of continuous or lifelong learning (Pang, Chua, & Chu, 2008) and are crucial to maintaining employability security (Dany, 2003) in a rapidly changing world. It has been contended that one's "career should now be viewed as the individual's lifelong progression in learning" (Watts, 2000, p. 261). Arguably continuous or lifelong learning may be today's metacompetency and critical in ensuring that one is equipped to navigate successfully contemporary shifting local and global economic landscapes.

Within tertiary institutions, a key person in this learning process is the international educator (IE), whose work has evolved, expanded, and professionalized. IEs comprise both scholars and practitioners (many spanning both spheres) working eruditely to advance comprehensive internationalization and to develop and implement meaningful international education programming. IEs have long transcended the point of simply facilitating student mobility, to becoming active stewards of student learning. IEs have endeavored to maximize the impact of EA by providing student training prior to, during, and after the international experience, in an effort to support student learning abroad and goal setting during the educative process. IEs have subsequently identified a range of skill sets and competencies that students can potentially acquire from the international experience (Deardorff, 2008) and, more recently, have established tools and methods for measuring and assessing intercultural and other development outcomes of an EA experience (Deardorff, 2015; Hammer, Bennett, & Wiseman, 2003; Savicki, 2008; Savicki & Brewer, 2015).

Nevertheless, this chapter introduces a new challenge for IEs, namely to further support students by leveraging EA to enhance their career readiness and employability. Essentially, we propose that IEs must communicate the relevance and impact of EA on career readiness and employability, especially given the increasing evidence that EA enhances motivation, confidence, and other soft skills. Thus, IEs should convey the convergence of experiential learning activities abroad with the development of continuous learning skills for students beyond graduation, especially regarding career aspirations, readiness, and employability. Moreover, employability should not be held as a finite end point, but rather viewed as an integral part of the lifelong learning continuum. From the contributors' experiences and observations, IEs increasingly are finding themselves at the intersection of higher education and the broader community. This is particularly true of IEs located in professional schools and in offices with staffing levels that permit outreach. Under these circumstances, IEs need to be cognizant of the central position that they hold and, in this knowledge, be able to execute their role with intentionality and purpose. This encompasses developing programs with explicit career readiness and employability desired outcomes and supporting students accordingly. It also requires being strategic in articulating these outcomes in alignment with the expectations of a multitude of internal stakeholders (including colleagues from various academic and service/support units) and external institutional stakeholders (e.g., corporate partners, government representatives and agencies).

Internationalization, EA, and Labor Markets

Internationalization is fast gaining traction and momentum in today's economy and society. Stakeholders are becoming more proactive and engaged due to their respective interests. For example, governments around the world must ensure that they supply human capital that will meet labor market demands in order to support economic advancement and sustain growth and prosperity. Employers are seeking to hire well-qualified and experienced staff, who are also highly trainable and have potential for continued learning and development. Similarly, forward-looking students, who are the next generation of workers, want to equip themselves with the requisite skills to position themselves to their best advantage before entering into a competitive labor market. Higher education institutions tasked with the responsibility to educate and train students holistically, both inside and outside of the classroom, are taking action to prepare students for the challenges that will confront them in their future careers.

The Organisation for Economic Cooperation and Development's (OECD) latest indicators on education show that "international students account for only 5.6% of total enrolment in tertiary programmes" (OECD, 2017, p. 286). This seemingly small percentage of students, apparently motivated and with the means to pursue a full-time degree in another country, may do so to improve their employability (OECD, 2017). However, the OECD figure excludes the many students who spend up to a year studying and/or working abroad as part of their home institution degrees. Institutions are increasingly providing extensive portfolios of semester-based exchanges, study tours and visits, international internships, global service-learning abroad, and language and cultural immersion programming.

Recognizing the importance of international experience to workforce development, governments worldwide have been gearing up efforts to internationalize tertiary education. Policies and financial support encourage greater student mobility for undergraduates in an attempt to provide them with the necessary exposure and opportunity to acquire requisite skills to engage effectively in a complex and diverse global economic environment.

The European Union (EU) has been an early starter in this respect, operating the European Action Scheme for the Mobility of University Students (or Erasmus) program since 1987. More recently, the EU implemented the Erasmus+ program in 2014. It goes beyond the student mobility of the original Erasmus program to provide funding for work placements and other forms of training abroad, and to support not just students, but the faculty, IEs, and other staff who facilitate student learning and mobility. The Hong Kong Special Administrative Region's Government publication *Aspirations for the Higher Education System* in Hong Kong (University Grants Committee, 2010) was a response to employer criticisms that new graduates in Hong Kong possessed insufficient knowledge about the outside world and were ill equipped to deal with the globalizing economy. One recommendation advocated the provision of more and varied international study opportunities for local students, with funding and credits to be attached to these programs. Meanwhile, the government of Australia introduced the New Colombo Plan in 2014, "a signature initiative . . . , which aims to lift knowledge of the Indo-Pacific in Australia by supporting Australian undergraduates to study and undertake internships in the region" (Australian Global Alumni, 2017).

In the United States, a key government initiative, USA Study Abroad, provides funding and programming to U.S. and international institutions for students and faculty to improve capacity to host EA programs. Further, the U.S. Department of State's Bureau of Educational and Cultural Affairs supports the annual Open Doors Report on International Educational Exchange, published by IIE. The annual enrollment increases reported in Open Doors suggest that EA is increasingly viewed as an effective means to enhance the knowledge and skills of U.S. students and their readiness to compete for jobs in the twenty-first-century workforce. Yet, the decentralized approach of the U.S. government delegates responsibility for internationalization strategies and policies to states and individual institutions, including around EA, and for the development of global competencies in students, faculty, and staff. As a result, there are no centralized goals or policy initiatives to mobilize increasing numbers of U.S. students to study abroad. This makes it increasingly important for IEs to understand and drive EA continued momentum at the local level.

Connecting EA and Employability: Emerging Evidence

Despite a relative dearth of research on the impact of EA on graduates' career outcomes, there is pervasive acceptance that EA participation enhances career readiness and employability by contributing to the development of relevant skill sets (flexibility and adaptability, communication and teamwork skills, etc.) and mind-sets (curiosity to explore the world, openness toward diversity and cultural differences, etc.). Fortunately, studies are emerging that lend credence to anecdotal evidence of the connection between EA and employability. Indeed, scholars and employers are beginning to recognize the greater competitiveness of graduates who have earned credit abroad as students. Shaftel, Shaftel, and Ahluwalia (2007) recommended that employers prioritize sending on international assignments those graduates who had participated in EA, since they coped better internationally, grew more, and were prepared for international teamwork. Likewise, Crossman (2010) reported that employers believe that graduates with international exchange experiences outperform other employees and are better able to adjust and contribute when posted abroad for work.

In Norway, Wiers-Jenssen (2008) compared the employment attainments of 2,300 graduates, between 3.5 and 5 years after graduation, to determine the extent to which EA participation resulted in the higher likelihood of securing employment abroad or with an international work assignment. The findings confirmed that formerly "mobile" students, who had either graduated abroad or studied abroad, worked abroad more frequently than "nonmobile" students. Furthermore, in the domestic labor market, mobile students held jobs with more international assignments than nonmobile students. This suggests that mobile students have more employment opportunities and options than nonmobile students, both within and beyond their domestic labor markets. The findings reinforce the belief that EA participation has a positive and measurable impact on graduates' employability, both internationally and locally.

An Australian study concluded that "international experience does enhance learning, the acquisition of competencies, the development of critical soft skills, and overall employability," by giving "graduates 'an edge' in the initial recruitment process" (Crossman & Clarke, 2009, p. 609). However, the relationship between international experience and longer term career progression was inconclusive in the study. Nonetheless, a different Australian study by Potts (2015) on early career impacts of EA indicated that almost two-thirds of respondents felt that EA had given them career direction and their first job, and anticipated EA would also have positive long-term impacts on career prospects. Most also claimed to have developed general personal skills.

The Erasmus Impact Study (2016) focused on the skills and employability of students. It reported that the opportunity to develop soft skills, such as adaptability, and to improve and widen career prospects in the future were motivating factors to study abroad for 92% and 90% of students, respectively. In addition, 87% of students sought to enhance their future employability abroad, while 77% wanted to enhance their future employability in their home country. Rather disappointingly, however, despite this evidence as well as "policy rhetoric on the importance of international learning mobility for a range of outcomes including future employment prospects, in most [European] countries only a minority of employers take international experience into account when making recruitment decisions" (Van Mol, 2017, p. 59).

In contrast, a QS Global Employer Survey report titled "Employers Value International Student Experience," found that 60% of respondents "value international study when recruiting talent" (Molony, Sowter, & Potts, 2011, p. 5). Responses came from 10,000 graduate recruiters in 116 countries and 5 continents. The results affirm "the increasing investment being made in the activity by the individuals, institutions, governments and industries" (Molony et al., 2011, p. 21).

A similar picture has been evolving in the United States. An alumni survey conducted by the EA provider Institute for International Education of Students (IES) found that 77% of respondents perceived that they had acquired skills that influenced their career paths, 63% believed EA had assisted or influenced their careers, and about a third claimed the global career door had been opened up for them (Norris & Gillespie, 2008). Further, an IES Abroad Recent Graduates Survey (Preston, 2012) reported nearly 85% of respondents felt that studying abroad helped them build job skills, and almost 80% indicated that studying abroad was (very) effective in helping them develop confidence to deal with new skills required for the first job. On the hiring side, Harder, Andenoro, Robers, Stedman, and Newberry (2015) found that employers declared a greater predisposition toward candidates with EA experience, all other things being equal.

In contrast, a study commissioned by the Association of American Colleges & Universities (Hart Research Associates, 2015) compared the perceptions of employers with those of college students regarding the most important learning outcomes and attributes for graduates, and whether they had been achieved. While 78% of employers agreed that irrespective of field all college graduates should have intercultural skills and an understanding of societies and countries outside the United States, 87% of students answered positively to this question. However, only 51% of employers stated that they were more likely to consider hiring recent college graduates who had studied abroad, in contrast to the 71% of students who considered studying abroad of value. As in Europe, the rhetoric of U.S. employers is not always evident in actual hiring practices.

Recently, IIE (Farrugia & Sanger, 2017) investigated the impact of EA on the development of skills that contribute to employment and career development. The key findings suggest that EA has an overall positive impact on the development of a wide range of twenty-first-century job skills, expands career possibilities, and has a long-term impact on career progression and promotion through skills gained. Moreover, EA impacts subsequent job offers and the development of most skills when the time abroad is of a longer duration, while short-term programs are most effective at developing teamwork skills. For science, technology, engineering, and mathematics (STEM) majors, EA allows students to gain highly valued skills outside of their majors; EA in a less familiar destination was positively associated with skill development and sense of career impact. In highly structured programs, student intentionality also contributed to skill development. This study, albeit based on student self-reports, suggests that EA participation, at least in the United States, can give students an employment edge in their careers.

Although not without contradictions and its own methodological consideration, the emerging research suggests a clear and compelling connection between EA participation and employability. The literature is consistent in finding that EA programming provides a unique and potentially transformative context to foster a mind-set and skill set students need to be successful in the global economy of today. The experience abroad potentially adds value to students' overall education and development by enabling them to acquire personal and professional qualities and competencies beyond what they can achieve in the classroom at home. For their part, employers express support for EA, but in practice do not always give priority to graduates with EA experience. This mixed message from employers may be attributable to the fact that students are not always able to articulate effectively what they learned abroad, nor the applicability of this learning to the professional workplace. To demonstrate convincingly the potential that EA participation has for career readiness and employability is no easy task (Mestenhauser, 2011). As discussed next, IEs, along with their colleagues in career (advisory) units, can play a critical role by advocating for the value EA adds to career readiness.

The Evolving Role of IEs: Stewards of International Education and Career Readiness Guides

An increasing body of knowledge and practice attests to international education being multifaceted, multidimensional, interdisciplinary, and global (Mestenhauser, 2011). Success is dependent on ongoing engagement of an array of stakeholders across institutions, sectors, and geographies with an approach toward development for the future (Ellingboe, 1996). Growth in international education has increased the complexity of the environments in which IEs operate and, as a consequence, expanded the scope of their work. In recognition of this development, international education organizations are paying ever more attention to the professional development of their members and establishing benchmarks for these. Thus, NAFSA has published a taxonomy of IE professional competencies (NAFSA, 2015) as well as a hiring guide for managers, the Association of International Education Administrators (AIEA) has established professional standards for IE leaders (AIEA, n.d.), and EAIA has begun to issue publications aimed at particular specialists within IE. The categories of competencies NAFSA has identified align with major areas of specialization within IE (comprehensive internationalization, EA, international enrollment management, international student and scholar services) and also indicate a need for cross-cutting competencies (NAFSA, 2015). Further, an IE may work in a one-person EA office, be a faculty member focused on teaching in the field of international education, or serve as a senior administrator in charge of a large multitasked unit.

Independent of environmental and contextual changes, the unequivocally constant and overarching function of the IE is that of steward of international education, who, as trusted adviser, teacher, and/or cocurricular designer, facilitates the advancement of student learning and development. To be effective, the IE must simultaneously engage with stakeholders of practice in curricular and cocurricular ways across the educational continuum, exemplified by career coaches, recruiters, student affairs counselors, faculty peers, alumni, and other community and board professionals. The need for such engagement is most pronounced in small IE offices with limited staffing. IEs in such cases must be able to refer students to colleagues outside their offices for support.

IEs as Lifelong Learners and EA Career Readiness Guides

IEs are central to advancing student development along the educational continuum, and to leveraging EA to enhance students' career readiness and lifelong learning. To successfully execute their roles as stewards of student learning that boosts graduates' employability, IEs must possess the ability to continuously learn and adapt in their shifting work roles. Just as students are supported to develop lifelong learning skills and become more flexible, adaptable, and globally minded employees, so too must IEs, as stewards of international education, attend to their own professional lifelong learning. Further, they must play an active role in helping their institutions and their faculty and staff colleagues continue to learn, evolve, and sustain EA's relevancy and value into the future. Therefore, continuous (lifelong) learning skills must be acquired not only by students but also the IE in order to remain relevant and effective. Thus, while students will emerge with a different consciousness about their EA experience, and likely struggle to articulate those experiences, IEs need to comprehend the broader needs of the labor market to ensure competitive, intelligent, and more globally minded graduates for the workforce of the future. Consequently, IEs, particularly those in professional schools, increasingly are engaging employers to move the understanding of EA from educational tourism to academic and experiential rigor. Methods include engaging employers in program design; visiting organizations abroad; and using live-case projects, virtual teaming and problem-solving, and reflection and goal setting (Gardner, Gross, & Steglitz, 2008). Also receiving attention are intercultural competence development and strategic design (Deardorff, 2008), and career-building skills.

IEs must reach out to other campus stakeholders, in career and employability centers, for example, or to recruiters and potential employers, to engage in discussions about what competencies are needed in future graduates and how EA can be leveraged to enhance and develop those competencies. IEs must support career services professionals to integrate EA into their processes, such as by résumé-writing classes and when teaching interviewing skills. Students can be taught to analyze EA through storytelling and to demonstrate competencies on résumés to help employers understand their international experience. In other instances, online coursework with integrated strategies, including reflection and goal setting, helps a students maximize the impact of learning and doing while abroad for a full semester (Paige, Cohen, Kappler, Chi, & Lassegard, 2009). IEs can work with students virtually to enhance awareness of what they are experiencing while abroad, provide opportunity to reflect and communicate about it, and help them articulate EA's value.

The development and cultivation of academic, career, and/or alumni office partnerships to enhance student development and advance institutional goals (Tillman, 2012) requires intentionality. IEs must be cognizant of and acknowledge the entire educational continuum within which they work to engage those along the continuum and to recognize interrelationships and patterns of change (Senge, 1990). Moreover, an increasing number of IEs are convening employers and alumni, often for recruitment purposes or during predeparture orientations or coursework, in order to share myriad stakeholder viewpoints about the value of EA and to clarify the importance of career and skills-based goals in advance of going abroad. Additionally, employers illustrate opportunities to reflect and adapt at the time of experience, in order to strengthen the ability for students to articulate their experiences upon return. Accordingly, IEs are fundamental to the development of access—for students to be exposed to organizational cultures of employers, whether through panel discussions, consulting, or internship opportunities, and for employers to become more knowledgeable partners during the process.

EA and Employability: Challenges for IE

A number of challenges exist for IEs as they navigate and articulate student perceptions of EA's value for employability, discrepancies between employer claims about this value, and actual employer hiring processes. Moreover, IEs are becoming integral to fund-raising as they seek financial support for EA and communicate metrics associated with career readiness and the needs of employers for the future workforce.

Student Perceptions

IEs recognize that when EA is not intentionally integrated into curricular and cocurricular initiatives for students, such as academic advising and career services, fewer students are compelled to participate. Moreover, students may perceive EA as difficult to pursue or even a barrier if coursework does not yield academic credit toward graduation. Student time, interests, and motivation for participating also vary significantly, from choosing programs based on location or because of family connections, to professional development goals or other reasons. With competing demands on students' time, without credit or integration of content or purpose with all other things they must do, student participation and often their understanding or opportunity to learn may be inhibited. In the face of these challenges, IEs must negotiate curricular and cocurricular integration and design impact interventions that maximize the EA experience (Paige et al., 2009). They may coordinate with other student development initiatives and/or serve as intercultural coaches for students and the student services staff who support them (Deardorff, 2008). The more easily staff and faculty can present EA and intercultural learning to students as enhancing employability and development along the educational continuum, the more students will be predisposed to participate and realize EA's value.

Employer Perceptions

Another challenge for IEs is the variance between the skills that employers declare they value, and the value they actually place on the impact of EA when hiring. This variance is demonstrated by survey results highlighting the disconnect between what employers express as their preference and the stark reality of their hiring practices or intentions (Hart Research Associates, 2015; Van Mol, 2017). The discourse on career integration, EA participation, and EA's learning outcomes as valuable for career readiness and employability has emerged in most international education conference agendas, including NAFSA, AIEA, EAIE, The Forum on Education Abroad, and IIE's Generation Abroad initiative. However, a broader strategic challenge is to ascertain how IEs can better influence employer practice in support of EA, and its alignment with broader talent development goals. While the previously discussed 2011 QS Global Employer Survey demonstrates strong support for international experience among CEOs, responses by human resource professionals are less strong (Molony et al., 2011). These data support anecdotal reports that recruiters focus solely on functional areas, such as business, engineering, and medicine, while international education cuts across sectors. IEs have an opportunity to convene recruiters who are instrumental in hiring practices but who do not necessarily seek direct international experience or the global or intercultural skill sets that CEOs and other experienced leaders acknowledge are necessary. Currently, career counselors and IEs work with students to assist them to discuss, in interviews and in cover letters, the ways in which EA has developed them for the positions for which they are applying. Yet the challenge remains as to how to better influence recruiter engagement and process, in order to realize the nature and value of EA.

Fund-Raising

As higher education institutions look to external funding to support their educational initiatives, so too can IEs become fund-raisers. More IEs are writing grant proposals for government and private foundations to support EA, especially its integration into curricular and cocurricular initiatives. Funds help support intercultural and global learning for students, and faculty and staff mobility and development. Thus, IEs are submitting proposals to the popular Erasmus and Erasmus+ initiatives in Europe and the New Colombo Plan in Australia, while there are opportunities in professional schools across the world to connect to corporate and individual donors. A recent BBC article heralded *cultural intelligence*, defined as a capability that can improve one's ability to function successfully across cultural contexts, as "the hidden talent that determines success" (Robson, 2017). IEs need to continuously link EA to institutional priorities. Doing so can help ensure that when their institutions undertake bold, strategic development campaigns, EA scholarships are incorporated as the vehicle and evidence for the institutions' ability to develop global-ready students.

Conclusion

As the internationalization of higher education continues to increase rapidly, higher education leaders, government officials, and employers are recognizing EA, more than ever before, as an important vehicle for future talent development in a fast-changing global economy. Research findings suggest that EA positively impacts students' (lifelong) learning and personal growth. Evidence is also emerging for a strong connection between EA participation and the development of key competencies and skills that have demonstrated value for career readiness, employability, and long-term professional development.

This chapter has highlighted that critical to the understanding and advancement of the convergence of EA and career employability are IEs and their complex and evolving roles as stewards of international education. While helping students learn and develop from EA, IEs need to interact with myriad stakeholders to collectively shape students' abilities to effectively navigate unfamiliar sociocultural contexts and adapt to new, ambiguous situations, both of which are critical for today's global workforce. In fact, IEs must themselves employ the lifelong learning competencies that EA seeks to instill in students, namely flexibility, adaptability, and (cultural) agility. As such, students and IEs are two sides of the same coin, distinct yet one; subject to similar forces, necessary and valuable.

References

Association of International Education Administrators (AIEA). (n.d.). *Standards of professional practice for international education leaders and senior international officers.* Available from http://www.aieaworld.org/standards-of-professional-practice

Australian Global Alumni. (2017). *New Colombo Plan.* Available from https://globalalumni.gov.au/NewColomboPlan/Home.aspx

Crossman, J. (2010). "Act them into a new way of thinking": Multiple stakeholder perspectives on developing international and cultural leadership (ICL) through experiential learning. *International Journal of Management Leadership*, *9*, 33–42.

Crossman, J. E., & Clarke, M. (2009). International experience and graduate employability: Stakeholder perceptions on the connection. *Higher Education*, *59*(5), 599–613.

Dany, F. (2003). "Free actors" and organizations: Critical remarks about the new career literature, based on French insights. *International Journal of Human Resource Management, 14*(5), 821–838.

Deardorff, D. K. (2008). Intercultural competence: A definition, model and implications for education abroad. In V. Savicki (Ed.), *Developing intercultural competence and transformation: Theory, research, and application* (pp. 32–52). Sterling, VA: Stylus.

Deardorff, D. K. (2015). *Demystifying outcomes assessment for international educators: A practical approach.* Sterling, VA: Stylus.

Ellingboe, B. J. (1996). *Divisional strategies on internationalizing the curriculum: A comparative, five-college case study of deans' and faculty perspectives at the University of Minnesota* (Master's thesis). University of Minnesota, Minneapolis, MN.

Erasmus Impact Study. (2016). *Effects of mobility on the skills and employability of students and the internationalization of higher education institutions.* Luxembourg: Publication Office of the European Commission. Available from http://ec.europa.eu/dgs/education_culture/repository/education/library/study/2016/erasmus-impact_en.pdf

Farrugia, C., & Sanger, J. (2017). *Gaining an employer edge: The impact of study abroad on 21st century skills & career prospects.* New York, NY: Institute of International Education.

Gardner, P., Gross, L., & Steglitz, I. (2008). Unpacking your study abroad experience: Critical reflection for workplace competencies. *Collegiate Employment Research Institute Research Brief, 1,* 1–11.

Hammer, M. R., Bennett, M. J., & Wiseman, R. (2003). Measuring intercultural sensitivity: The Intercultural Development Inventory. *International Journal of Intercultural Relations, 27*(4), 421–443.

Harder, A., Andenoro, A., Robers, T. G., Stedman, N., & Newberry M. P. III, (2015). Does study abroad increase employability? *NACTA Journal, 59*(1), 41–48.

Hart Research Associates. (2015). *Falling short? College learning and career success.* Washington, DC: Author.

Mestenhauser, J. (2011). *Reflections on the past, present, and future of internationalizing higher education: Discovering opportunities to meet challenges.* Minneapolis: Global Programs and Strategy Alliance, University of Minnesota.

Molony, J., Sowter, B., & Potts, D. (2011). QS Global Employer Survey. London, UK: QS Intelligence Unit.

Morrison, R. F., & Hall, D. T. (2002). Career adaptability. In D. T. Hall (Ed.), *Careers in and out of organizations* (pp. 205–233). Thousand Oaks, CA: SAGE.

National Association of College and Employers (NACE). (2018). *Career readiness defined.* Available from http://www.naceweb.org/career-readiness/competencies/career-readiness-defined/

NAFSA: Association of International Educators. (2015). *NAFSA international education professional competencies.* Washington, DC: Author.

Norris, E. M., & Gillespie, J. (2008). How study abroad shapes global careers: Evidence from the United States. *Journal of Studies in International Education, 13*(3), 382–397.

Organisation for Economic Co-operation and Development (OECD). (2017). *Education at a glance 2017: OECD indicators.* Paris, France: OECD Publishing.

Paige, R. M., Cohen, A. D., Kappler, B., Chi, J. C., & Lassegard, J. P. (2009). *Maximizing study abroad: A student's guide to strategies for language and culture learning and use* (2nd ed.). Minneapolis: Center for Advanced Research on Language Acquisition, University of Minnesota.

Pang, M., Chua, B. L., & Chu, C. (2008). Learning to stay ahead in an uncertain environment. *International Journal of Human Resource Management, 19*(7), 1383–1394.

Potts, D. (2015). Understanding the early career benefits of learning abroad programs. *Journal of Studies in International Education, 19*(5), 441–459.

Preston, K. (2012). *Recent graduates survey.* IES Abroad. Available from https://www.iesabroad.org/system/files/resources/recentgraduatessurvey_0.pdf

Robson, D. (2017, October 13). The "hidden talent" that determines success. *BBC.* Available from http://www.bbc.com/capital/story/20171013-the-hidden-talent -that-determines-success

Savicki, V. (2008). *Developing intercultural competence and transformation: Theory, research, and application in international education.* Sterling, VA: Stylus.

Savicki, V., & Brewer, E. (2015). *Assessing study abroad: Theory, tools, and practice.* Sterling, VA: Stylus.

Selby, K. M. (2014). Study abroad storytelling for interviews. In C. Anderson, J. Christian, K. Hindbjorgen, C. Jambor-Smith, M. Johnson, & M. Woolf (Eds.), *Career integration: Reviewing the impact of experience abroad on employment* (Vol, 1, pp. 75–83). Minneapolis, MN: University of Minnesota Learning Abraod Center.

Senge, P. M. (1990). *The fifth discipline: The art and practice of the learning organization.* London, UK: Random House.

Shaftel, J., Shaftel, T., & Ahluwalia, R. (2007). International education experience and intercultural competence. *Journal of Business & Economics, 6*(1), 25–34.

Tillman, M. (2012). Employer perspective on international education. In D. K. Deardorff, H. De Wit, J. D. Heyl, & T. Adams (Eds.), *The SAGE handbook of international higher education* (pp. 191–206). Thousand Oaks, CA: SAGE.

University Grants Committee (UGC). (2010, December). *Aspirations for the higher education system in Hong Kong: Report of the University Grants Committee.* Hong Kong: Author.

Van Mol, C. (2017). Do employers value international study and internships? A comparative analysis of 31 countries. *Geoforum, 78,* 52–60.

Watts, A. G. (2000). The new career and public policy. In A. Collin & R. A. Young (Eds.), *The future of career* (p. 259–275). Cambridge, UK: Cambridge University Press.

Wiers-Jenssen, J. (2008). Does higher education attained abroad lead to international jobs? *Journal of Studies in International Education, 12*(2), 101–130.

12

FACULTY ROLES IN ADVANCING STUDENT LEARNING ABROAD

Joan Gillespie

Acampus gives priority to internationalization through such measures as its strategic plan, hiring criteria for faculty and administrators, allocation of resources, recruiting and services for international students, and advising and support for education abroad students. Faculty play a central role in the planning of these campus-wide efforts to internationalize, as they coincide with traditional faculty roles of teaching, research, and service to the campus community (Childress, 2010). However, the intersection of internationalization initiatives with faculty roles cannot be left to accident; it requires a structure.

The structure is framed around the common definition of *internationalization*: "integrating an international, intercultural, or global dimension into the purpose, functions, and delivery of higher education" (Knight, 2004, p. 11). Within this frame, unique campus culture is supported by the complex fabric of institutional mission; student, faculty, and staff demographics; teaching practice; governance and policy-making; and variables in the local environment (Hudzik, 2015). Horizontal lines connect faculty, staff, and students; vertical lines organize departments and offices; and diagonal lines link departments in multidisciplinary studies, creating and sustaining an academic environment of inquiry and exploration in a global context.

This chapter focuses on the central role of faculty in advancing student learning abroad, first by contributing to the internationalization of the curriculum, and second by directing the curriculum toward the integration of education abroad into teaching and learning on campus (and, for some, into teaching students abroad). Teaching complements research, advising, and other faculty service to the campus. A community of practice creates a forum for faculty and staff to develop pedagogy, assessment methods, and advising strategies that advance the campus commitment to education abroad. This advocacy leads to a point where the roles of teaching, research, and service converge as interdependent activities. However, for practical organizational purposes, in this chapter each role is addressed separately.

Faculty as Teachers

Faculty make the greatest potential contribution as teachers, integrating education abroad into the undergraduate experience. All faculty can claim space for themselves and their disciplines in shaping academic experiences that promote a campus mission. Further, facilitating global learning cannot be the purview of a single department, multidisciplinary major, or office.

Association of American Colleges & Universities Global Learning VALUE Rubric

The Global Learning Valid Assessment of Learning in Undergraduate Education (VALUE) Rubric is one of a number of Association of American Colleges & Universities (AAC&U) rubrics relevant to the education continuum that were created by faculty for faculty. Others are civic engagement (local and global), integrative and applied learning, and intercultural knowledge and competence. While all four present opportunities to foster connections between education abroad and the campus teaching and learning, in this analysis, the Global Learning VALUE Rubric is most helpful. The AAC&U (2014) rubric defines *global learning* as

> a critical analysis of and engagement with complex, interdependent global systems and legacies (such as natural, physical, social, cultural, economic, and political) and their implications for people's lives and the earth's sustainability. Through global learning, students should (1) become informed, open-minded, and responsible people who are attentive to diversity across the spectrum of differences, (2) seek to understand how their actions affect both local and global communities, and (3) address the world's most pressing and enduring issues collaboratively and equitably.

Further, the global learning VALUE rubric describes six categories in which curriculum and cocurriculum intersect: global self-awareness, perspective taking, cultural diversity, personal and social responsibility, global systems, and knowledge application. Learning in each category progresses in four stages, from novice to capstone. By focusing attention on what defines a *global learner* at each stage in terms of knowledge, skills, and action, and providing assessment measures, the rubric invites a campus community to design curricular and cocurricular experiences directed toward the stages of learning in each category (Hovland, 2014).

A plan based on this rubric implicates faculty in all stages of developing global learners. It establishes that a single offering, such as education abroad, is not simply a box to check off but is one of many educational experiences during the undergraduate years. "Factors that impact study abroad outcomes (sojourner, host culture, program design)" are part of a trajectory of experiences that begin on campus and expose students to cultural differences (Twombly, Salisbury, Tumanut, & Klute, 2012, p. 44). Many of these experiences can take place on campus or in the local community. Thus, some advocate that domestic off-campus study has potential for global learning as powerful as an international experience; such study "also expand[s] students' horizons, their knowledge of global issues and processes, their familiarity and experience with cultural diversity, their intercultural skills, and their sense of citizenship" (Sobania, 2015, p. 16). Faculty for whom the community represents new territory for teaching and learning are advised to look for campus allies among "constituencies that increasingly have initiatives focused on diversity, multi-culturalism, community-based learning . . . [to] build stronger partnerships across what are too often seen as institutional boundaries" (Sobania, 2015, p. 31).

Internationalizing the curriculum through curricular design and course content is an obvious priority in a global learning agenda (Childress, 2010; Hudzik, 2015). Many existing courses can accommodate global learning objectives. The strategy of backward design with discipline-specific outcomes can be applied, using the end point of the course—the knowledge that students will have gained and be able to demonstrate—as the starting point for the "selection of materials, learning activities, and pedagogies" (Bronstein, Jones, & Neuwirth, 2014, p. 17). As relevant, materials might require students to examine their own social and cultural assumptions and biases and begin to consider different cultural and non-Western perspectives.

Experiential and Transformative Learning Pedagogies

Pedagogical choices also can begin to prepare students to process information in new ways and learn in an unfamiliar context such as that presented by education abroad. The faculty role of teacher expands beyond being an expert in a particular subject to contributing to a student's identity formation as a learner. This identity is self-directed and self-aware, with the cognitive and emotional skills required to critique and reflect on observations and experiences that disrupt a previous line of thought.

Three pedagogies intersect as strategies that are learner centered and relevant to the educational continuum: experiential learning, transformative learning, and intercultural learning. Each theory asks faculty to give students control of their learning while guiding them in meaning-making and requires a great effort from students to assume that control, in spite of challenging encounters with different worldviews and identities. Including one of these practices or a combination of them in an on-campus course benefits all students, regardless of their learning style and intent to study abroad. Students who do plan to study abroad will benefit while abroad from having become practiced in reading the environment and its cultural cues and processing their intellectual and emotional responses.

A large bibliography exists on each one of these theories and its application to study abroad. The following discussion briefly introduces each theory and examples of practice on-campus.

Experiential Learning

David Kolb's seminal work on the demanding cycle of experiential learning was based on theories of the role of experience in human learning (Passarelli & Kolb, 2012). Among the prominent thinkers were John Dewey, who described learning "as a process, not . . . outcomes," and Jean Piaget, who saw learning "result from synergetic transactions between the person and the environment" (as cited in Passarelli & Kolb, 2012, p. 139). Kolb's expansion on previous theories defined *learning* as "the process whereby knowledge is created through the transformation of experience" (Passarelli & Kolb, 2012, p. 139). Experiential learning theory identifies four learning modes: thinking (abstract conceptualization), experiencing (concrete experience), reflecting (reflective observation), and acting (active experimentation) (Passarelli & Kolb, 2012). Learners generally prefer one mode for taking in information and one mode for analyzing and acting on that information. Situations may demand flexibility in switching modes in order for learning to occur, a transition premised on the learner's awareness of their preferred learning style and other possible styles.

Faculty become experiential educators in part by seeing their environment as a rich opportunity for teaching innovation and students' self-directed learning. Kolb identifies four distinctions of the experiential educator's philosophy: "Educating is a relationship . . . [that] honor[s] students as complex, relational beings. . . . Educating is holistic . . . , facilitating integrated development in affective, perceptual, cognitive, and behavioral realms. . . . Educating is learner-oriented. . . . Educating is learner-centered" (Passarelli & Kolb,

2012, pp. 149–150). A learner-oriented approach reflects the emphasis on the process "of inquiry, critical thinking, and . . . creation of values" (Passarelli & Kolb, 2012, p. 150). A learner-centered approach takes into account the learner's background and previous knowledge and how these will contribute to new experiences in the course. The pedagogy of experiential learning asks faculty to see their students in what may be a new or different way.

The high level of uncertainty with this pedagogy, given the emphasis on process, not outcomes, implies risk taking for both faculty and students. One strategy to mitigate student anxiety is to start small and design a learning activity that encompasses all learning modes, for example, a group field excursion, be it to a museum exhibit, meeting of a community organization, or city park, with a guide or an interpreter. In preparation, faculty might ask students what they expect of this activity and what strengths or experiences they can offer the group. Prompts ask students to respond in writing to what they observe and hear, who they meet, and how that information ties to their course reading. Further assignments that give students ownership of their learning can extend to an independent small-group excursion and, eventually, to an individual self-guided excursion with a written reflection or creative response.

Transformative Learning

Another pedagogy that begins to prepare students to engage new ideas, cultural and social norms, and value systems is transformative learning. Its seismographic shifts in the understanding of a particular issue lead to a wholly new perspective on oneself and the world that shapes subsequent experiences (Mezirow, 1991). The markers of disorientation, dissonance, uncertainty, and questioning one's assumptions may be prompted by encounters with those who hold divergent views or introduce students to a different reality, whether those encounters be with a person, a place, or an imagined world of fiction or cinema. Recognizing these markers is essential for faculty who adopt this pedagogy.

> When transformational disorientation strikes and the cascade effect begins [evaluation of the dilemma, exploration, and recalibration], one task of the facilitator is to help students sort out what aspects of the self are still intact and which are open to evolution. (Fuller, 2015, pp. 67–68)

Faculty who adopt the methods of transformative learning not only plan the initial stages that push students beyond their received and untested knowledge but also create an intermediate stage for them to explore and test other options, that is, other ways of thinking and being. Debriefing with students about an encounter succeeds if the classroom is recognized as a safe space and trust exists among the teacher and students. A challenge of debriefing is that students may consider the discussion prompts as probes into their private thoughts or personal lives. Depending on the student group dynamic, an intermediate stage for a less public debriefing gives students creative options through writing, photography, or movement to explore their responses.

As detailed in chapter 9 in this volume, reflection exercises paired with instructor feedback are central to student learning, particularly with pedagogies that ask students to construct knowledge via their direct interaction with the environment. Reflection invites students to use first-person narrative to explore their cognitive and emotional response to an event or experience. This is completely different from a straight academic exercise in which the writer's persona and feelings have no place. However, critical inquiry is key to reflection; written reflection must be purposeful and thoughtful to round out the learning cycle. Prompts that direct the student to answer "why" and "how" as well as the details of "who, what, where" may succeed in eliciting a nuanced perspective that offers a starting place for the next reflection exercise.

Intercultural Learning

Another approach to preparing students for learning in a new environment introduces the vocabulary of intercultural learning and development. Because it addresses students' personal growth, intercultural learning may be the strategy that asks the most of faculty in setting learning objectives that use benchmarks such as respect for diverse backgrounds and perspectives, interrogation of one's own cultural identity, and openness. These benchmarks should also validate soft skills such as tolerance for ambiguity, respect for others, and flexibility. Colleagues who staff the office of international education or teach intercultural communication are resources for faculty exploring this pedagogy.

Facilitating intercultural development requires going beyond course delivery via experiential and transformative learning pedagogies. However, faculty seeking to expand their repertoire in this direction might begin with the milieu in which they are already comfortable: the academic culture. Cultural practices, economic and social disparities, historical moments, and political priorities that students are likely to question abroad are embedded in universities, beginning with the physical classroom, its layout and implied relationship between faculty and students. Pedagogical choices, the potential for interaction among students, course content and reading, and assessments all represent specific traditions of higher education. Disciplinary approaches likewise vary, depending on the intellectual tradition. Virtual classrooms enable faculty across time zones and national borders to share courses, students, and academic cultures. A virtual classroom does not require a high level of technology or know-how; open-source software allows students to post assignments to shared folders and create chat rooms. As a small experiment in cross-cultural connections, a virtual classroom creates a venue for conversation about cultural differences.

Some faculty partner one-on-one with colleagues overseas to create a shared course or connect their students in the discussion of a common topic. On a much larger scale, the Global Liberal Arts Alliance (GLAA), established in 2009 by the Great Lakes Colleges Association, facilitates partnerships between faculty whose institutions are GLAA members through an initiative called Global Course Connections (liberalartsalliance.org/programs-and-opportunities/global-course-connections/program-description). The collaboration offers an example of like-minded institutions, in this case, missions driven by the liberal arts, drawing mutual benefit from student and faculty interactions across the curriculum. The program's primary purpose is to add "an authentic international dimension" to courses, along with the opportunity for cross-cultural learning, because

> planned classroom interactions as well as the unplanned, informal exchanges that occur make a difference in how students think about parts of the world that are very different from their own and about which they know little. This can be especially powerful when it leads to insights that challenge student misperceptions. (GLAA, n.d.)

As this description makes clear, the aim is to give students experience with another culture. Simon Gray, GLAA director, explains that most learning activities are asynchronous because of time differences and academic calendars, but occasionally the course partners meet together, outside their regularly scheduled time, for a guest lecture. Small virtual groups offer the main opportunity for students to work together and serve as an important venue for cross-cultural learning. As part of their final assessment of the course, faculty look at evidence of cultural change and perception in their students (S. Gray, personal communication, January 23, 2018).

In the 2017–2018 academic year, 42 faculty created course connections in such fields as communications, dance-choreography, development economics, history, literature, math, migration studies, and French and German. Gray notes that faculty development has proved "very strong" in terms of learning to use course management software and understanding what liberal arts and disciplinary studies look like in another country, the demographics of student populations, cultural differences around concepts of a deadline, the etiquette of responding to e-mail, and communication with students (S. Gray, personal communication, January 23, 2018).

An institution might adapt the GLAA model to create its own list of partners, drawing on existing staff and faculty international connections. According to Gray, having a faculty liaison at each member college is key; the liaison puts out a call for interested faculty, who are then referred to GLAA, a structure that could be replicated. Another essential, replicable component, with funding, is a summer workshop at an international site. Teaching teams could convene to work through their objectives in pairing courses; resolve inconsistencies in content level; address logistical problems, particularly technological, and engage in their own cross-cultural learning at the hosting partner (S. Gray, personal communication, January 23, 2018). Or team members could convene on their own campuses, follow the same curriculum, and schedule check-ins with partners.

Case Studies in Pedagogy

These strategies can help faculty build their teaching portfolios. According to the Scholarship of Teaching and Learning (SoTL), instructors apply the same practice of critical inquiry that they have perfected in their discipline to their teaching practice and the evidence of student learning (Robinson, 2012). *Integrating Study Abroad Into the Curriculum: Theory and Practice Across the Disciplines* (Brewer & Cunningham, 2009) and *Putting the Local in Global Education: Models for Transformative Learning Through Domestic Off-Campus Programs* (Sobania, 2015) contain case studies of courses and pedagogy with ambitious learning objectives paired with thoughtful and creative strategies. One example that combines all three pedagogies discussed previously while also applying the principle of SoTL is Culture, Religion, Nationality, team taught by faculty in religion and anthropology at Kalamazoo College. Designed around the knowledge, attitudes, and skills needed to engage with another culture, the course uses experiential, transformative, and intercultural learning theories (Anderson & Cunningham, 2009). In field notebooks, students link readings, field notes from site visits, and personal reflection, with one reflection prompt explicitly asking students to discuss "learning related to study abroad (in hindsight [for juniors] or in anticipation [for sophomores])" (Anderson & Cunningham 2009, p. 68). An analysis of students' first and last reflective essays, according to levels of transformative learning, found that students fell into three groups along the learning continuum.

In response, the authors redesigned their course to move all students farther along the continuum by being explicit about the kinds of learning embedded in the course, including understanding of self. The authors also concluded that the course would be more successful in achieving its learning goals if offered as a sophomore seminar, in preparation for a semester of study abroad: "(a) students need to be taught how to learn experientially, and (b) they need a great deal of practice doing it before they become proficient experiential learners" (Anderson & Cunningham, 2009, p. 81).

Another example uses the model of community-based learning and acknowledges "the role of faculty . . . not only in using a teaching pedagogy, but also in developing and sustaining long-term, reciprocal relationships with community partners" (Castillo, Freer, Guillen, & Maeda, 2015, p. 288). Occidental College's Center for Community-Based Learning works with faculty to incorporate community-based learning into its courses. An example of a resulting course is the team-taught, multidisciplinary Living Los Angeles. Developed with community organizations in four neighborhoods, students study gentrification through academic readings, after which they conduct personal interviews with local residents and business owners. The lead instructor wrote, "The course challenged students to re-think what is considered to be 'good' and 'bad' . . . [and] enabled students to see national and global contexts that shape the city and its communities" (Castillo et al., 2015, p. 296).

Faculty as Researchers

Faculty expertise in conducting research in their discipline figures in the educational continuum as they apply it to their own projects and as they supervise students, in either independent or group projects. Undergraduate research, a high-impact practice, is built into the curriculum at some institutions as a capstone or senior project, with stepping-stones guiding students to successful completion. How research methods are taught varies by discipline and may include good practice in data collection, the ethics of human subject research, ethnographic fieldwork, archival work, or explorations in the arts. Some institutions offer students research opportunities during the summer to jump-start senior projects, with stipends to cover living expenses. Opportunities vary widely, from a science lab on campus to fieldwork or archival research at a domestic or international location, from close supervision in a group project to an independent study. In all these instances, faculty, to a greater or lesser extent, help structure students' research and their analysis and dissemination of findings.

Students who study abroad as juniors or in the first term of their fourth year may intend to collect data for a senior project. Early faculty involvement is key to helping to set student expectations for what might be accomplished abroad. Considerations include logistics, national laws governing research and the ethical review of human subjects research, equipment and technology, translators, and on-site support.

Some faculty may involve student teams in a research project, closely supervising them in a hands-on experience. The advantages to a student of working on such a team extend beyond the satisfaction of contributing to the findings of the project at hand. Enabling the student to pursue research at a high level, a faculty-led team offers an accurate picture of an academic life in certain disciplines. No matter whether the student enrolls in graduate studies, the student may be able to add a publication to a curriculum vitae. More importantly, participation in a research team develops skills that serve the student regardless of future field: organizing and managing a project, collaborating with team members, building an argument based on credible findings. With research across borders, the student tests abilities to work across cultures.

An option available to students and faculty at a campus that runs its own education abroad programs is to incorporate research supervised by either local faculty members or faculty from the home institution. In a program administered by Macalester, Pomona, and Swarthmore colleges at the University of Cape Town, South Africa, an independent research project, supervised locally, is required. William Moseley, professor of geography at Macalester who directed the program in 2006 and 2007, opted to involve students in his research. Having worked in development in Mali, first as a Peace Corps volunteer and later professionally, he wrote:

> For any student attempting research in a different culture, I knew that it was important for them to have the necessary time to learn about the history and culture of the place before they considered becoming involved in a research project. . . . The context of a study abroad program provides the necessary infrastructure for acculturation. (Moseley, 2009, p. 234)

Faculty also can facilitate opportunities for students to present their research from an off-campus program, advising them on professional conferences or cooperating with colleagues to organize a student symposium on campus. These events serve the important purpose of celebrating students' academic accomplishments and contributions to the field. Just as significant is the invitation to students to present their intercultural learning in an off-campus setting. Presentations can begin with the significance of the research question to the local population and the principles of ethical research that guided the collection of data. A discussion of the research process can follow, including strategies for collaborating with on-site research guides, adapting to field conditions, and working in a second or third language. An on-campus symposium might bring students together to discuss their research, share their experiences during formal and informal programming abroad, or discuss adjustment to their lives back on campus.

Faculty Service

Faculty can support the integration of learning abroad into the educational continuum through service to the campus community, such as advising students and working with administrative staff who impact internationalization. As participation in education abroad has increased, faculty involvement in students' decisions about their options has changed. The major reason is represented by the campus office of international education. In the past, this office may have existed in the person of a single faculty member, charged with managing a portfolio of education abroad programs in return for a course release. The professionalization of the field led to hiring full-time staff with knowledge of and experience in the field (Twombly et al., 2012). This introduced campus policies and processes that recognize and are responsive to the complexities of the enterprise of education abroad, including safety, security, and risk management. Additionally, professional staff may offer students more informed choices, given their familiarity with the institution's approved options, including consortial agreements, direct enrollment, student exchanges, and third-party providers.

Faculty remain critically involved in advising on campus-operated programs; reviewing third-party programs for approval for student enrollment; and, on some campuses, leading programs themselves. However, an unintended consequence of professionalization removed faculty on many campuses from advising students about program options. This change represents a loss of expertise to students and staff. Faculty have much to offer by coordinating efforts with offices of international education, global initiatives, and diversity and inclusion—the horizontal line of institutional structure that intersects with global learning objectives. Conversely, study abroad professionals are advised to build allies among faculty who might "support having an off-campus option or two that is more appropriate for majors in their disciplines whose focus is in the United States" yet can further the goals of global learning (Sobania, 2015, p. 30).

The Forum on Education Abroad's (2015) *Standards of Good Practice's* section titled "Student Selection, Preparation, and Advising" implies that faculty participate in these processes. The queries that expand on each standard can help institutions assess their practices in these areas as well as guide the external evaluation of an education abroad office or program. They include queries about academic preparation; predeparture training and on-site orientation around achieving program goals, including academic goals; and academic planning. Each of these queries presumes faculty engagement with students long before they meet with a staff adviser to discuss education abroad.

Faculty advisers can fill a gap for international office staff, particularly a bare-bones office on a small campus that has ambitions to develop program options. While international office staff may be better positioned to advise students about program options, faculty bring the advantage of familiarity with large numbers of students, some of whom may lack awareness of or information about education abroad, which is "a limitation to participation" (Twombly et al., 2012, p. 44). Students underrepresented in study abroad—men, athletes, racial minorities, students in science, technology, engineering, and mathematics (STEM) fields—would particularly benefit from an advising session with a faculty member that addresses education abroad. Faculty can articulate its value to the academic interests of a student who may not have considered it relevant to advance their education. On the strength of this new knowledge, the student may be encouraged to make an appointment with a staff adviser to learn more. Faculty who keep informed on education abroad options may identify a student as early as a first-year seminar as a possible candidate for a specialized program and begin conversations about an academic plan that includes the program. This early intervention may be particularly important in the sciences and social sciences that carry lockstep requirements in the major, but can also be helpful for students in the humanities who arrive on campus with a well-developed academic focus.

Faculty also help set student expectations about a term of education abroad and create conditions for student learning.

> Problematizing the experience of study abroad by raising questions about race, class, and gender or the concept of global citizenship comes into direct conflict with the need to package, present, and sell study abroad as a positive, life-changing adventure of discovery that will lead to intercultural competence and to positive career outcomes. (Twombly et al., 2012, pp. 102–103)

Articulating the challenges as well as the positive academic outcomes related to the educational continuum is the shared responsibility of faculty and staff advisers.

Finally, faculty in leadership roles may serve the larger goals of global learning by helping to plan and implement campus-wide efforts, including education abroad. Some may serve on strategic internationalization committees or committees that approve program options. While student learning will be the core focus, faculty serving on such committees will also support education abroad by attending to administrative issues, such as resource allocation, institutional partnership selection and management, risk assessment, and student health and welfare. Such service provides faculty with professional development opportunities, while also ensuring that education abroad is embedded into the educational continuum.

Faculty Development for Integrating Education Abroad Into Undergraduate Education

The American Council on Education's survey *Mapping Internationalization on U.S. Campuses* "indicates that internationalization continues to gain momentum among U.S. colleges and universities" with "improving student preparedness for a global era" (Helms, 2017, p. 5) the highest priority. According to the survey findings, the first priority of institutional activities for internationalization is increasing education abroad participation rates. However, faculty development is the fifth and last priority. Indeed, "for each type of on-campus faculty development opportunity included in the survey, not more than 30 percent of respondents indicated it is offered by their institutions" (p. 23), and "only slightly over one-fifth of respondents indicated that faculty development is among the institution's top three internationalization priorities" (p. 22). These findings "raise questions about the recognition of faculty as key drivers of internationalization" (p. 23). It is essential that faculty, who advance institutional goals related to education abroad in their roles as teachers and advisers, both have firsthand international perspectives and experiences and can share these with students to help them anticipate what they may encounter abroad.

Similarly, research conducted with 224 faculty at liberal arts colleges who have led domestic and international off-campus programs of 3.5 weeks to 15 weeks in duration found that 59% of respondents believed "to a great extent" that "global learning is a priority for my institution." However, only 22% believed "to a great extent" that "supporting faculty members who lead global programs is a priority for my institution" (Gillespie, Glasco, Gross, Jasinsksi, & Layne, forthcoming).

Faculty awards for international activity and international work include recognition in tenure decisions, and funding for conference attendance. However, according to the liberal arts faculty who were surveyed, and of relevance to this volume, the most important faculty development activities to them are leading students on an education abroad program (55% in 2015; 64% in 2016), studying or conducting research abroad (30% in 2011; 40% in 2016), and internationalizing courses (25% in 2011; 30% in 2016).

Faculty who lead domestic and international off-campus programs cite multiple benefits that accrue to the campus community:

- Faculty who understand the off-campus learning experience of students are better prepared to enable students to make the most of that experience through preparation and postprogram curricular and cocurricular activities.
- Faculty who embrace the pedagogies of experiential learning and transformative learning serve as role models for how—not what—to learn, contributing to students' development as lifelong learners.
- Faculty who are trained to lead off-campus programs not only affect the learning and development of students enrolled in their particular program but also apply what they learned by doing so to their teaching when they return to campus. Thus, they may build new course content, engage with local experts, and/or explore field sites.
- Faculty develop skills and confidence in other high-impact practices: mentoring student research, supporting community engagement, and conducting problem-based inquiry.
- Faculty appreciate the critical importance of students' personal development during their undergraduate years.
- Faculty are willing to support campus-wide internationalization initiatives outside the classroom, for example, by acting as hosts to international students and serving on dedicated committees (Gillespie et al., forthcoming).

The positive outcomes reported by liberal arts faculty represent significant campus investments in faculty-led off-campus programs, in terms of planning, preparation, training, on-site coordination, and program implementation. However, of the models in the spectrum of development opportunities, the faculty-led program carries one of the highest learning potentials.

The "Mapping Internationalization on U.S. Campuses" study found that the percentage of campuses offering workshops on internationalizing the curriculum decreased from 29% in 2011 to 26% in 2016, although workshops on global learning assessment saw modest growth from 11% in 2011 to 15% in 2016 (Helms, 2017). These two kinds of workshops likely took place on campus, sponsored perhaps by a center for teaching and learning or center for assessment. Here lies potential for specific faculty development opportunities designed to support student learning.

Conclusion

The contribution of faculty to an institutional mission of internationalization draws on their existing responsibilities of teaching, research, and service. While these roles are familiar, the perspective of the educational continuum may be new, as it asks faculty to engage with staff members across campus and with students in the larger context of their lives outside the classroom. The benefits of this engagement accrue to the campus community and to faculty themselves, who enlarge their pedagogical practice, connect with new colleagues, and potentially introduce opportunities to students who would not have sought them on their own. These benefits require an institutional investment in training, workshops, and other activities for faculty consistent with the campus structure of the educational continuum.

References

Anderson, C. S., & Cunningham, K. (2009). Culture, religion, and nationality: Developing ethnographic skills and reflective practices connected to study abroad. In E. Brewer & K. Cunningham (Eds.), *Integrating study abroad into the curriculum: Theory and practice across the disciplines* (pp. 63–84). Sterling, VA: Stylus.

Association of American Colleges & Universities (AAC&U). (2014). *Global Learning VALUE Rubric.* Available from www.aacu.org/resources/global-learning

Brewer, E., & Cunningham, K. (Eds.). (2009). *Integrating study abroad into the curriculum: Theory and practice across the disciplines.* Sterling, VA: Stylus.

Bronstein, M., Jones, S., & Neuwirth, S. (2014). Awakening global awareness in the humanities. *Diversity & Democracy: Civic Learning for Shared Futures, 17*(2), 16–18.

Castillo, C., Freer, R., Guillen, F., & Maeda, D. (2015). Faculty development and ownership of community-engaged teaching and learning. In N. Sobania (Ed.), *Putting the local in global education* (pp. 288–297). Sterling, VA: Stylus.

Childress, L. K. (2010). *The twenty-first century university: Developing faculty engagement in internationalization.* New York, NY: Peter Lang.

The Forum on Education Abroad. (2015). *Standards of good practice* (5th ed.). Carlisle, PA: Author. Available from https://forumea.org/resources/standards-of-good-practice/

Fuller, A. E. (2015). Where experience meets transformation: Pedagogy and study away. In N. Sobania (Ed.), *Putting the local in global education* (pp. 52–72). Sterling, VA: Stylus.

Gillespie, J., Glasco, S., Gross, D., Jasinski, L., & Layne, P. (forthcoming). Faculty matter: Faculty support and interventions integrated into global learning. In N. Namaste, A. Sturgill, M. Vande Berg, & N. Sobania (Eds.), *Mind the gap: Framing global learning in the university experience.* Sterling, VA: Stylus.

Global Liberal Arts Alliance (GLAA). (n.d.). *Program description.* Available from http://liberalartsalliance.org

Helms, R. M. (2017). *Mapping internationalization on U.S. campuses.* Washington, DC: ACE and Center for Internationalization and Global Engagement. Available from https://www.acenet.edu/news-room/Documents/Mapping-Internationalization-2017.pdf

Hovland, K. (2014). *Global learning: Defining, designing, demonstrating.* AAC&U & NAFSA: Association of International Educators. Available from www.nafsa.org/GlobalLearning; www.aacu.org/GlobalLearning

Hudzik, J. K. (2015). *Comprehensive internationalization: Institutional pathways to success.* Oxon, UK: Routledge.

Knight, J. (2004). Internationalization remodeled: Definitions, rationales, and approaches. *Journal of Studies in International Education, 8*(1), 5–31.

Mezirow, J. (1991). *Transformative dimensions in adult learning.* San Francisco, CA: Jossey-Bass.

Moseley, W. G. (2009). Making study abroad a win-win for pre-tenure faculty. *Frontiers: The Interdisciplinary Journal of Study Abroad, 18,* 231–240.

Passarelli, A. M., & Kolb, D. A. (2012). Using experiential learning theory to promote student learning and development in programs of education abroad. In M. Vande Berg, R. M. Paige, & K. H. Lou (Eds.), *Student learning abroad: What our students are learning, what they're not, and what we can do about it* (pp. 137–161). Sterling, VA: Stylus..

Robinson, J. M. (2012). Learning abroad and the scholarship of teaching and learning. In M. Vande Berg, R. M. Paige, & K. H. Lou (Eds.), *Student learning abroad: What our students are learning, what they're not, and what we can do about it* (pp. 239–257). Sterling, VA: Stylus.

Sobania, N. (2015). The faraway nearby: Putting the local in global education. In N. Sobania (Ed.), *Putting the local in global education* (pp. 16–35). Sterling, VA: Stylus.

Twombly, S. B., Salisbury, M. H., Tumanut, S. D., & Klute, P. (2012). Study abroad in a new global century—renewing the promise, refining the purpose. *ASHE Higher Education Report, 38*(4), 1–152.

13

LOCAL PARTNERS AS TEACHERS AND LEARNERS IN EDUCATION ABROAD

Introducing a Local Partner Engagement Process Model

Julie M. Ficarra

This volume argues that education abroad research often focuses on U.S. students' experiences abroad, disconnected from how that experience fits into their broader education, before they go abroad and after they return to their home campus. It calls on U.S. home institutions and local partners abroad to help ensure that education abroad is firmly connected to students' other educational experiences. However, before partners can be asked to assist in that effort, it is crucial to recognize *their* role in education abroad, both as teachers and as learners. These roles are often overlooked in education abroad programming despite pervasive discourse within the professional community of the value of bilateral relations for promoting intercultural learning and exchange. Yet they play crucial roles in the education of U.S. students and are greatly impacted, in a variety of ways, by the presence of those students. Unfortunately, the evaluation of education abroad usually takes the form of assessing fluctuations in student enrollment or tallying the number of new partners or programs developed each year. Student-level evaluations often ask students to self-report their satisfaction with a number of program elements (e.g., orientation, housing, food, and excursions), as well as, increasingly, their academic and cultural learning.

This chapter, therefore, invites readers to pivot back toward the in-country experience to explore how local partners are embedded within education abroad programming, both as teachers and as learners. This chapter begins by defining *local partners* and provides some context for that choice of term. Because the vast majority of the research on community impact in education abroad focuses on service-learning programs, the chapter briefly reviews two recent local community impact studies to provide some context for how community impact is currently defined and studied. The chapter then argues that the ways that community impact is currently framed, primarily in terms of outcomes, is limited. It then introduces an alternative organizational framework, the local partner engagement process model, for seeing community impact in a different way, one that goes beyond local partners' perceived *outcomes* to a *process* within which local partners exercise agency as both teachers and learners. To illustrate the utility of the model, data from a third study conducted by the author is introduced and analyzed through the lens of the model. This study does not focus on service-learning, but rather a broader and more traditional (nonservice-learning-focused) education abroad context. The local partner engagement process model as an organizational framework for reading the data illustrates the ways that many current community impact studies, by focusing on particular types of "impact" (economic, material, political, cultural), are incomplete. Instead, it advocates for taking a more holistic, process model approach to understanding the experiences of local partners' engagement with U.S. students, from their motivation to engage with visiting students to how they make meaning of these experiences for themselves and their communities. Finally, the chapter ends with a call to action for finding ways to engage more intentionally with the experiences and perspectives of local partners within the education continuum.

Who's Who? Defining *Local Partners*

The overall lack of engagement with the nonstudent side of the education abroad equation has resulted in a proliferation of terms to describe those overseas who contribute in some way to students' education abroad experiences. *On-site partner, provider, overseas partner, local partner, host community,* or *host community member* are sometimes used interchangeably. The term *host community* can itself be problematic—first because it insinuates something monolithic and unchanging. It may also oversimplify the ways in which we all are always part of several communities at once (Andreotti, 2007). Distinguishing between "the" host community monolith and host community "members" can be helpful. However, an important distinction within host community members that is rarely, if ever, discussed is that of *intentional* and *unintentional* hosts. Intentional hosts are partners who intentionally choose to engage with visiting students: local professors teaching visiting students, local university or educational organization administrators, or local families hosting visiting students. Unintentional hosts, by contrast, are those who encounter U.S. students by way of proximity but may not specifically choose to actively engage with them. Engagement is, at least in theory, mutually intentional, whereas an encounter suggests two or more parties interacting with each other, but not necessarily with the same mutual intentionality as engagement. As Larsen (2016) points out, many times research on host communities "work[s] from the assumption that individuals working in partner (NGO) organizations, as well as third-party International Service Learning providers *are* the community" (p. 11). The intentional/unintentional host community-member distinction helps to clarify that difference.

While unintentional hosts, such as local business owners or neighbors, may very well play an educative role in U.S. students' time abroad, and certainly make meaning of their encounters with U.S. students, intentional hosts play a much more active role as teachers and learners within the education abroad context. More commonly used terms for intentional hosts are *overseas providers* or *overseas partners*. The former implies an intermediary person or organization that acts as a link among a U.S. institution, its students, and local communities, whereas *overseas partners* implies a more direct connection. As the field of education abroad continues to unpack and complicate these terms, this chapter uses the term *local partners* to mean individual, intentional, host community members whose engagement with visiting U.S. students is facilitated by their association with a local education provider organization or university. Using the term *local partners* as opposed to *overseas partners* helps to decenter the United States as the frame of reference to which the local partner is always "overseas."

Current Local Impact Research in Education Abroad Limited to International Service-Learning

The ways that locals engage with visitors has been a subject of study in the disciplines of anthropology, sociology, and tourism studies for many years. U.S.-based *service-learning and community engagement*, which can be defined as "a form of experiential education in which students engage in activities that address human and community needs together with structured opportunities for reflection designed to achieve desired learning outcomes" (Jacoby & Associates, 1996, p. 5), has been a site of largely student-focused, scholarly research. Only relatively recently has local partner impact been a focus of study within service-learning literature (Blouin & Perry, 2009; Caldwell & Purtzer, 2015; d'Arlach, Sanchez, & Feuer, 2009; Friedman et al., 2016; Reynolds, 2014; Toms Smedley, 2016; Worrall, 2007).

While this is a growing area of interest within international service-learning, it has been virtually ignored within more traditional (nonservice-focused) education abroad research. This has the potential to create a paradigm in which there is a false impression that visiting students are only "impacting" those they choose to impact through service. Surely students studying abroad on traditional education abroad programs, which lack service or intensive community engagement, are also having community impacts.

Because local impact research is currently taking place primarily within international service-learning research, it is important to first understand what some of that research looks like and how the somewhat narrow construction of community impact specifically within service-learning is limited. Particularly if we are interested in gauging how local partners engage with the process of education abroad both as teachers and as learners, we need to think more broadly about community impact as process.

Community Impact as Process: Local Partner Engagement Process Model: Costa Rica Case Study

The lack of local partner (host community) impact research in traditional education abroad contexts was a starting point for a study that resulted in the development of the local partner engagement process model presented here. For the purposes of the study, traditional education abroad contexts refer to programs that are based at a local university or educational institution and that revolve around classroom-based, nonservice-orientated, academic learning facilitated primarily by local instructors. Although research on local partner impact within international service-learning may not be generalizable across education abroad program types, it and the model presented here suggest some ways forward.

Much of the current research on local impact in international programs focuses on partners' *impressions* of students and programs, and *outcomes* of their experience as a partner. What seems to be underexplored is the *process* of engagement from the perspective of local partners—the methods they use when interacting with visiting students, and how this fits into a more holistic understanding of the local partner experience. Further, if we are interested in questions of reciprocity and mutuality, we first need to know more about how local partners make meaning of their engagement with visiting students. This is something that does not often appear in the current literature in this area.

When the "end goal" is to better understand local perspectives of education abroad programs for the purposes of improving them and increasing reciprocity, there is a methodological inclination to concentrate on inputs (how are programs designed?) and outputs (what do local partners get from their participation?). But in doing so we often miss out on a holistic, local, partner-centered view of the entirety of their engagement with visiting students. A local partner engagement process model provides a framework for complicating or accommodating complex inputs and outputs, by making room for longitudinal *processes* of engagement with a distinct orientation toward local partners' experiences. Taking the time to better understand local partner experiences at different stages in the engagement process may provide important insights beyond the types of host community impact and outcomes currently found in the international service-learning literature.

The model illustrated in Figure 13.1 was developed during the data analysis phase of a qualitative study aimed at better understanding the experiences of local education abroad partners, including faculty, administration, staff, and host families, at two traditional education abroad sites based at local universities in San Jose, Costa Rica. Semistructured interviews were conducted in person with 26 local partners in March 2017, and over 35 hours of interview data were recorded and transcribed. After coding and interpreting themes from the data, the process illustrated in the model emerged.

Figure 13.1. Local partner engagement process model.

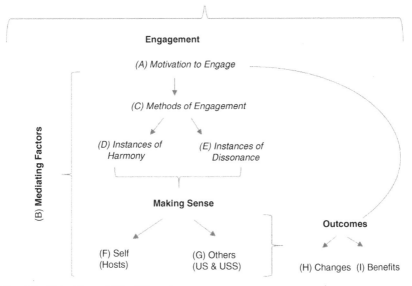

Note. US = United States; USS = U.S. student

The section to follow outlines the process model, largely summarizing data in the interest of space, but delving deeper at the points where local partners' roles as teachers and learners within education abroad come to the fore.

Local Partners' Motivation to Engage

A natural "entry point" in the model is local partners' motivations (A) to engage with U.S. students. In these Costa Rican cases, motivations varied widely by partner type, meaning whether a partner was an education abroad administrator, university staff member, professor, or host mother. Among the Costa Rican study participants, primary motivations for engaging with U.S. students included their own international experiences, as was the case for almost all of education abroad administrators and professors; a chance to use and/or improve English language skills; economic benefits; and, for many of the host mothers, having the chance to "have kids again." In many ways, the desire to be a teacher and a learner is central to the motivation of many local hosts. Learning more about the motivation of local partners to engage with visiting students helps to better understand the goals that local partners bring to the table.

Methods of Engagement—Local Partners as Teachers

Methods of engagement (C) is the first point in the process where we begin to see how local partners play an important role in the educative process of U.S. students. Almost all participants, when asked specifically if they see themselves as teachers or as part of the educational experience for visiting students responded, that indeed they do consider themselves as an important piece of students' education process. However, as one might expect, there is great variance in how different types of hosts understand their roles and explain their methods of engagement. Following is an explanation of some of the ways local partners engaged differently with U.S. students during their time in Costa Rica, and in some cases challenges they faced in the process of educating U.S. students.

Of the four intentional host types identified in this research (education abroad administrators, university staff, professors, and host families), education abroad administrators made the fewest references to themselves as "teachers." Rather, many of them saw their teaching role as having more to do with educating colleagues at the university and members of the community on the benefits of internationalization. One education abroad administrator explained how she and her colleagues attempt to educate the university community about international education through meetings and presentations with deans and department chairs.

Some professors emphasized how important they feel it is for them to give U.S. students opportunities in the classroom that they do not get at home. A professor of marine biology lamented that many of the U.S. students he teaches in Costa Rica complain about how large lecture halls are at home, and how even by the time they are juniors or seniors they have not made meaningful personal or academic connections with faculty. He went on to describe how he takes students to the ocean each semester to tag sea turtles and how he has coauthored published journal articles with U.S. undergraduate students who spent one semester in Costa Rica.

The primary method of educative engagement shared by host mothers was providing cultural guidance. In one host mom's case, this took the form of assisting U.S. students with their homework after dinner and making suggestions for other books to read, places to visit, and different foods to try. Other host mothers encouraged their U.S. students to keep a notebook with them at the table so that they could write down unfamiliar words that came up in conversation during dinner. At the end of the meal, the words could be reviewed, and their meaning shared. Both host mothers also shared that when U.S. students make mistakes in their spoken Spanish they correct them. One host mom suggested,

> Sometimes I feel like I could be a tourist guide already because of all the information I give out to the students. But I also help them with their language. I do this thing where I give them a new word of the day, but I try to make it a hard word for them to learn.

These host mothers do not know each other; two different Costa Rican universities employ them, yet they use similar pedagogical tactics.

Instances of Harmony and Dissonance

Discussion around how local partners intentionally engage with visiting students organically led to participants sharing instances of harmony (D) that often stood in contrast to specific instances of dissonance (E). Instances of harmony shared by participants far outweighed instances of dissonance across host types. In particular, host mothers described in detail the long-lasting, international relationships that they have formed and maintained, in some cases over the course of decades, with U.S. students. One mother, for example, shared that the year before, she broke her arm while hosting a student. The student stayed in Costa Rica beyond the program to help her as she healed. On the other hand, a different host mother shared a story of a student coming home so drunk one night that having apparently lost the house key the student attempted to climb on-to the roof in order to enter the house. The juxtaposition of such stories was particularly stark.

Local Partners as Learners—Making Sense of Self

How local partners make sense of this engagement, and how it makes them reflect on themselves (F) is another point in the process model where their role as learners is prominent. A local professor put it well: "To me it's very interesting to see my own culture, my own country, through their [U.S. students'] eyes. The average Costa Rican is pura vida, everything is pura vida, and here in class, they tell me their experiences, good and bad, so it opens my eyes to a different perspective of my own reality."

Participants identified their collectivist nature and orientation toward family, indirect communication style, unpunctuality, risk aversion, and lack of patriotism or national pride as elements of Costa Rican culture that they have come to reflect on more deeply as an effect of engaging with U.S. students, many of whom seem to exhibit opposite cultural characteristics. Several participants noted the general differences in communication style between Costa Ricans and U.S. students. A professor who teaches Spanish to U.S. students explained, "We are not a direct people, there are certain ways to say things in Costa Rica—you either say nothing, or say it using lots of nice words, a lot of explanations. People in the U.S. are used to efficiency and that's something that we're not."

Further, an education abroad administrator and a university staff member at two different institutions described how working with U.S. students makes them think differently about Costa Rican perceptions of time. One shared that U.S. students like to be punctual, whereas in Costa Rica, "We have this problem—we call it Tico Time, I'm really embarrassed by it because some professors are not here at 8:00 a.m. when their class starts, and they [the U.S. students] are already here at 7:30 a.m., and so I'm so embarrassed about that." Similarly, another education abroad administrator said, "I am Costa Rican and I know my culture, so most of the time people will be doing things late—U.S. students will be doing things in advance, so they want everything to be secure . . . so of course the customer service that I have to deliver is a really high level."

The last aspect of self-reflection that presented as a theme in participant interviews was Costa Rican lack of U.S.-style patriotism or national pride. A professor of Spanish noted, "U.S. students are so proud of their culture, their flag, their military." Likewise, an education abroad administrator shared that U.S. students' "obsession" with freedom makes her think about how or if the United States is actually "more free" than Costa Rica. A philosophy professor shared that teaching U.S. students, especially during the time leading up to the U.S. presidential election in 2016, made him realize how "inward facing" the United States currently is, and how that draws attention to how "outward facing" Costa Rica is. He commented, "Costa Rican culture is xenocentrist by nature. We are always looking toward the outside, I actually think that a bit of patriotism wouldn't hurt us." Similarly, an education abroad administrator suggested, "It's like people think that if there's something from the outside it's better than what we have here, it's a Latin American thing."

Local Partners as Learners—Making Sense of Others

Of course, through engaging with U.S. students, local partners do not just reflect on themselves and their culture, but they make sense of others (G), in most cases U.S. students, or other people from the United States. Local partners shared how they make sense of U.S. student visitors—their culture, orientations, and behaviors while abroad. They offered a number of different things that they learned about U.S. history, geography, food, and culture from the U.S. students whom they host.

One education abroad administrator shared that she thinks that in the United States education abroad in Costa Rica is romanticized in such a way that students are disappointed when they arrive and realize that Costa Rica, like any other place, has its problems. They also are not prepared for the different situations that they may encounter, and this participant attributed some of this to education abroad messaging in the United States. She said, "I don't know how the communication is in the States when it comes to study abroad, always happy? Always fun? Always great opportunities? And maybe not talking about the academics, the work, the potential for issues to arise? The need to be flexible?" A number of education abroad administrators discussed their interest in contributing to deeper predeparture preparation for U.S. students.

Participants also reflected on U.S. students' drinking, which was at the heart of many of the instances of dissonance that they described. A university staff member offered one particularly interesting interpretation of why U.S. students drink and party so heavily in Costa Rica:

> Their [U.S. students] drinking makes me sad. There must be something wrong, something so terrible happening in their life, that they are self-medicating with alcohol. I think it is connected to the lack of family support, of people who are around you to care. They must feel very alone.

Yet, other participants said that they attribute U.S. student drinking to nothing more than them being young and wanting to have fun. Some claimed that they believe the problem of U.S. student drinking is overstated.

Interpretations of U.S. student drinking are mixed, but increasingly local hosts are connecting U.S. student behavior to the freedom that they experience being separated from their families, both at home and in Costa Rica. Likewise, one professor described drinking as "self-medicating" for deeper issues that students are experiencing—an explanation that may be quite different from how students themselves might characterize their behavior. Nonetheless, this is a prime example of how hosts are not only noticing student behaviors but also making meaning of it.

Outcomes and Mediating Factors

Participants were asked what they see as outcomes (I, J) of the experience of engaging with U.S. students, for themselves, their families, and their communities. In most cases, outcomes echoed the instances of harmony that they shared—however, some evidenced deeper levels of reflection. One host mother, who had talked earlier about helping U.S. students learn English, identified her children's exposure to English through hosting U.S. students as a major benefit. She spoke further to the democratization of access to "the global" that hosting students brings with it. Many local partners shared the sentiment that when locals and visitors are brought together, over an extended period of time, truly mutual, intercultural exchange can happen. Another, more surprising outcome mentioned by a majority of local partners was that hosting U.S. students increased security in the area around the host institutions. Because of visitors, there is now an increase in police presence, and money to pay local security guards. They shared more negative outcomes as well, including the rising cost of everything due to the increase in U.S. student and visitor presence.

Mediating factors (B) are discourses or systems that sit outside of or, perhaps more accurately, blanket the entire process model and that seem to color the engagement between local partners and U.S. students. The primary mediating factors in this case were U.S. cultural and economic imperialism, and the politics of language and North American identity. Thus, many reflections on engagement were in some way mediated by the massive cultural and economic presence of the United States in Costa Rica—participants are acutely aware of the dependence of Costa Rica on U.S. companies and, increasingly, U.S. tourism. Some participants likened the increase in U.S. student presence to an extension of that dependence. This is exacerbated by another mediating factor, the politics of language and identity—the local partners' perception that U.S. students who come to Costa Rica not only do not speak Spanish but also do not try to speak Spanish; that has an undeniable impact on both the logistics and spirit of communication.

Applying the Model and Implications for Education Abroad

This volume's call for further attention to the connection between education abroad and undergraduate education serves as a great opportunity to think more deeply about important stakeholders, both on campus and abroad, who contribute in meaningful ways to student learning. Too often, we focus on student learning abroad in a vacuum, disconnected from those local partners abroad from whom they are learning—or we tend to move past engagement between students and local partners to outcomes. Community impact and student learning should not be seen as distinct, but rather as an intricately interconnected process. The local partner engagement process model can help us do that by organizing our thinking and analysis at various stages of local partner engagement.

In terms of program design, better understanding of the motivation of local partners to engage with visiting students and their various methods of engagement can help us see the many types of instruction that are happening outside of the traditional classroom and work toward assessing them. Having more knowledge of instances of harmony and dissonance from local hosts' perspectives can both help us better prepare students to go abroad and serve as a foundation for understanding what, if anything, is mutual about the engagement between students and local hosts. Finally, knowing what local hosts see as benefits of engaging in education abroad can help us to design programs and environments that increase local partner-identified benefits and mitigate drawbacks.

Conclusion

Those in the profession of education abroad already know how critical local partners are to the success of programs, and internationalization efforts already promote mutual understanding and intercultural exchange. Yet, research on local partners and host community impact continues to be limited to international service-learning contexts, which leaves out a broad swath of the education abroad experience. The data used to illustrate the utility of the local partner engagement process model, drawn from a traditional (nonservice-focused) education abroad environment, is intended to promote further scholarly engagement with community impact work outside of international service-learning. Of course, time and resources are always a constraint, but the model and case studies introduced previously provide a glimpse into the depth of understanding that can be achieved when we turn the evaluative lens toward local partners. This understanding can begin moving us in the direction of more explicitly acknowledging the role local partners play as teachers and learners within education abroad and, by extension, within undergraduate education.

References

Andreotti, V. (2007). *The contributions of postcolonial theory to development education* (DEA Think Piece). Available from http://clients.squareeye.net/uploads/dea/documents/dea_thinkpiece_andriotti.pdf

Blouin, D. D., & Perry, E. M. (2009). Whom does service learning really serve? Community-based organizations' perspectives on service learning. *Teaching Sociology, 37*, 120–135.

Caldwell, P., & Purtzer, M. A. (2015). Long-term learning in a short-term study abroad program: Are we really truly helping the community? *Public Health Nursing, 32*(5), 577–583.

d'Arlach, L., Sanchez, B., & Feuer, R. (2009). Voices from the community: A case for reciprocity in service-learning. *Michigan Journal of Community Service Learning, 16*(1), 5–16.

Friedman, M. A., Gossett, D., Saucedo, I., Weiner, S., Young, M. W., Penco, N., & Evert, J. (2016). Partnering with parteras: Multi-collaborator international service-learning project impacts on traditional birth attendants in Mexico. *International Journal of Research on Service-Learning and Community Engagement, 4*(1), 1–13.

Jacoby, B., & Associates (Eds.). (1996). *Service-learning in higher education: Concepts and practices*. San Francisco, CA: Jossey-Bass.

Larsen, M. (2016). Introduction. In M. Larsen (Ed.), *International service learning engaging host communities* (pp. 3–18). New York, NY: Routledge.

Reynolds, N. (2014). What counts as outcomes? Community perspectives of an engineering partnership. *Michigan Journal of Community Service Learning, 20*(1), 79–90.

Toms Smedley, C. (2016). Women, development, and international volunteerism. In M. Larsen (Ed.), *International service learning: Engaging host communities* (pp. 65–79). New York, NY: Routledge.

Worrall, L. (2007). Asking the community: A case study of community partner perspectives. *Michigan Journal of Community Service Learning, 14*(1), 5–17.

14

FROM TRANSACTION TO RELATIONAL

Realigning Partnerships Between Higher Education Institutions and International Education Organizations

Kris Holloway, Lisa Chieffo, Rich Kurtzman, and Anthony C. Ogden

Higher education institutions (HEIs) and international education organizations (IEOs) have distinct and important roles to play in advancing U.S. education abroad programming and practice. As discussed in chapter 1, formal U.S. education abroad began in the early twentieth century, and from the outset, providers (IEOs) have worked alongside universities and colleges. IEOs initially emerged as helpful collaborators in developing and facilitating education abroad programs. As the popularity of education abroad programming grew over the ensuing decades, their role as indispensable partners was secured.

Today, IEOs provide a wide range of specialized resources, programming, and services that continue to contribute to advance international education in the United States. IEOs may be degree-granting colleges and universities, regional and national consortia, independent nonprofit organizations, or for-profit businesses (The Forum on Education Abroad, n.d.a). All have in common a primary mission of supporting students who are matriculated elsewhere. Although the number of IEOs in operation today and the proportion of students enrolling in IEO-affiliated programming is unknown, it is certain IEOs' role in facilitating education abroad programming is intertwined with U.S. HEIs'.

Widely acknowledged and accepted, the long-standing collaboration between HEIs and IEOs has nonetheless at times been strained. Some HEIs have opted against working with external IEOs, while others engage solely on a transactional basis, with the IEO as vendor and the HEI as consumer. In turn, there has been unease about IEOs blatantly bypassing institutional protocols and academic regulations to recruit students directly. Further, legal concerns have been raised about possible collusion and unethical practices between HEIs and IEOs (Fischer, 2008; Glater, 2008). As education abroad programming continues to grow and diversify, however, it is time for the relationship between HEIs and IEOs to move beyond transaction to partnership. Such partnership can mobilize HEI and IEO collective strength and positions to support student learning and development across the educational continuum.

This chapter begins by summarizing the history of IEOs, then discusses the value and benefit of HEIs and IEOs partnering together. Next, brief perspectives from the vantage point of HEIs and IEOs provide additional context for further enhancing the potential of the partnership. The chapter concludes with a forward-looking view of the partnership, and a brief discussion of two challenges to education abroad and the partnership.

Historical Overview of IEOs

The number of IEOs operating within U.S. education abroad has grown in recent decades. Yet the history of such organizations arguably stretches back to the very beginnings of U.S. education abroad. Education abroad in the United States likely began at Indiana University in the 1870s when faculty encouraged students to enroll in summer courses taught in Switzerland, France, England, Germany, and Italy. However, credit-bearing education abroad for U.S. students only began in the 1920s when the University of Delaware began offering this option (Hoffa, 2007; Institute for Global Studies, n.d.). Under the Delaware Foreign Study Plan (which came to be known as the junior year abroad), the first group sailed for France in 1923. The program was such a success that Delaware began enrolling students from other colleges and universities, among them Brown, Columbia, Harvard, Pennsylvania State University, Princeton, Smith, Wellesley, and Wesleyan. Thus, the University of Delaware became one of the first "providers" of education abroad.

Only in the mid-1940s did the first wave of contemporary IEOs emerge, however. After World War II, the U.S. government began to prioritize developing international understanding and establishing trust between nations. Student travel was considered an effective way to achieve these priorities. Not surprisingly, the Fulbright Program was established in 1945 with the aim of promoting international learning through the exchange of students

(Bureau of Educational and Cultural Affairs, n.d.). Shortly thereafter, the Council on International Educational Exchange (CIEE) was founded in 1947 as a nonprofit, member organization promoting international education and exchange. CIEE remains today a leader in international education (IEE, n.d.). Founded in 1950, for over 65 years the Institute for the International Education of Students (IES Abroad) has provided education abroad programming via its academic consortium of U.S. institutions (IES Abroad, n.d.). Consortia, such as CIEE and IES Abroad, offer U.S. colleges and universities the means to actively collaborate in the development, implementation, and oversight of education abroad programming without requiring sole ownership, risk, and responsibility.

The first major wave of IEOs emerged in the 1960s. In contrast to their predecessors, they were not consortia, instead admitting students from a wide range of U.S. colleges and universities (see Figure 14.1). First among these was the Danish Institute for Study Abroad (DIS), initially established at the University of Copenhagen in 1959 (DIS Study Abroad in Scandinavia, n.d.). Founded in 1964, SIT Study Abroad began by offering training programs for Peace Corps volunteers and today retains its focus on intercultural and field-based learning (School for International Training, n.d.). Other emerging IEOs at this stage included university-facilitated programs such as Arcadia University's Center for Education Abroad (now the College of Global Studies), founded in 1965, and the innovative Semester at Sea program, established in 1963 to offer education abroad programming while circumnavigating the globe.

Beginning in the early 1980s, the next 20 years welcomed dramatic and consistent education abroad enrollment growth (Farrugia & Bhandari, 2017). Not surprisingly, this period also saw a massive proliferation of IEOs. Unique to this second wave were numerous for-profit organizations, including The Education Abroad Network (1995), International Studies Abroad (1987), Academic Programs International (1997), Cultural Experiences

Figure 14.1. Evolution of international education organizations.

| 1920/1930s "Campus Programs" | 1960/1970s "Early Providers" | 2000s "Short-Term" |

| 1940/1950s "Early Consortia" | 1980/1990s "Companies" | 2010s "Custom Programs" |

Abroad (1997), Knowledge Exchange Institute (1997), and CISabroad (1999). Such IEOs firmly established the "industry" of education abroad through enhanced marketing and promotion efforts; innovative education abroad programming; expanded student affairs and orientation programming; sophisticated enrollment management processes; and advances in best practices in health, safety, and security.

The next wave began at the turn of the twenty-first century, at a time when education abroad enrollments were growing annually by more than 10%. During this time, there was also increasing awareness of the need to expand the notion of education abroad programming from the traditional junior year abroad and semester-length programs to include summer and short-term programming, especially in regard to international internships, undergraduate research, global service-learning, and so on. IEOs were quick to respond by offering summer and short-term programming that appealed to student interests. Additionally, new specialized IEOs emerged, such as the Academic Internship Council (2011), which exclusively offers internships, and EuroScholars (2005), which focuses on undergraduate research. Because many institutions were not equipped to facilitate such short-term programming on their own, IEOs were essential partners in providing it.

As education continues to evolve, the number of IEOs based outside of the United States that cater to changing U.S. student needs and HEI priorities is increasing. Examples include Barcelona Study Abroad Experience (founded in 2009), which is representative of IEOs focused on one location, and Customized Educational Programs Abroad (CEPA; founded in 1997), which offers programs and services in multiple locations. Both offer supports for faculty-directed, short-term, and customized programs; other IEOs are moving in this direction. Programs of less than eight weeks in duration currently account for 63% of all U.S. students who earn credit abroad (Institute of International Education [IIE], 2017). Among modes of short-term programs, faculty-directed programs are likely growing most rapidly, that is, programs in which a faculty member (or members) from the home campus accompanies students abroad (Chieffo & Spaeth, 2017). U.S. universities and colleges, even those that have long resisted such partnerships, are more readily turning to IEOs for assistance with customizing faculty-directed programming. When IEOs provide customized programming support, faculty members are less bound geographically by their own networks, language proficiency, and disciplinary expertise. Partnerships with IEOs enable institutions to expand faculty-directed programming to new disciplines and whole world destinations.

Today, IEOs are increasingly expected to contribute to education abroad's advancement in areas related to student scholarships and grants, diversity, and program design, as well as areas related to research and scholarship, best practices in instructional pedagogy, and outcomes assessment. Notable examples include the ISA Diversity Abroad Scholarship developed in partnership with the University of Kentucky; the LGBTQ Ally training programming offered by CISabroad across the United States; and the well-known research and scholarship conducted by such providers as IES Abroad, CAPA International Education, and AIFS Study Abroad.

Though the total proportion and number of students participating in IEO-facilitated education abroad is unknown, there is no doubt that IEOs have had an essential and influential role in shaping the development of education abroad programming in the United States. Although many IEOs have emerged over the years only to quietly disappear or be absorbed by other entities, partnerships between IEOs and HEIs suggest that looking forward IEOs that partner with HEIs will continue to offer new advances in education abroad programming and practice. This in turn will strengthen both IEO and HEI education abroad efforts.

Leveraging the Partnership

IEOs are not uniquely a U.S. phenomenon. However, it is undeniable that IEOs have contributed greatly to shaping the history and development of U.S. education abroad, and have thrived in the space where education abroad is a component of undergraduate education. By all accounts, IEOs will likely remain central to advancing new directions in the years ahead. However, as indicated in the introduction to this chapter, it will be essential that the relationship between HEIs and IEOs move beyond mere transactional terms (IEOs supply a service that HEIs solicit) to true partnership, wherein mutual reinforcing positions are well understood and shared initiatives are strategically advanced. HEIs and IEOs can achieve more together as true partners than on their own. Consider the following brief examples:

1. *Portfolio Diversification.* Student demand is calling for education abroad programming beyond traditional study abroad experiences. Students are increasingly interested in international internships (combined or not with other studies), global service-learning, undergraduate research, student teaching placements, and so on. Such programming is difficult for any single institution to develop and facilitate broadly. In providing such offerings, IEOs enable HEIs to diversify their program portfolios and thereby respond to changing student needs and interests.

2. *Program Development and Design.* With the shift toward ever shorter programs and the popularity of faculty-directed programming, HEIs are increasingly turning toward their IEO partners for program customization, wherein the IEOs provide tailored academic and student services support for their HEI partners. For some institutions, this support has launched a broader range of programming, thus enabling students to pursue study in destinations, disciplines, and at certain institutions that may have once been out of reach. In turn, IEOs rely on their HEI partners to generate sustainable enrollment that allows them to offer innovative and creative programming.

3. *Enrollment Management.* Although enrollment management platforms have greatly advanced in recent years, IEOs, because they simultaneously support multiple institutions and are well positioned to provide a wide range of enrollment management and technological support, including enhancements in student communication, enrollment reporting, and data collection. IEOs can also provide a reliable platform through which HEIs can recruit and enroll external students in home institution programs, such as faculty-directed programs customized by an IEO. In turn, IEOs are better positioned to reach enrollment targets.

4. *Student Services.* IEOs have proven to be valuable partners in meeting the evolving needs and expectations of a diversifying student population. Frequently with more developed on-site infrastructures, IEOs are better positioned to support students who need physical and learning accommodations; facilitate ongoing orientation programming tailored to U.S. students; and provide assurances for health, safety, and security. In fact, many HEIs have come to rely on their IEO partners for 24/7 emergency response and comprehensive student support. This level of enhanced student services can enrich the space in which students learn and engage while abroad. It can also reassure students who might otherwise hesitate to study abroad, including underrepresented students.

5. *Operational Management.* Education abroad is increasing in popularity, just as public support for higher education is declining. In response, some institutions are turning to their IEO partners to help them sustain and enhance their daily operational capacity. For example, IEOs may provide assistance with student advising and orientation, program development, curriculum integration, staff professional development, faculty engagement, and so on. In turn, IEOs are able to enroll better-informed and prepared students.

6. *Partnerships and Linkages.* As more institutions seek to establish and maintain international partnerships and linkages, some are tapping into

their IEO partners' extensive international networks and expertise. IEOs have similarly proven to be strong partners in establishing cross-border delivery programming, assisting with international student recruitment, and developing regional hubs for education abroad programming.

7. *Faculty and Staff Engagement.* Faculty and staff development and international research are critical to internationalizing higher education. It is not surprising, then, that HEIs are turning to their IEO partners to help advance their curriculum integration initiatives, strengthen international networking and exchange potential, and enhance international engagement opportunities for faculty and staff through program site visits, faculty development seminars, and disciplinary partnerships. IEOs, in turn, become better known to faculty and staff.

8. *Outcomes Assessment.* In an era of increasing accountability, it is strategically important that education abroad professionals be able to produce data that give insight into student learning abroad; show how education abroad contributes to student learning and development (and can be adapted to improve these); and demonstrate how international education potentially enhances and extends institutional missions, values, and priorities. Not surprisingly, HEIs are turning to their IEO partners for assistance documenting students' learning and development through education abroad. In turn, this helps IEOs gather and disseminate evidence of the success of their programs.

Both HEIs and IEOs unquestionably benefit operationally by such mutually reinforcing partnerships. More importantly, such partnerships enhance education abroad programming and practice. In turn, students benefit from expanded program offerings, enhanced student services, and more. However, given the challenges inherent in establishing and sustaining partnerships, it is important to consider somewhat in depth the perspectives of both HEIs and IEOs. The following two sections do just that, with the aim of providing additional context for enhancing the potential of the HEI/IEO partnership.

The Higher Education Institution Perspective

It can be challenging for even the most experienced education abroad professional to differentiate IEOs, to determine with whom to partner, and how to get started (Ogden, 2015). Before deciding whether to work with an IEO, an HEI must determine its short- and long-term education abroad goals, and its capacity to meet those goals given existing resources. An institution can then decide if partnering with one or more IEO can help to realize those goals. If so, planning can focus on with whom and how to move forward. This sounds easy in principle but, in practice, is often more complex and time consuming than one might imagine.

Ideally, a critical look at an institution's education abroad offerings and practices should precede any search for possible IEO partners. This self-study should be guided by questions such as the following:

- What are the institution's educational goals for its students, and how does education abroad presently fit into these? In what areas do current education abroad operations fall short?
- How do education abroad enrollments align with the campus student profile in regard to academic major, ethnic and gender demographics, socioeconomic status, and other relevant statistics? Is there a plan in place to achieve better alignment? Are resources adequate to do so?
- What is the institution's education abroad model and campus tradition? Is there a desire or willingness to expand or change these?
- How are the institution's education abroad operations currently resourced in regard to staffing, funding, facilities, and so on? Can resources be increased or realigned to better meet institutional needs?
- Does the range of program options adequately serve students' needs based on institutional goals and values? This may mean, for example, offering direct enrollment and study-center-based academic models, short- and long-term programs, fieldwork and internship experiences, and programs in traditional and less traditional locations.

Answering questions such as these will help education abroad decision-makers obtain a clear understanding of the status quo, a feasible timeline for achieving goals, and a realistic picture of present and future capacity before considering how, or whether, to involve one or more IEOs.

Many, if not most, colleges and universities will discover that partnering with an IEO will enhance the capacity of their education abroad offices to meet institutional goals. The challenge is to identify one or more suitable matches such that the relationships are not simply transactional. It is fairly easy to create an approved list of well-respected IEOs, each with dozens of programs, and thus offer a huge array of opportunities to students. Such an approach can become unmanageable and risks misaligning with an institution's educational goals.

However, a self-reflective education abroad office that knows its strengths and needs can intentionally seek partners positioned to help it extend its capacity in multiple and focused directions. For example, as stated previously,

IEOs are often more flexible than colleges and universities in developing innovative program designs. They are often better equipped than an HEI's education abroad office to broadly publicize programs, attract more diverse applicants, and provide program-specific scholarships. Identifying the right partners to augment campus capacity requires time and research.

A fundamental task early in the vetting process is to ascertain the values and priorities of potential partners. Just like colleges and universities, IEOs have varying missions and institutional cultures. Some place great importance on immersive experiences and may offer only direct-enrollment options at local universities. Others embed experiential fieldwork and language study in all programs to promote independence and host-country contact. Still others prioritize low staff-to-student ratios to enable a very high level of support, but this often comes with a higher price, while low cost and accessibility are paramount for some IEOs. Education abroad offices must ascertain which IEO values align with those of their institutions and will resonate with senior leadership, faculty, staff, students, and other key stakeholders.

Beyond an alignment of core values and purpose, some measure of operational synergy between HEI and IEO partners is necessary. Often IEOs can be more flexible than colleges and universities on deadlines, billing, and other procedural matters, but this may not always be the case. Thus, having a shared and realistic understanding of the operational priorities of each organization is crucial before commitments are made. For most education abroad offices, the challenge is to find IEOs whose values and organizational culture align with those of the institution and the needs of its students. Without this, a successful partnership is improbable.

Similar to HEIs, IEOs generally have multiyear strategic plans for growth and development. When HEIs and IEOs seek long-term, sustainable partnerships, it is important that they determine a shared sense of mission and strategic direction. Mutually reinforcing partnerships gives advantage to both when each expands into new areas of programming. For example, when an IEO with robust internship program offerings adds preservice teacher placements, the HEI partner in response can offer student teaching opportunities for its education majors.

Some IEOs boast specific goals for student learning and development and have formal assessment plans in place to measure various aspects thereof. Partnering with such an organization can be advantageous to an education abroad office at an institution whose administration is calling for data to justify the enterprise. Moreover, an education abroad office that itself has a robust assessment initiative can consider collaborating with a partner IEO on studies of student learning abroad, with the ultimate goal of contributing jointly to the field in the form of presentations and/or publications. Of course, before committing to such a partnership the education abroad office will want to see the IEO's assessment data to ascertain areas of strength and weakness and the IEO's level of success in achieving student learning and development goals.

Once established, sustaining a partnership is similarly challenging. HEIs and IEOs both face periodic changes in senior administration, staff turnover, fluctuations in enrollment, shifts in capacity, changes in funding prioritization, and so on. Such changes can impact the nature and scope of partnerships. Consequently, as a partnership matures both partners will need to be attentive and mindful of internal changes and developments and maintain clear communication and realistic expectations. Negotiating a renewable affiliation agreement that outlines the structure and orientation of the partnership is essential to ensuring that the partnership remains viable, current, and mutually beneficial. It is similarly important to recognize when the partnership may have reached a natural end, and then to respectfully part ways.

The International Education Organization Perspective

In much the same way as HEIs seek to partner with IEOs, IEOs are looking for productive and sustainable partnerships with HEIs. Their success and viability rests on IEOs being intentional with whom and how they work with their HEI partners. While some IEOs orient themselves around affiliated partnerships or institutional member consortia, other IEOs are guided by the input and direction of advisory boards composed of representatives from their closest partner institutions. All IEOs, however, seek HEI partners similarly motivated to establish and sustain mutually beneficial partnerships that will advance education abroad programming and support student learning and development. Of particular importance to IEOs pursuing HEI partnerships are commitment to (a) ensuring sustainable enrollment, (b) preparing and orienting students, and (c) providing high standards of professionalism and quality.

It is a common and shortsighted misconception that IEOs partner with HEIs solely to increase enrollment. While IEOs rely on income derived from student enrollment, many IEOs also enroll students outside of any partnership arrangements. As has been the intention of IEOs throughout history, most are structured to work in tandem with HEIs as part of a committed and mutually reinforcing partnership that is grounded in establishing and facilitating sustainable and high-quality programming. As indicated earlier, IEOs initially emerged to complement and extend the capacity of HEIs by providing specialized resources, programming, and services. This raison d'etre persists today.

When entering a partnership, HEIs must recognize their responsibility to ensure student enrollment when IEOs extend them services and support. IEOs rely on such revenue for the services and support they offer. Thus, when an HEI engages its IEO partner to customize a program, the IEO commits significant time and resources to development and design. Should the program ultimately fail to enroll a sufficient number of students to operate, the IEO is unable to recoup on its efforts. Whereas the HEI may have capacity to absorb the loss of its own committed time and resources, the IEO often does not. As such, it is essential that the HEI recognize and mitigate the potential financial risk and exposure that each new initiative may have on its IEO partner. One recommendation is to think beyond "the study abroad fair" to find innovative ways to attract student interest—webinars, classroom visits, campus-wide talks, and sponsored student events. A second recommendation is to develop long-term partnerships with well-established and mutually supportive goals, clear strategies, and shared commitment to program quality. Both help ensure greater likelihood that the partnership will thrive.

Further, IEOs are held to high standards, as they should be. The same must be true of HEIs. Beyond using the language of higher education, both should be expected to know and implement the *Standards of Good Practice* (The Forum on Education Abroad, n.d.b.). When both rise to this level of best practice, it helps the partnership become greater than the sum of its parts. Examples of best practice include HEI partners developing a rigorous prescreening process before sending students abroad. A careful process for selecting faculty to lead programs likewise helps ensure they are trained in health and safety measures, risk mitigation and management, mental health issues, and managing groups. In particular, the HEI should be able to provide compelling answers to the following questions:

- What is the institution's emergency response plan and risk management protocol?
- How are proposed programs vetted to ensure they further students' academic and cultural objectives?
- How does the institution prepare its faculty?
- How does the institution manage the orientation needs of its students?
- How are the students vetted academically, emotionally, and behaviorally before being accepted to study abroad with the IEO partner?
- Will the institution provide ongoing support before and after the program, just as the IEO is expected to do while the students are abroad?

The best scenario is for IEOs and HEIs to work together to create robust training and predeparture manuals as well as re-entry workshops so that the responsibility does not fall to only one or the other.

HEIs and IEOs very often share the same goals of creating programs that are academically sound, culturally enriching, professionally relevant, and safe. Both are committed to leveraging education abroad programming to support learning and development throughout students' undergraduate careers, and to helping students graduate with the international knowledge, skills, and experiences needed to be successful in their future careers and further learning. By working together in a true partnership, communicating openly, and approaching the partnership with mutual respect, HEIs and IEOs can do more together than apart.

Conclusion

This chapter has argued that partnerships between HEIs and IEOs make education abroad possible, amplify its value, and strengthen education abroad's contributions to undergraduate education. Such partnerships help both explore and maximize collective talents, knowledge, and resources. However, the discussion of the partnership cannot end without reference to two important considerations.

First, the number of students traveling abroad to study has been on the rise. Internationally mobile students now exceed over 4.6 million students annually, a trend expected to continue (IIE, 2017). However, in the United States growth in credit-bearing education abroad is slowing. This is in part because of changing student demographics; as discussed elsewhere in this volume, the traditional audience for education abroad (White, middle-/upper class students) is shrinking. More inclusive policies and practices are needed if education abroad is to retain even its current low participation rate of roughly 10% of U.S. undergraduates. Cost control is one pressure point; another is the perception of whom education abroad is for. Yet other concerns focus on risk (health, safety, security), and questions of investment: Will time and money (and loans) invested in education pay off? Initiatives such as Generation Study Abroad (IIE, n.d.), in recognition of these challenges, are proposing noncredit-bearing international experience as one solution. How will this alternative to credit-bearing education abroad be integrated into undergraduate education? Is it a valuable tool for recruitment of underrepresented students? Can HEI/IEO partnerships play a role, and if so, which and how?

Second, what higher education does at its best is to educate leaders who reduce conflict and resolve issues of power and privilege at home and abroad.

Civic life, or being connected to and concerned with the life of a community, a nation, and the larger world, means students must develop their abilities to reason, think critically, empathize with others, be aware of privilege and bias, and be able to take ethical action. Education abroad, by engaging students with difference, helping them make sense of it, and giving them the knowledge, skills, and motivation to act on what they have learned, already plays a role in equipping students for positive contribution to society writ large. Can it play even a bigger role in doing so? HEIs and IEOs must work synergistically, the chapter authors would argue, if education abroad is to justify the investment it requires on the part of students and their families, sending institutions/organizations, and all of the actors who support it.

As argued throughout this chapter, transactional roles must continue to give way to partnerships that address challenges and ensure that education abroad programming supports the ongoing learning and development of students, and the values and goals of higher education. When such synergies exist, they increase student access to a world of new educational opportunities, strengthen comprehensive internationalization efforts, and ultimately benefit higher education. The bar must be set high. As Peter N. Stearns (2015), retired provost of George Mason University, so aptly stated,

> Global is hard work. It involves lots of discussions that do not bear fruit, lots of visits that lead to nothing, and probably a certain amount of internal resistance. But it's a great calling. It links education to the world we live in, and that our students will live in. It pushes the institution to greater contemporary relevance.

Education abroad, and the IEOs and HEIs that facilitate it, must be at the forefront of this relevance.

References

Bureau of Educational and Cultural Affairs. (n.d.). *Fulbright program history.* Available from https://eca.state.gov/fulbright/about-fulbright/history

Chieffo, L., & Spaeth, C. (Eds.). (2017). *The guide to successful short-term programs abroad* (3rd ed.). Washington, DC: NAFSA: Association of International Educators.

Council on International Educational Exchange (CIEE). (n.d.). *History.* Available from https://www.ciee.org/about/what-we-stand-for/history

DIS Study Abroad in Scandinavia (n.d.). *Our history.* Available from https://disabroad.org/dis/history/

Farrugia, C. A., & Bhandari, R. (2017). *Open Doors 2017 report on international educational exchange.* New York, NY: Institute of International Education.

Fischer, K. (2008, January 21). Cuomo expands investigation of study abroad programs to colleges. *The Chronicle of Higher Education*. Available from https://www.chronicle.com/article/Cuomo-Expands-Investigation-of/420

The Forum on Education Abroad. (n.d.a). *Forum glossary.* Available from https://forumea.org/resources/glossary/

The Forum on Education Abroad. (n.d.b). *Standards of good practice.* Available from https://forumea.org/resources/standards-of-good-practice/

Glater, J. (2008, January 21). Investigation of study abroad program widens. *New York Times*, p. A10.

Hoffa, W. (2007). *A history of US study abroad: Beginnings to 1965*. Carlisle, PA: The Forum on Education Abroad.

IES Abroad. (n.d.). *The IES difference*. Available from https://www.iesabroad.org/about/ies-abroad-difference

Institute for Global Studies. (n.d.). *Our history.* Available from https://www1.udel.edu/global/studyabroad/information/brief_history.html

Institute of International Education (IIE). (2017). *Project Atlas: Trends and global data*. New York, NY: Author.

Institute of International Education (IIE). (n.d.). *IIE generation abroad*. Available from https://www.iie.org/en/Programs/Generation-Study-Abroad

Ogden, A. (2015). *Ten quick tips for working with education abroad provider organizations*. Association of International Education Administrators (AIEA). Available from www.aieaworld.org/assets/docs/Issue_Briefs

School for International Training (SIT) (n.d.). *Why SIT.* Available from https://studyabroad.sit.edu/why-sit/

Stearns, P. N. (2015, August). Pride and regret: Reflections on global education from a retired provost. *Trends & Insights*. Available from http://www.nafsa.org/Professional_Resources/Research_and_Trends/Trends_and_Insights/Trends___Insights/

15

FUTURE PERSPECTIVES ON EDUCATION ABROAD

Elizabeth Brewer and Anthony C. Ogden

L ooking forward to the future of education abroad, 5 to 10 years out, the editors of this volume invited 10 influential education abroad leaders and scholars engaged in research on international education to share their perspectives. 3 themes stand out and resonate with the questions this volume seeks to address. First, rather than focus on participation numbers, the discussion of education abroad must focus on its purpose and contributions. To this end, international educators must become more adept scholars who can ask critical questions as well as contribute to the research needed to understand such questions as the relationship between outcomes and program design. Second, education abroad must respond to changes in student demographics with innovations that make it more affordable and inclusive. Frameworks such as global learning can help connect it to learning across the curriculum, and strengthen students' abilities to address complex problems collaboratively. This connects to a third theme: Partnerships (on campus, with community members, and abroad with universities and others) are critical to developing education abroad as a high-impact practice interconnected with other learning activities to prepare students for both careers and social responsibility.

Opening the World: Quality, Scope, and Access

Esther Brimmer
Executive Director and CEO of NAFSA: Association of
International Educators

A high-quality, well-designed education abroad experience can enrich undergraduate education, across a variety of disciplines. Whatever the major, students can learn about human understanding of a topic, field, or discipline. Exposure to how experts in other places interpret a discipline can improve students' understanding of it. Whether philosophers or physicists, scholars understand that debating and sharing ideas with people in other places advances human knowledge. Long before there were modern states with clear borders, there were great universities advancing academic inquiry with scholars from far away.

Today, both scholars and students can benefit from education abroad. A greater understanding of how people think and work in other parts of the world is important to being a well-educated person, an informed citizen, and a well-prepared member of the workforce, given that foreign direct investment can mean well-paying jobs. Many people will work for companies based in other countries, or with complex, multinational supply chains. Even when working in one's hometown, an appreciation of other cultures can help one succeed.

Given the potential benefits to students, workers, and society, programs must be well crafted and tailored to meet students' needs. Three areas merit attention: quality, scope, and access. Whether it is a semester or a short-term program abroad, academic quality is important. NAFSA encourages administrators who manage and faculty who may facilitate such experiences to delve deeper into ways to design programs to integrate the goals of the curriculum into learning outcomes. NAFSA also encourages educators to widen the scope of disciplines that incorporate education abroad into the course of study and to broaden the range of countries to which students travel. Four countries in western Europe receive 40% of U.S. education abroad students.

The issue of access is especially challenging. A complex web of factors may inhibit students from studying abroad. Cost is one, but not the only, factor. Forfeiting income that helps pay tuition or meet family obligations can be a deterrent. Students may not know anyone who has traveled abroad; parents may fear their children will be mistreated in an unfamiliar setting. Educators must reach out to these students with messages that education abroad is possible. NAFSA encourages international educators to share model practices in overcoming direct and indirect restraints on greater access to education abroad. However, this is a responsibility for higher education and policymakers, not just international educators. Students' home institutions and foundations, as well as federal and state sources, can help fill financial gaps. In an era of tight budgets, public-private partnerships should be explored. All students need to be able to take advantage of what their institutions offer—including education abroad. International education benefits students and society. Innovative program management and insightful research can help improve quality, scope, and access and contribute to the field of international education.

The Future of Education Abroad: Will the Ducks Still Quack?

Hans de Wit

Director, Center for International Higher Education, Boston College

Education abroad is probably the activity that people most often connect to international education, certainly in the United States. It is predominantly a Western concept, and it takes many different forms and shapes, as I described in 1998 in "Ducks Quack Differently on Each Side of the Ocean" (de Wit, 1998). There is a big difference internationally in how education abroad is perceived and what it focuses on. The practice of credit mobility predominantly takes place in the United States and in Europe—but even between these two regions, there are substantial differences in funding schemes, organization, the role of external providers, levels of study, and rationales.

What does the future hold for education abroad? First, an increasing expansion globally. Countries that have primarily focused on inbound degree mobility such as Australia, Canada, and the United Kingdom are realizing the importance of outbound credit mobility for their own students. Other regions and countries, for instance, the Association of Southeast Asian Nations (ASEAN), and Brazil, with its "Science Without Borders" program (now stalled due to economic and political factors), are advocating the benefit of study abroad. Second, the shift in education abroad from study to international service-learning and internships will require different policies and arrangements. Third, education abroad will no longer be the exclusive domain of universities: It is already practiced at other levels of education, such as in community colleges and, increasingly, high schools and even primary education. Fourth, technological developments create opportunities for virtual and hybrid models of education abroad, also referred to as "virtual exchange" or "collaborative online international learning." Fifth, education abroad may be positively influenced by trends toward dual and joint degrees, becoming an integral part of the curriculum, teaching, and learning—thus limiting the risk of "academic tourism." And sixth, education abroad now has to take into consideration the changing political climate fueled by anti-international feelings. Study and work abroad and global citizenship development will face more political and security challenges than before.

Institutions of higher education need to adopt a more innovative and inclusive approach than is currently the case. National governments and programs, institutions of higher education, and senior international officers have to rethink its future, not only looking at increasing the numbers but also considering the rationales, the "what" and the "how," and the outcomes and impact of their policies. "Education abroad" has to become an inclusive part of "study at home." Otherwise, the ducks will still quack, but will their noise be heard?

Education Abroad: Hope for Its Future

Mary Dwyer
President and CEO, IES Abroad

As the British American theoretical physicist and mathematician Freeman Dyson said, "The purpose of thinking about the future is not to predict it but to raise people's hopes" (as cited in Jaeger, 2011, p. 59). Despite the increasing complexities in education abroad, there is genuine hope for the future. Here are six examples:

1. *More Impactful Utilization of Educational Technology.* Due to educational technology advancements, it is feasible and imperative to enhance instruction worldwide and make active learning the standard bearer. Educational software and online learning can improve the education abroad experience before, during, and after studying abroad. Increased, effective use of educational technology will bring active learning to classrooms around the world. Technology also makes it possible to inexpensively share varied cultural perspectives with students who are unable to study abroad through linking classrooms in different locations synchronously.

2. *Increasing Research.* There has been a dearth of research in the field relative to other academic disciplines. As international education graduate programs proliferate, the quantity and quality of research will improve. Programs' graduates will ensure it. Rigorous findings will take precedent over personal opinions. This will allow for more effective decision-making about program design, more and better designed longitudinal impact studies, examination of every element of the education abroad experience, and so on. Acting on the results will be critical for the welfare of students and the credibility of the profession. Program design and implementation will need to reflect results that are proven statistically reliable and generalizable.

3. *Reinforcing Curricular Integration.* The concept of curricular integration of the education abroad experience with the home institution curriculum has existed for over two decades. To the extent that education abroad is truly integrated into students' total academic experiences and recognized by the academy, the impact and value of the experience will increase.

4. *Growing Participation Rates of Underrepresented Students.* The growing number of traditionally underrepresented students desiring to study abroad, as well as male student participation, will be addressed. Achieving participation rates reflecting today's and tomorrow's college demographics is vital. Making education abroad equitably accessible is simply the right thing to do.

5. *Making Education Abroad More Affordable.* Sophisticated economic modeling of the total costs of education abroad resulting in an innovative pricing model will make education abroad more financially accessible to not only more students but also a broader spectrum of students. Doubling the number of college graduates studying abroad is a manageable, aspirational goal.

6. *Advancing the Profession.* The field will continue to mimic the evolution of other academic fields. More graduate programs, increased and improved research, and the curricular valuing of education abroad will enhance professionalization of the field. It will result in the development of more specialists in areas such as program planning, marketing, recruiting, managing/leadership, educational technology, policymaking, crisis management, fund-raising, and economic modeling.

These are six areas for hope in the future of the field. There are many others. It behooves us to make these and other changes occur. Join me.

Technology

Kevin Kinser
Professor of Education, Pennsylvania State University

Education abroad is on the edge of transformation. Technology is the reason. We are at the receiving end of a technological tailwind that has created a golden age for international experiences. It is changing the field. Consider some of the things that have happened in the last quarter century. They have already impacted internationalization of higher education in general and have the potential to dramatically change education abroad in the years to come.

First, the Internet has made the global sharing of information simple. No more waiting for the brochure to be delivered or seeking out printed books and guides for basic data on another country or a program at a host institution. Now students can easily find information about opportunities for education abroad and other international activities. And even better, they can be targeted with messages related to their interests. Visa requirements, local conditions and customs, and other details about the destination are readily available whenever and wherever international staff and students need them.

Second, communication is now essentially free. We have Skype, WhatsApp, WeChat, among others, that provide the ability to connect with others no matter where they are. Videoconferencing that used to require dedicated facilities and expensive equipment is now available at the push of a button. From this perspective, managing education abroad programs at a distance is easier—and cheaper—than it has ever been. Mobile platforms— combined with free communication technology—mean you never have to be disconnected from people, places, and current events during an education abroad experience.

Third, translation technology changes how we think about language. Education abroad does not have to be limited by fluency in the host country language. For example, my high school French is easily outpaced in Paris, but apps on my phone serve as a virtual tutor that reminds me of the right word or phrase whenever I need it. The world is open to education abroad opportunities even when our students' language skills are subpar.

The technological advances keep coming, too, both defining the university of today and challenging its future. How might virtual reality help our students experience other cultures without needing months away from home? How will real-time translation diminish the role of language barriers in identifying education abroad opportunities? How does travel to education abroad locations change because there will be faster and cheaper ways of getting around?

Some might look at this future and wonder whether education abroad can maintain its ability to foster immersion in another culture, especially as technology makes it increasingly difficult to truly step away. Some traditional justifications for education abroad, like language acquisition or pushing students outside of their comfort zones, may be difficult to sustain. Other worrisome trends that technology may enable, such as the privileging of English and cultural homogenization, deserve specific attention from international educators.

Bottom line: Technological realities will influence how students are prepared for education abroad, and the kinds of experiences they encounter. Get ready for the future!

Back to the Future: Collaboration as Global Mobility Solution

John Lucas
President and CEO, ISEP

The Gordian knot of U.S. student mobility is the problem of scale. The United States has increased the number of undergraduates it sends abroad for academic credit consistently for a decade (Farrugia & Bhandari, 2017). These students achieve global competencies through studies, work, internships, and volunteering. Yet, at best only 15% of U.S. undergraduates earning a BA or BS degree study abroad. Efforts to double the number of U.S. students studying abroad are achievable, however, if institutions and organizations mitigate obstacles they have put in their way.

Bilateral and multilateral exchange partnerships have demonstrated success, in Europe and elsewhere, by approaching them with humility and in the spirit of mutual respect. In contrast, in the United States, such partnerships are often viewed as outdated. U.S. institutions often insist on their teaching methods, models of credit transfer, and pedagogical interventions. When their partners cannot or will not yield, they develop complex and costly work-arounds, including creating U.S.-style experiences overseas. This is not scalable. If institutions expect their students to navigate difference, they must do so as well. Collaboration will keep them honest.

Flexible models of curricular integration are key. Dual and multilateral degree programs will continue to grow. This is a heavy lift for faculty on the front end. Agreement on such programs, however, builds in curricular integration. Increasingly, universities will be a set of experiences, not a place; this will improve the chances that mobility can achieve greater scale.

Faculty increasingly look to short-term exchanges to address a concrete set of learning outcomes (as opposed to course equivalencies). Educational technology, such as collaborative online international learning, allows faculty to embed a field experience into a semester-long course. Blended learning programs use technology to facilitate the human connection that occurs when we share the same (virtual) space.

The Erasmus program was developed to manage a massive European Union investment and serve as a clearinghouse for European students. Launched in 1987, by 2014 it was providing mobility opportunities for almost 275,000 students annually (European Commission, 2015). Its successor, Erasmus+, is both taking the European program to a global scale and incorporating practical training. All of this took place through collaboration and multilateral agreements that managed economic disparity among nations.

The United States has such models available, but they challenge its cultural norms. Multilateralism requires students to accept that learning abroad may be different from learning at home. U.S. institutions must similarly accept their partners' pedagogies and the institutional cultures.

American individualism has been a springboard to many of the United States' achievements, from technological innovations to social justice movements that value individual difference. Collaboration is a collective approach and presents U.S. students, faculty, and administrators with a true learning opportunity if they are willing to seize it.

The Train Is Leaving and We're Not on It

Mark Salisbury
Founder and CEO, MC4L

Remember the excitement we all felt during the mid-2000s when we thought passage of the Senator Paul Simon Study Abroad Program Act would finally give education abroad the legitimacy, priority, and funding it deserved? Remember when the U.S. Senate unanimously designated 2006 as the "Year of Study Abroad"? Remember swooning at the possibility of substantial federal resources invested to achieve a goal of one million students studying abroad annually by 2016–2017? For most of the second half of the last decade, the litany of pronouncements about the importance of education abroad seemed to suggest a rare consensus throughout the higher education sector.

So what happened?

Congressional willingness to put real money behind the Senate's resolution couldn't survive a tumultuous legislature and an imploding economy. The 2012 Institute of International Education initiative, Generation Study Abroad, stepped into the void and set a goal of 600,000 undergraduates studying abroad annually by 2020. But the trajectory of this well-intended effort seems already far too flat to achieve its original goal. Even though education abroad participation continues to grow ever so slowly in absolute numbers (just over 325,000 in 2015–2016), it remains a steadily tiny proportion of overall postsecondary enrollment and participation demographics have changed little. Further, internships and undergraduate research as experiences, as necessary for every college student, are replacing study abroad, a necessity touted by educational organizations and the higher education press.

And why shouldn't they be? There is an ample body of evidence to suggest that these experiences do, in fact, correlate strongly with improved learning outcomes. Moreover—and this is a key reality as family incomes continue to flatline while the costs of college increase—internships and undergraduate research appear directly linked to improved postgraduate outcomes in the form of jobs and graduate school admission.

Even though the metaphor is tired and old, we have to embrace the urgency that it should engender. The higher education train is pulling out of the station and education abroad is still arguing with the conductor about its seat assignment. We are still hooked on participation numbers as our metric of success, even though we know that participation is a poor proxy for the learning that we continue to believe, almost desperately sometimes, that education abroad is supposed to provide. We must entirely flip our focus from participation to learning outcomes and partner with every campus office that shares a passion for creating interculturally literate college graduates. We must advocate, and then collaborate, with faculty and student affairs professionals to weave an off-campus study into the series of learning experiences that culminate in graduation. Furthermore, we must champion the idea that these learning experiences are explicitly linked and are not merely a list of boxes to be checked off. Otherwise, education abroad may go the way of the small rural liberal arts college—idyllic for those who can afford it, but increasingly difficult to justify as a necessary part of preparing for life as a college graduate.

From Centralization to Decentralized Ownership and Integration

Kathleen Sideli
Associate Vice President for Overseas Study, Indiana University

Given that I have been involved in the field of education abroad for four decades, it is commonplace for me to look back. Therefore, I appreciate the invitation to look forward, to see where the field might be in the next decade.

I have been fortunate to spend my career at an institution that has been a pioneer from the start—sending students abroad on faculty-led programs in the late nineteenth century not only for language and culture but also to discover the natural world. Our multicampus research institution has always benefited from administrators who have understood that a complete university education should include an international dimension. And with each year, that aspiration has become a reality as program models have evolved for different purposes. From once offering traditional immersion programs, we've witnessed the growth of embedded programs; discipline-specific field study courses; and experiential activities, including service-learning and internships. All units are now trying to get their majors abroad.

I predict this metamorphosis will continue into the future, with education abroad activity continuing to devolve to campus units. There is an irony to this; our office was centralized almost 50 years ago precisely to facilitate education abroad, from program development to student/faculty preparation to program administration, crisis management, and integrated systems. What changed, why will the change continue, and how will we adapt?

Adept at centralizing policies and systems, education abroad professionals have nonetheless hankered for faculty engagement and support since student learning is at the core of our efforts. We became experts in aspects of education abroad that needed professionalization but relied on faculty to design program curriculum or embrace curriculum our students completed abroad. It has been transformative to see every academic unit today develop its own programs; hire staff; engage faculty; and, most importantly, turn to the education abroad office for professional advice, guidance, and training.

Therefore, it is essential to rethink the mission and efforts of the study abroad office from administering programs and sending students abroad through providers and exchanges to now working hand in hand with units that seem to replicate what we do. However, instead of resenting them or diminishing their efforts, we need to share our expertise, invite them to join us at conferences and meetings, and show our leadership at all times. The education abroad office can still set the gold standard and provide quality control without micromanaging all international efforts across the institution.

I remember when I felt that my only peers were those in parallel positions at other institutions. Any chance to discuss the trials and tribulations of education abroad took place at conferences, workshops, and meetings. Today, I am pleased to say that I can have those conversations with colleagues at my own institution as well.

I look forward to the ongoing expansion of education abroad activity across other colleges and universities. This is, after all, the ultimate success of curriculum integration that we have long considered the holy grail of education abroad!

The Great Unbundling

Richard Slimbach
Professor of Global Studies, Azusa Pacific University

> If I were to redesign the American college experience, students would spend their entire four years in different civilizational cultures, gathering a wealth of international experience that can be applied to addressing similar problems in communities and cities back home. (Nick Kristof, personal communication, Sonagachi, Kolkata)

Education abroad confronts many of the same challenges as its campus "mother ship": soaring tuition costs; student indebtedness; economic and racial homogeneity; Title IX rules; mental health issues; grade-grubbing; marginal learning; and a general atrophying of students' ability to see things from the perspective of someone on the other side of some cultural, national, or ethnic divide. Also, like domestic campuses, many overseas programs bundle real estate, housing, dining, health services, cocurricular activities, and career counseling.

Education abroad has a long history, but has taken a distinctly nontraditional turn. A quarter of today's students are older than 25. A similar percentage are single parents. The new normal is to be a student of color from a low-income family and work at least 20 hours a week. Precious few such students can afford to quit work, leave their families, pay thousands of dollars in program fees, and discharge several tons of CO for a semester (or less) abroad. This begs the question: How will the global learning needs of this new majority be met, especially as wealth disparities widen and the climate system continues to warm?

To help a rising generation learn how to live well on a precarious planet, education abroad will need to do five things:

1. Reduce the overall cost (be affordable).
2. Produce powerful, interdisciplinary learning outcomes (be educative).
3. Minimize harm to the biosphere (be sustainable).
4. Shape lives of meaning and consequence (be formative).
5. Prepare students for vocations that intelligently respond to the world's toughest problems (be socially responsible).

Achieving this will require a great unbundling.

Imagine education abroad, no longer served up as a side dish to the main meal on a sequestered campus compound, but as a four-course (year), accredited, degree-granting, and progressive (multi-civilizational) feast deployed through an international network of community-based "centers." Imagine this four-year internationalized education made radically affordable by "unbundling" it from splashy facilities, "smart" classrooms, seat time, sports teams, and superfluous amenities and program administration. What if infrastructure had to be justified in terms of student and community competency development?

What if spaces for learning were then "rebundled" to include vernacular communities of diverse peoples working together on the "grand challenges" of the twenty-first century? What if families replaced dorms? Local eateries replaced swank restaurants or cafeterias? Internet cafes replaced brick-and-mortar libraries? Project-based student teams, jamming intellectually with local experts and organizations, replaced one-off "service experiences"? Students themselves decided what to learn, where to learn it, when, and with whom?

In the coming years, the dominant model of education abroad—high priced, elite serving, geographically distant, fossil fuel dependent, and input (versus outcome) oriented—will need to be fundamentally rethought. Whatever forms its new ecology takes, we can hope it will generate the scholarship and competencies needed for graduates to launch careers serving the common good.

The Future Is Collaborative: Making University Partnerships Do Even More

Susan Buck Sutton
Emerita Associate Vice President of International Affairs,
Indiana University

Starting with the University of Delaware and the Sorbonne nearly a century ago, university-to-university partnerships have been a key component of U.S. education abroad. Ninety percent of U.S. institutions responding to a recent survey have such partnerships, sometimes managed by a provider organization but most often by the institutions themselves (The Forum on Education Abroad, 2018). While these linkages have focused on student mobility and learning, they have also constructed an emergent international network that holds transformative potential not only for students who pursue education abroad but also for the institutions they represent and the nature and practice of higher education itself. Leveraging partnerships requires expanding our understandings of what they offer and revisiting how to build sustainable structures on which they depend.

Such endeavors can benefit from greater conversation between education abroad and the growing literature on international academic partnerships. Even though education abroad has deep experience with partnerships, such relationships do not animate the field's research literature, which has focused on student learning outcomes, among other issues. An increase, in the United States and elsewhere, in international academic partnerships for research, curricular collaboration, capacity building, and so on, has sparked significant analysis concerning the impact of such linkages more generally, what makes some work, and why so many do not.

This literature reveals what more partnerships might offer, if developed in certain ways. Borrowing from the discussion of university-community partnerships by Enos and Morton (2003), the power of partnerships is being seen less as transactional than generative and transformative (Sutton, 2016). In transactional partnerships, institutions engage because each has something the other finds useful. Transformative or generative partnerships emphasize collaboration, with partners opening themselves to change, and giving birth to new ideas and possibilities. The difference is that between buying a product and pursuing a creative process. Transformative linkages are concerned with management, exchange, and quality control but are equally concerned with trust and equity, sustaining the relationship, fashioning new projects, and finding common purpose.

Seen this way, university partnerships offer education abroad opportunities other partnerships may not: certainly faculty-level instruction as well as the possibility of collaborative global learning embedded within a larger framework of generative institutional cooperation. Partnerships connect entire academic institutions in ways that can interweave student learning at home and away, expand to disciplines not normally associated with education abroad, transform disciplinary knowledge, develop faculty and staff capacities, spark research and other sorts of collaborations, and stand as a model from which students draw many lessons.

In this light, and in terms of this volume's theme, university partnerships can be developed to create a continuum of global learning, with the same partner involved in education abroad, on-campus instruction, online global dialogues, civic engagement projects, and cocurricular campus programming, all encased in a framework that enables students to connect theory, knowledge acquisition, application, personal reflection, and intercultural competence. With such amplification, the partnerships long built by education abroad practitioners enter into more general discussions on the kind of collaborative academic internationalization and institutional global citizenship needed for the twenty-first century.

High-Impact Practices as Tools for Integration of Education Abroad for All

Dawn Whitehead
Senior Director for Global Learning and Curricular Change
Association of American Colleges & Universities

In today's complex, interconnected, and fascinating times, it is more important than ever, many argue, that college students are global ready upon graduation. This doesn't happen simply because an undergraduate studies abroad at some point. It requires intentional, well-structured experiences before, during, and after education abroad rooted in other high-impact practices (HIPs). As HIPs become more commonplace at institutions of all types, the integration of education abroad with other HIPs may be a way to ensure quality learning experiences and encourage increases in participation in education abroad. While HIPs are becoming ubiquitous at many institutions, a commitment to internationalization vis-à-vis institutional mission statements is also becoming quite common. This should be an indication of the emerging priority of global learning skills for all students. In the quest to increase participation in education abroad, we must also push strongly for global learning for all students.

When colleges and universities require global learning for all students—through institutional learning outcomes and robust professional development for all campus educators—it impacts all students. Preparation for global readiness involves multiple opportunities for engagement, analysis, and attempts to address complex challenges that may be local with global implications and that cannot be solved by a single discipline or nation. When institutions integrate global dimensions, students gain global experiences in course-based, community-based, and cocurricular activities across all majors and disciplines. Integrative global learning resonates with the emphasis of this book and the intentional use of the term *education abroad* instead of *study abroad*. Education abroad, as Brewer and Ogden clearly articulate, implies a relationship between the international experience and multiple aspects of student learning, including HIPs. As institutions seek to find ways to improve student success, many have adopted HIPs. These practices for teaching and learning have been shown to benefit college students from many backgrounds, but especially historically underserved students (Finley & McNair, 2013). Many institutions are offering multiple HIP experiences for students across their educational experience, and some are bringing HIPs together as they expand offerings and seek to increase student participation in HIPs.

When education abroad is combined with other HIPs, student learning deepens. With global service-learning, global internships, and globally focused research taking place in international settings, students have experiences with diversity where they must wrestle with circumstances and individuals who are unfamiliar. Ideally, they also have periodic opportunities to engage in structured reflection and to integrate their formal, academic learning with the lessons they are learning from colleagues in the lab, in the community, and at their placement sites to enhance their understanding. Finally, students are also empowered to apply their learning and skills to the real world through experiential learning.

Research on what makes HIPs high impact can help ensure that education abroad is more than an amazing experience.

References

de Wit, H. (Ed.). (1998). Ducks quack differently on each side of the ocean. International education in the US and Europe. In *50 years of international cooperation and exchange between the United States and Europe: European views. Essays in honour of NAFSA.* Occasional Paper 11 (pp. 13–20). Amsterdam, The Netherlands: EAIE.

Enos, S., & Morton, K. (2003). Developing a theory and practice of campus-community partnerships. In B. Jacoby (Ed.), *Building partnerships for service learning* (pp. 20–41). San Francisco, CA: Jossey-Bass.

European Commission. (2015) *Erasmus: Facts, figures & trends, 2013–2014.* Brussels, Belgium: Unit B1 "Higher Education" Directorate-General for Education and Culture.

Farrugia, C. A., & Bhandari, R. (2017). *Open Doors 2017 report on international educational exchange.* New York, NY: Institute of International Education.

Finley, A., & McNair, T. (2013). *Assessing underserved students' engagement in high-impact practices.* Washington, DC: Association of American Colleges & Universities.

Jaeger, C. (2011). *Wachstum: Wohin?* Munich, DE: Oekom.

The Forum on Education Abroad. (2018). *State of the field 2017.* Available from https://forumea.org/wp-content/uploads/2018/03/ForumEA-State-of-the-Field-18-web-version.pdf

Sutton, S. B. (2016). Mutual benefit in a globalizing world: A new calculus for assessing institutional gain through international academic partnerships. In C. Banks, B. Siebe-Herbig, & K. Norton (Eds.), *Global perspectives on strategic international partnerships: A guide to building sustainable academic linkages* (pp. 175–186). New York, NY: Institute of International Education.

CONTRIBUTORS

Roger Adkins is the senior international officer at Gustavus Adolphus College in Minnesota and directs its Center for International and Cultural Education. His current research considers decolonizing pedagogies and applications of queer theory in intercultural education, and he periodically teaches folklore and social justice to Gustavus students in the United Kingdom. Adkins held a 2016–2017 Association of International Education Administration Presidential Fellowship, is a member of several campus working groups, and serves on advisory boards and committees for education abroad consortia and nonprofits. His PhD in comparative literature is from the University of Oregon; he previously worked there and at California Polytechnic University in San Luis Obispo.

Giselda Beaudin has worked in education abroad for more than 10 years and currently directs the Office of International Programs at Rollins College. She has presented at numerous conferences including NAFSA: Association of International Educators regionals, AIEA, and The Forum on Education Abroad. She currently serves on the CAPA Academic Advisory Board and the SIT Partnerships Council and publishes regularly in the field of education abroad. Beaudin served on the NAFSA Trainer Corps and the NAFSA Consular Liaison Subcommittee, and has led workshops at NAFSA regional and national conferences. Her BA in comparative literature is from Brown University, and her MA in English and creative writing is from Binghamton University.

Elizabeth Brewer directs international education at Beloit College, Wisconsin, where her work has focused on internationalizing the curriculum and deepening education abroad's impacts on students and the campus. Brewer coedited *Assessing Study Abroad: Theory, Tools, and Practice* (Stylus, 2015), *Integrating Study Abroad Into the Curriculum: Theory and Practice Across the Disciplines* (Stylus, 2010), and *Study Abroad and the City: Bringing the Lessons Home* (a special edition of *Frontiers: The Interdisciplinary Journal of Study Abroad*, 2011). She has also written on comprehensive internationalization, international partnerships, and curriculum internationalization. Active in international education organizations, she has held positions at

Boston University, the University of Massachusetts at Amherst, and the New School for Social Research. Her PhD is in German literature.

Paige E. Butler is an assistant professor in the MA program in international education management at the Middlebury Institute of International Studies, Monterey, California. She teaches development theory, education abroad, and program design and assessment, and a course in Spain that explores on-site perspectives on education abroad. Previously, at CEA and Arizona State University, she managed faculty-led programs and academic operations for study abroad centers around the world. Butler's research examines student development and outcomes assessment in international education. A Forum Certified Education Abroad Professional and QUIP reviewer, Butler earned her MEd and EdD from Arizona State University in educational leadership and policy studies in higher education.

Lisa Chieffo is associate director for study abroad in the University of Delaware's Institute for Global Studies. Overseeing nearly 100 global programs enrolling about 1,400 students annually, she is responsible for program development, crisis management, policy development and implementation, and assessment. With 25 years of experience in education abroad, Chieffo has presented at multiple conferences and published widely, most recently coediting NAFSA's *Guide to Successful Short-Term Programs Abroad*, third edition. She spent an undergraduate semester in Vienna, Austria, and one year as a Fulbright scholar in Tübingen, Germany. Her MA in German and EdD in educational leadership are from the University of Delaware.

Anne M. D'Angelo is assistant dean of Global Initiatives at Carlson School of Management, University of Minnesota, where she leads strategic partnerships, education abroad, and global executive programs. D'Angelo serves as adjunct faculty in the College of Education and Human Development; chair of NAFSA's Teaching, Learning, and Scholarship Community; board director for Minnesota's World Affairs Council; and a certified leadership coach. She lived and worked in Japan and the Republic of Georgia, and earned a PhD in organizational policy, leadership, and development from the University of Minnesota. D'Angelo received a U.S. State Department Meritorious Honor Award, U.S. Fulbright-Nehru Award, and University of Minnesota Distinguished Award for Global Engagement.

Julie M. Ficarra is the associate director of study abroad, SUNY Cortland. She earned her PhD in cultural foundations of education at Syracuse University.

She holds an MA in international education policy (Harvard University), and worked in international education at the U.S. Department of State's Bureau of Educational and Cultural Affairs, the U.S. Embassy in Swaziland, the University of South Florida, and the SUNY COIL Center. Recipient of the 2013 NAFSA Region X Rising Professional Award, she has held multiple consultancies. Her research on the application of critical theories to policy and practice in education abroad has appeared in *Issues in Teacher Education*, *The SoJo Journal: Education Foundations and Social Justice*, and *Frontiers: The Journal of Study Abroad*.

Joan Gillespie has worked in international education for 20-plus years. An instructor in Northwestern University's graduate program in higher education administration and policy, she held senior positions at the Associated Colleges of the Midwest and IES Abroad. Her current research, sponsored by the Elon University Center for Engaged Learning, examines impacts on faculty of leading study away programs. She has published and presented on quality standards, program evaluation, and the assessment of student learning and development. Gillespie served on The Forum on Education Abroad Council and chaired the working group that developed standards for undergraduate research abroad. Her MA and PhD in English literature are from Northwestern University.

Anthony Gristwood is faculty chair and principal lecturer at CAPA The Global Education Network in London, where he teaches interdisciplinary urban studies and directs the Global Institute of Community Engagement. He has taught in higher education since 1994 and since 2000 has specialized in education abroad at CAPA, Queen's University (Canada), and the University of Connecticut in London. His research and teaching interests include contemporary urban studies, global cities, and modern London; politics, identity, and culture in modern Europe; public geographies; and participatory approaches to teaching and learning, including the use of Web 2.0 technologies. Coeditor and regular contributor of CAPA Occasional Publications, he holds an MA, PGCE, and PhD in geography from the University of Cambridge.

John P. Haupt is a graduate student in the doctor of higher education program at the University of Arizona. His research focuses on issues in comparative and international higher education abroad. Previously, he served as the curriculum integration specialist in Michigan State University's Office for Education Abroad and taught English as a second language at Ohio University and Rice University. He has published research in both education abroad and second language acquisition. Haupt's MA in linguistics is from Ohio University and his MA in diplomacy and international commerce, and his graduate certificate in international education are from the University of Kentucky.

Kris Holloway is president of the Center for International Studies (CISabroad, Northampton, Massachusetts), an education abroad organization. She is author of two nonfiction books: the award-winning personal ethnography *Monique and the Mango Rains: Two Years With a Midwife in Mali* (Waveland Press, 2007), based on her experience as a Peace Corps Volunteer; and *Shores Beyond Shores: From Holocaust to Hope* (White River Press, 2018), cowritten with Holocaust survivor Dr. Irene Butter. A frequent speaker on international service, women's health, and international development issues, Holloway is a founding board member of the Global Leadership League, whose mission is to empower and train women leaders. Her MPH is from the University of Michigan.

Darren Kelly began teaching U.S. undergraduates in Ireland with the Institute for the International Education of Students in 2002. He has designed and taught experiential learning courses for several U.S. education abroad providers and colleges, including at Beloit College, where he was Fulbright Scholar-in-Residence in 2007. Much of Kelly's theoretical discourse and pedagogy derives from his (interdisciplinary) PhD in geography (Dublin City University), and his work as a community educator in inner-city Dublin neighborhoods. Kelly's current work includes service-learning, place-based education, and intercultural education. He developed CAPA's Global Internship Program and teaches on the postgraduate diploma in further education and training at Trinity College, Dublin.

Rich Kurtzman has worked on the provider side of international education for over two decades in the United States and in Barcelona, Spain. As an undergraduate he studied abroad (St. Petersburg, Russia; Madrid, Spain), interned (Milan, Italy), and volunteered (the Philippines). Since 2002, he has served as an intercultural consultant in Barcelona and taught intercultural communication, global learning, and Spanish civilization and culture. In 2009 he founded Barcelona Study Abroad Experience to offer programming focused on Barcelona. He regularly presents on increasing cultural awareness, improving personal and professional development abroad, and enhancing orientation and re-entry workshops. He recently published a chapter in NAFSA's guide to short-term programming.

Bruce La Brack is professor emeritus of anthropology and international studies in the School of International Studies at University of the Pacific, Stockton, California. Trained as a South Asian specialist and interculturalist, he led Pacific's innovative and integrated study abroad orientation and re-entry programs for over three decades. He also directed the Pacific Institute for Cross-Cultural Training and chaired the MA program in intercultural relations. He is the primary author and editor of the What's Up With Culture? website, a free Internet resource for preparing U.S. students for an international educational experience. In 2012, he was awarded NAFSA's Teaching, Learning, and Scholarship (TLS) Knowledge Community Award for Innovative Research & Scholarship in Internationalization. During his career, he traveled to over 85 countries and conducted field research in England, India, Japan, Uganda, and North America.

Rosalind Latiner Raby teaches at California State University, Northridge, in the Educational Leadership and Policy Studies Department and at the Southern California Campus of University of Phoenix. She is also the director of California Colleges for International Education, a non-profit consortium of California community colleges. Raby received her PhD in comparative and international education from University of California, Los Angeles. Since 1984 she has worked with community college faculty and administrators to help them internationalize their campuses. Raby has been publishing in the field of community college internationalization since 1985.

Bryan Messerly is assistant director of Study Away Programs in the Center for International and Cultural Education, Gustavus Adolphus College. Messerly manages faculty-led January-term study away programs and three semester-length flagship programs. Previously, he worked in the U.S. Department of State's Bureau of Educational and Cultural Affairs, first as a member of the outreach team for the Fulbright Program, and later as a Fulbright Program officer for the Middle East and North Africa. His MA in English is from Boston College, and his MA in ethics, peace, and global affairs is from American University's School of International Service. He taught Italian at the University of Kansas and led students on KU's summer language institute in Florence, Italy.

Anthony C. Ogden is associate vice provost for global engagement and assistant professor at the University of Wyoming. Previously, he worked for IES Abroad, Pennsylvania State University, the University of Kentucky, and Michigan State University. A two-time Fulbright recipient, Ogden has published widely on education abroad, including the widely read essay "The View From the Veranda: Understanding Today's Colonial Student." Coeditor of a volume on international education's scholar-practitioners in international education, he is currently working on a coedited volume on research and practice in education abroad (Routledge, forthcoming). As a visiting professor at the Middlebury Institute for International Studies, he teaches comprehensive internationalization. Ogden earned a PhD in educational theory and policy with a dual title in comparative and international education from Pennsylvania State University.

Mary Pang is concurrently associate dean (internationalization) in the City University of Hong Kong's College of Business and associate professor of management. Pang has spearheaded the internationalization drive in the business school for the past 15 years, building up and leading the student mobility operations. She is a member of the International Advisory Board of HHL Leipzig Graduate School of Management and a recipient of the City University of Hong Kong's Teaching Excellence Award. Pang's research focuses on career development and student learning, and she has published and presented widely. Pang's PhD in sociology is from the University of Warwick, and her BSc (Hons) in economics (business administration) is from Cardiff University.

Michele V. Price is emeritus director of Study Abroad and International Exchanges, Western Oregon University. At WOU, she participated in many international site visits and evaluations, implemented photo-blogging and digital storytelling projects for a required study abroad capstone course she taught, and with Victor Savicki established an ongoing research and assessment project of student reflective writing. She and Savicki are continuing this research, working with a study abroad provider, and have published their work in several journals. Price strives to help other education abroad professionals find solutions to improve programs and to enhance student learning. Her MA is from Western Oregon State College.

Victor Savicki, professor emeritus of psychology at Western Oregon University, has taught university students eight times in Austria, Germany, Greece, Argentina, and the United Kingdom. Twenty-eight of his peer-reviewed publications emphasize some aspect of culture, including the research-based book *Burnout Across Thirteen Cultures: Stress and Coping in Child and Youth Care Workers* (Praeger, 2002), the edited book *Developing Intercultural Competence and Transformation: Theory, Research, and Application in International Education* (Stylus, 2008), and the coedited book

Assessing Study Abroad (Stylus, 2015). His entry in the *SAGE Encyclopedia of Intercultural Competence* (SAGE, 2015), "Stress, Coping, and Adjustment in Intercultural Competence," synthesizes his views on study abroad student development. His current research interest is the influence of study abroad on student identity, and the role that reflection plays from a constructivist viewpoint.

Brian J. Whalen is chief academic officer and dean of education at Atlantis, a leading provider of international health care education. He serves as a director and advisory partner at Academic Assembly, Inc., a Dean's Fellow at Dickinson College, and an International Education Leadership Fellow at the University at Albany. For 12 years Brian was the president and CEO of The Forum on Education Abroad, and was founding editor of *Frontiers: The Interdisciplinary Journal of Study Abroad.*

Michael Woolf is deputy president for Strategic Development at CAPA Global Education Network. Woolf has spent much of his career in an international context. Prior to working in mainstream international education, he taught American literature at the University of Hull, Middlesex University, University of Padova, and University of Venice and worked as a researcher-writer for BBC radio. Woolf has held leadership roles in international education for many years with, among others the Foundation for International Education (FIE), the Council on International Educational Exchnage (CIEE), and Syracuse University. Woolf has written extensively on international education and cultural studies.

Katherine N. Yngve, a "recovering" senior international officer, codirects Purdue's Center for Intercultural Learning, Mentoring, Assessment and Research (CILMAR), where she oversees institutional research relating to intercultural learning and delivers faculty/staff training in support of Purdue's intercultural competence requirement. She founded e-mentoring for Purdue study abroad participants in 2015 and as a doctoral student was among the first in the United States to e-mentor study abroad students. Prior to Purdue, she served as founding director of International Programs at the American University of Beirut, Lebanon, and has been an active NAFSA member. Her PhD is from the University of Minnesota and her MA from the University of Chicago.

Study Abroad/International Learning books from Stylus

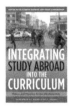

Integrating Study Abroad Into the Curriculum
Theory and Practice Across the Disciplines
Edited by Elizabeth Brewer and Kiran Cunningham
Foreword by Madeleine F. Greene

Integrating Worlds
How Off-Campus Study Can Transform
Undergraduate Education
Scott D. Carpenter, Helena Kaufman, and Malene Torp
Foreword by Jane Edwards

Leading Internationalization
A Handbook for International Education Leaders
Edited by Darla K. Deardorff and Harvey Charles
Foreword by E. Gordon Gee
Afterword by Allen E. Goodman

Making Global Learning Universal
Promoting Inclusion and Success for All Students
Hillary Landorf, Stephanie Doscher, and Jaffus Hardrick
Foreword by Caryn McTighe Musil

Assessing Study Abroad
Theory, Tools, and Practice
Edited by Victor Savicki and Elizabeth Brewer
Foreword by Brian Whalen

Becoming World Wise
A Guide to Global Learning
Richard Slimbach

Leadership & Administration books from Stylus

Conducting an Institutional Diversity Audit in Higher Education
A Practitioner's Guide to Systematic Diversity Transformation
Edna Chun and Alvin Evans
Foreword by Benjamin D. Reese Jr.

Enhancing Assessment in Higher Education
Putting Psychometrics to Work
Edited by Tammie Cumming and M. David Miller
Foreword by Michael J. Kolen

High-Impact Practices in Online Education
Research and Best Practices
Edited by Kathryn E. Linder and Chrysanthemum Mattison Hayes
Foreword by Kelvin Thompson

Facilitating Intergroup Dialogues
Bridging Differences, Catalyzing Change
Kelly E. Maxwell, Biren Ratnesh Nagda, and Monita C. Thompson
Foreword by Patricia Guirin

A Good Job
Campus Employment as a High-Impact Practice
George S. McClellan, Kristina L. Creager, and Marianna Savoca
Foreword by George D. Kuh

Building the Field of Higher Education Engagement
Foundational Ideas and Future Directions
Edited by Lorilee R. Sandmann and Diann O. Jones

Leadership & Administration books from Stylus

Learner-Centered Teaching
Putting the Research on Learning Into Practice
Terry Doyle
Foreword by Todd D. Zakrajsek

Of Education, Fishbowls, and Rabbit Holes
Rethinking Teaching and Liberal Education for an
Interconnected World
Jane Fried With Peter Troiano
Foreword by Dawn R. Person

Creating Wicked Students
Designing Courses for a Complex World
Paul Hanstedt

Dynamic Lecturing
Research-Based Strategies to Enhance Lecture Effectiveness
Christine Harrington and Todd Zakrajsek
Foreword by José Antonio Bowen

Designing a Motivational Syllabus
Creating a Learning Path for Student Engagement
Christine Harrington and Melissa Thomas
Foreword by Kathleen F. Gabriel

Course-Based Undergraduate Research
Educational Equity and High-Impact Practice
Edited by Nancy H. Hensel
Foreword by Cathy N. Davidson

Leadership & Administration books from Stylus

Creating Engaging Discussions
Strategies for "Avoiding Crickets" in Any Size Classroom and Online
Jennifer H. Herman and Linda B. Nilson
Foreword by Stephen D. Brookfield

The Neuroscience of Learning and Development
Enhancing Creativity, Compassion, Critical Thinking, and Peace in Higher Education
Edited by Marilee J. Bresciani Ludvik
Foreword by Ralph Wolff and Gavin W. Henning

Overcoming Student Learning Bottlenecks
Decode the Critical Thinking of Your Discipline
Joan Middendorf and Leah Shopkow
Foreword by Dan Bernstein

Creating Self-Regulated Learners
Strategies to Strengthen Students' Self-Awareness and Learning Skills
Linda B. Nilson
Foreword by Barry J. Zimmerman

A Concise Guide to Teaching With Desirable Difficulties
Diane Cummings Persellin and Mary Blythe Daniels
Foreword by Mary-Ann Winkelmes

Hitting Pause
65 Lecture Breaks to Refresh and Reinforce Learning
Gail Taylor Rice
Foreword by Kevin Barry

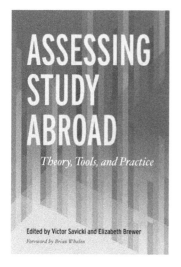

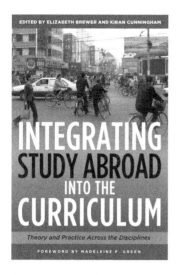

Integrating Study Abroad Into the Curriculum

Theory and Practice Across the Disciplines

Edited by Elizabeth Brewer and Kiran Cunningham

Foreword by Madeleine F. Green

"How can colleges and universities take the immense potential of study abroad and integrate what students are learning and experiencing abroad into the wider curriculum on the home campus? This is the central question Elizabeth Brewer and Kiran Cunningham address in their timely edited volume. Especially now, when greater numbers of institutions of higher education are searching for ways to internationalize their profile and offerings, this book presents a wide range of strategies aimed at effectively integrating the benefits of time spent abroad with developments in the home campus curriculum. Drawing on a wealth of study abroad experience, this book focuses on the intentional integration of students' educational and personal experiences abroad for transformational learning and development at home." — ***Comparative Education Review***

Making Global Learning Universal

Promoting Inclusion and Success for All Students

Hilary Landorf, Stephanie Doscher, and Jaffus Hardrick

Foreword by Caryn McTighe Musil

"From the pioneers of global learning, a much-welcomed guide to this new terrain, written for any postsecondary educator concerned with equity and quality. Landorf, Doscher, and Hardrick offer global learning as an inclusive, participatory process for every student. Unlike traditional international education, global learning dissolves the false binaries of U.S. and global, 'we' and 'other,' study abroad and study at-home, so that students learn in and of the world, and not merely about it."—**Heather H. Ward**, *Associate Director, Center for Internationalization and Global Engagement, American Council on Education*

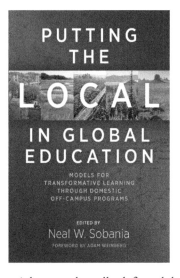

Putting the Local in Global Education

Models for Transformative Learning Through Domestic Off-Campus Programs

Edited by Neal W. Sobania

Foreword by Adam Weinberg

"*Putting the Local in Global Education* reminds us of how important it is to focus more on what students are learning than where they are studying. By linking complex questions of local and global impact, identity, power, and justice, the authors contribute to critical conversations about how we might more broadly define global learning. As a result, this book will encourage curricular and pedagogical experimentation and, I hope, lead to new ways that faculty and students may come to recognize the global in their communities and deepen their appreciation for the complexities of their interconnected lives." —**Kevin Hovland**, *Senior Director, Academic Programs, NAFSA*

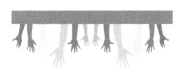

Building Cultural Competence

Innovative Activities and Models

Edited by Kate Berardo and Darla K. Deardorff

Foreword by Fons Trompenaars

"*Building Cultural Competence* makes a valuable contribution to intercultural trainers by presenting 50+ innovative activities designed specifically for the development of intercultural competence and framing the use of these activities in terms of

intercultural facilitation and intercultural development." —*R. Michael Paige*, *author of Education for the Intercultural Experience and Professor of International and Intercultural Education, University of Minnesota*

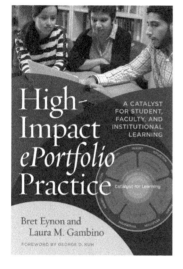

High-Impact ePortfolio Practice

A Catalyst for Student, Faculty, and Institutional Learning

Bret Eynon and Laura M. Gambino

Foreword by George D. Kuh

"Challenging the noisy legion of digital gurus who see job-specific training as the best choice for first-generation learners, Eynon and Gambino provide compelling evidence that ePortfolios can help underserved students achieve those distinctively twenty-first century liberal arts: agency as motivated learners, creativity in connecting myriad kinds of formal and informal learning, and reflective judgment about their own roles in building solutions for the future. An invaluable resource for all." —*Carol Geary-Schneider*, *Fellow, Lumina Foundation; President Emerita, Association of American Colleges & Universities*

22883 Quicksilver Drive
Sterling, VA 20166-2019

Subscribe to our e-mail alerts: www.Styluspub.com

This book is a copublication of NAFSA: Association of International Educators and Stylus Publishing, LLC.